LIBRARY OF NEW TESTAMENT STUDIES

608

Formerly Journal of the Study of the New Testament Supplement Series

Editor
Chris Keith

Editorial Board
Dale C. Allison, John M.G. Barclay, Lynn H. Cohick, R. Alan Culpepper,
Craig A. Evans, Robert Fowler, Simon J. Gathercole, Juan Hernandez,
John S. Kloppenborg, Michael Labahn, Love L. Sechrest, Robert Wall,
Steve Walton, Catrin H. Williams

SHARING IN THE SON'S INHERITANCE

Davidic Messianism and Paul's Worldwide Interpretation of the Abrahamic Land Promise in Galatians

Esau McCaulley

LONDON • NEW YORK • OXFORD • NEW DELHI • SYDNEY

T&T CLARK
Bloomsbury Publishing Plc
50 Bedford Square, London, WC1B 3DP, UK
1385 Broadway, New York, NY 10018, USA
29 Earlsfort Terrace, Dublin 2, Ireland

BLOOMSBURY, T&T CLARK and the T&T Clark logo
are trademarks of Bloomsbury Publishing Plc

First published in Great Britain in 2019
Paperback edition first published 2021

Copyright © Esau McCaulley, 2019

Esau McCaulley has asserted his right under the Copyright,
Designs and Patents Act, 1988, to be identified as Author of this work.

For legal purposes the Acknowledgements on p. vii constitute
an extension of this copyright page.

Cover design: Eleanor Rose
Cover image © Vince Cavataio/Getty Images

All rights reserved. No part of this publication may be reproduced or
transmitted in any form or by any means, electronic or mechanical,
including photocopying, recording, or any information storage or retrieval
system, without prior permission in writing from the publishers.

Bloomsbury Publishing Plc does not have any control over, or responsibility for,
any third-party websites referred to or in this book. All internet addresses given
in this book were correct at the time of going to press. The author and publisher
regret any inconvenience caused if addresses have changed or sites have
ceased to exist, but can accept no responsibility for any such changes.

A catalogue record for this book is available from the British Library.

A catalogue record for this book is available from the Library of Congress.

ISBN: HB: 978-0-5676-8592-6
PB: 978-0-5677-0029-2
ePDF: 978-0-5676-8593-3
eBook: 978-0-5676-8595-7

Series: Library of New Testament Studies, ISSN 2345678X, volume 608

Typeset by Forthcoming Publications (www.forthpub.com)

To find out more about our authors and books visit
www.bloomsbury.com and sign up for our newsletters.

Contents

Abbreviations	vii

Chapter 1
THE LAND AND MESSIAHSHIP IN GALATIANS — 1
   1.1. The State of the Question — 1
   1.2. Overview — 2
   1.3. History of Research on the Land in Paul's Letters — 5
   1.4. History of Research on Pauline Messianism and the Land
        Inheritance in Galatians — 28
   1.5. Conclusion of Chapter 1 — 46

Chapter 2
ROYAL FIGURES, DAVIDIC MESSIAHS, AND THE LAND AS KINGDOM
IN THE PSEUDEPIGRAPHA — 47
   2.1. Introduction — 47
   2.2. *Psalm of Solomon* 17 — 49
   2.3. *Second Baruch* — 56
   2.4. *4 Ezra* — 64
   2.5. 1 Maccabees 13–14 — 70
   2.6. Conclusion of Chapter 2 — 75

Chapter 3
DAVIDIC MESSIAHS AND THE LAND IN THE DEAD SEA SCROLLS — 76
   3.1. Introduction — 76
   3.2. 4QFlorilegium (4Q174) — 79
   3.3. 4Q252 (4QcommGen[a]) — 84
   3.4. 4QIsaiah Pesher[a] (4Q161) — 88
   3.5. 1QSb (Blessings) — 94
   3.6. Conclusion of Chapter 3 — 97

Chapter 4
THE END OF THE CURSE AND THE BEGINNING OF THE INHERITANCE:
DAVIDIC MESSIANISM, THE SPIRIT, AND THE ABRAHAMIC LAND PROMISE
IN GALATIANS 3:1-14 — 100
   4.1. Introduction — 100
   4.2. Galatians 3:1-5 — 102

4.3. Galatians 3:6-9	108
4.4. Galatians 3:10-14	115
4.5. Conclusion of Chapter 4	142

Chapter 5
SHARING IN THE SON'S INHERITANCE:
DAVIDIC MESSIANISM AND THE ABRAHAMIC LAND PROMISE
IN GALATIANS 3:15–4:7; 5:21

	144
5.1. Introduction	144
5.2. Galatians 3:15-19	145
5.3. Galatians 3:26-29	159
5.4. Galatians 4:1-7, 5:21	170
5.5. Conclusion of Chapter 5	190

Chapter 6
CONCLUSION

	191
6.1. The Land and Messiah in Pauline Scholarship on Galatians Revisited	191
6.2. The Evidence of Qumran and the Pseudepigrapha	193
6.3. The Curse, the Inheritance, and the Spirit in Galatians 3:1-14	195
6.4. The Messianic Seed, His Inheritance, and the Kingdom in Galatians 3:15–4:7 and 5:21	197
6.5. Implications of this Study	198

Bibliography	203
Index of References	217
Index of Authors	224

ABBREVIATIONS

AB	Anchor Bible
ABD	David Noel Freedman (ed.), *The Anchor Bible Dictionary*. New York: Doubleday, 1992
ABRL	Anchor Bible Reference Library
AcBib	Academia Biblica
BBR	Bulletin for Biblical Research
BECNT	Baker Exegetical Commentary on the New Testament
BETL	Bibliotheca Ephemeridum Theologicarum Lovaniensium
BHS	*Biblia hebraica stuttgartensia*
Bib	*Biblica*
BiBInt	Biblical Interpretation
BNTC	Black New Testament Commentary
BSac	Bibliotheca Sacra
BZNW	Beihefte zur Zeitschrift für die neutestamentliche Wissenschaft
CBET	Contributions to Biblical Exegesis and Theology
CBNTS	Coniectanea Biblica New Testament Series
CBQ	*Catholic Biblical Quarterly*
CTM	*Concordia Theological Monthly*
CurBR	*Currents in Biblical Research*
DSD	Dead Sea Discoveries
ErIsr	*Eretz-Israel*
ExpTim	*Expository Times*
FAT	Forschungen zum Alten Testament
FRLANT	Forschungen zur Religion und Literatur des Alten und Neuen Testaments.
HKNT	Handkommentar zum Neuen Testament
HR	*History of Religions*
HthKNT	Herders Theologischer Kommentar Zum Neuen Testament
JQR	*Jewish Quarterly Review*
JBL	*Journal of Biblical Literature*
JETS	*Journal of the Evangelical Theological Society*
JJS	*Journal of Jewish Studies*
JSJSup	Journal for the Study of Judaism in the Persian, Hellenistic, and Roman Periods Supplement Series
JSNT	*Journal for the Study of the New Testament*
JSNTSup	Journal for the Study of the New Testament Supplement Series

JSOTSup	Journal for the Study of the Old Study Testament Supplement Series
JSP	*Journal for the Study of the Pseudepigrapha*
JSPL	*Journal for the Study of Paul and His Letters*
JSPSup	Journal for the Study of the Pseudepigrapha Supplemental Series
JSS	*Journal of Semitic Studies*
JRS	*Journal of Roman Studies*
KEK	Kritisch-exegeticher Kommentat über das Neue Testament
LNTS	Library of New Testament Studies
LSJ	Liddell, Henry George, Robert Scott, Henry Stuart Jones. *A Greek-English Lexicon*. 9th ed. with revised supplement. Oxford: Clarendon, 1996
NAC	New American Commentary
Neot	*Neotestamentica*
NIB	New Interpreter's Bible
NICNT	New International Commentary on the New Testament
NICOT	New International Commentary on the Old Testament
NIGTC	New International Greek Testament Commentary
NovT	*Novum Testamentum*
NovTSup	Supplements to Novum Testamentum
NSBT	New Studies in Biblical Theology
NTS	New Testament Studies
OCD	*Oxford Classical Dictionary*. Edited by Simon Hornblower and Antony Spawforth. 4th ed. Oxford: Oxford University Press, 2012
OTL	Old Testament Library
RevQ	*Revue de Qumrân*
SBT	Studies in Biblical Theology
SHBC	Smyth & Helwys Bible Commentary
SNTSMS	Society for New Testament Studies Monograph Series
SP	Sacra Pagina
StBibLit	Studies in Biblical Literature
STDJ	Studies on the Texts of the Desert of Judah
TJ	*Trinity Journal*
TynBul	*Tyndale Bulletin*
TZ	*Theologische Zeitschrift*
VT	*Vetus Testamentum*
WBC	Word Biblical Commentary
WMANT	Wissenschaftliche Monogaphien zum Alten und Neun Testament
WTJ	*Westminster Theological Journal*
WUNT	Wissenschaftliche Untersuchungen zum Neuen Testament
ZAW	*Zeitschrift für die alttestamentliche Wissenschaft*
ZNW	*Zeitschrift für die neutestamentliche Wissenschaft und die Kunde der älteren Kirche*

Chapter 1

THE LAND AND MESSIAHSHIP IN GALATIANS

1.1. *The State of the Question*

It should be surprising to learn that there has never been a major study of Paul's interpretation of the Abrahamic land promises in Galatians. The lack of attention to the land inheritance is puzzling given that Paul refers to the Abrahamic narrative in Gal. 3:6, 8, 9, 14, 15-18; 3:26-29, 4:21, and 4:25-31. It is uncontroversial to state that the Abrahamic promises include at least the land of Canaan, the multiplication of Abraham's offspring, and the blessing of the Gentiles.[1] Given that most scholars agree that Paul is concerned with the large family promised to Abraham and the Gentile blessing, it is somewhat surprising to assert that Paul shows so little concern for the land inheritance, especially when his climactic statements describe the Galatians as heirs (3:26-29; 4:7, 30-31). The few who do discuss the land in Galatians argue that Paul abandons or spiritualizes the land promise.[2]

This book argues that recent discussions of the inheritance in Galatians are flawed because they do not link Paul's interpretation of the Abrahamic land promises to another hotly debated question in Pauline scholarship: the role of Jewish or early Christian messianism in his thought. Scholars

---

1. Even though Paul never uses the language of γῆ when referring to the Abrahamic promises, he does recognize that God promises Abraham physical space in Rom. 4:13, which includes the lexemes: Ἀβραάμ, ἐπαγγελία, κληρονόμος, and κόσμος. This justifies wondering if Paul displays an expanded understanding of the inheritance in other letters including Galatians. See the discussion below.

2. The seminal work on the land promise is Davies 1979. In that work he argues that Paul abandons any geographic land promise. Bruce (1982: 172) represents the consensus when he says, "the reference to the land...plays no part in the argument of Galatians." See also Burton 1980 [1921]: 185; Witherington 2004: 245–6, 292; Das 2014: 390; Martyn 1997: 342–3; Williams 1997: 96–7; de Boer 2011: 185; Garlington 2007: 206–7. These authors maintain that the Spirit replaces the land.

rarely consider the influence of messianism on Paul's interpretation of the Abrahamic land promises because most assume that Davidic messianism plays little to no role in any aspect of Paul's theology.[3] That assumption is mistaken. This volume contends that there is a link between Paul's affirmation of Jesus's status as the Davidic Messiah and his interpretation of the Abrahamic land promise. I argue that, rather than abandoning the Abrahamic land promise, Paul expands it to encompass the whole earth because he believes that Jesus, as the seed of Abraham and David (Gal. 3:16), is entitled to the peoples and territories of the earth as his inheritance and kingdom (Ps. 2:7-8). According to Paul, believers will receive their inheritance through sharing in the worldwide inheritance of the messianic son who rules over the earth. This work, then, argues that the scholarly consensus about Pauline messianism is incorrect, and for that reason the consensus about his understanding of the Abrahamic land inheritance is also mistaken.

1.2. Overview

This chapter considers the history of research on land and messianism in Paul. Here I show that the majority of scholars assume, without sufficient exegetical warrant, that Paul abandons or spiritualizes the land promises. Alongside this claim that Paul spiritualizes the land promises, I highlight a neglected group of scholars who assert that Paul replaces the geographical land of Israel with the eschatological reception of the whole world or kingdom. I show that their advocacy for a worldwide interpretation of the land promises is more accurate than proposals that ignore or spiritualize the land promises. Nonetheless, I contend that these scholars' proposals can be strengthened by a reading of Gal. 3:1–4:7 that highlights the connection between the removal of the covenant curses and the eschatological reception of the inheritance. I will also build upon these previous proposals by clarifying the relationship between Davidic messianism and Paul's affirmation of the worldwide inheritance in Galatians.

The review of messianism in the second half of this chapter will reveal that scholars neglect the central point of contact between Jewish, early Christian, and Pauline messianism in Galatians. This is their shared belief that royal or messianic figures would enable the final realization of the

---

3. Lee (2016: 375) says "traditionally, the majority of scholars maintained that Χριστός in Paul should be understood as Jesus's surname rather than a title, and that the Messiahship of Jesus *carries little or no significance in Paul's thought*" (italics added).

land promises through their rule.[4] This neglect causes scholars to ignore the worldwide kingdom of the Messiah as the answer to the question of how Paul interprets the inheritance in Galatians.

In Chapters 2 and 3, I review a selection of Second Temple texts (4Q161, 4Q174, 4Q262, 1QSb, *Pss. Sol.* 17, *2 Baruch*, *4 Ezra*, and 1 Maccabees). These texts show that Second Temple authors often claim that royal figures would enable the final realization of the land promises.[5] The scope of the land varies.[6] Sometimes the land encompasses the whole world and at other times it includes the area in and around Jerusalem. Nonetheless, the claim that royal figures act as agents of restoration is a stable and coherent element of much Second Temple discourse.

Chapters 4 and 5 show that Paul presents Jesus as the Davidic Messiah whose death for sins exhausts the covenant curses and thereby enables the final realization of the Abrahamic promises through believers sharing in the Messiah's inheritance of the whole earth. According to Paul, the inheritance that begins with the Spirit will find its ultimate fulfillment when believing Jews and Gentiles enter the Messiah's kingdom. Thus, the goal of Paul's argument—namely, the king inheriting the world and the people sharing in that inheritance—is recognizable as one Second Temple option among many.

The phrase "land promises" should be clarified before we progress further. In this book, the land promises refer to the repeated declarations found in various strands of biblical texts that say that God will provide a place for his people. Narratively, this promise first occurs during the Abrahamic narrative when God promises to give the land of Canaan to Abraham's offspring (Gen. 12:1-3; 15:1-21). God also promises the land to the nation of Israel during the Exodus narrative (Exod. 13:11). We can also observe declarations that God will restore Israel to this land after the exile in Israel's prophetic literature (Isa. 11:11-16; Ezek. 37:11-14). When I refer to the land promises, then, I refer to the idea that the land of Canaan (and in some post-exilic and Second Temple texts, the world) belongs to Israel as its inheritance. I do not claim that all later references to the land explicitly allude to the promises made to Abraham in Genesis. Some do; some do not. I do claim that there is a general idea that the land is Israel's by right as a gift of God.

---

4. See the definition of land promises offered below.
5. On the term "royal figures," see the methodology discussion below.
6. Lied (2008: 199), speaking of the land in *2 Baruch*, says, "land may refer to smaller areas," rather than the historic boundaries of Israel. Therefore, it can also refer to larger areas in *2 Baruch* and other Second Temple texts.

How then do Second Temple royal figures relate to the land promises? Second Temple authors often associate royal and messianic figures with the final realization of the land promises as defined above. Stated differently, for these Second Temple authors, Israel does not have what God promised to them, namely the land. They claim God will give Israel what he promised to them through the agency of royal and messianic figures. In these accounts, sometimes what Israel receives is not merely Canaan. Instead, the restoration of Israel climaxes in a worldwide kingdom.[7] Chapters 2 and 3, then, support the wider claims of this book by showing that royal and messianic figures are indeed associated with the final realization of the land promises in Second Temple texts. In Chapters 4 and 5, I argue that Paul's claim that believers stand to share in the worldwide inheritance of the Messiah Jesus is a manifestation of Second Temple messianism because Paul argues that when believing Jews and Gentiles inherit the world alongside Christ, then the promise of an inheritance that God made to Abraham will be fulfilled. For Paul, this fulfillment takes the form of believing Jews and Gentiles living under the reign of the Messiah Jesus in the new creation. This is not a spiritualization of the land promises because Paul envisions bodily resurrected believers living in a physical space.

Paul's explicit focus on Abraham does stand out among Second Temple authors. While other authors periodically evoke Abraham in the course of their declarations that royal figures will restore the people of God to the land, Paul makes God's promises to Abraham a central pillar of his argument. Why does Paul focus on the land promised to Abraham, while others refer to other iterations of the promises? Paul focuses on Abraham because he sees in God's promise that he would bless the nations through Abraham, a promise that God will allow Gentiles to share in the inheritance promised to Abraham's seed. For Paul, the Messiah Jesus is this seed of Abraham (and David) who has invited believing Jews and Gentiles to share in what belongs to him. Abraham, then, functions theologically to emphasize the Gentiles' place in the purposes of God. This expansion of the Abrahamic land promises to encompass the whole earth is not, to my mind, fundamentally different from Second Temple authors who highlight the promises of the land found in other strands of biblical material. Their theological agendas did not necessitate a focus on the Abrahamic land promises. Nonetheless, these authors are in different ways arguing that God will act through royal and messianic figures to restore Israel to the inheritance promised to them. With these clarifications in place, we now turn to a review of research on land and messianism in Pauline scholarship.

---

7. For example, see the discussion of *2 Baruch*, *4 Ezra*, and *Pss. Sol.* 17.

1.3. History of Research on the Land in Paul's Letters

Scholars neglect the question of the land in Pauline studies in general and Galatians in particular. Most discussions of the land in Paul's thought occur in the context of larger studies on the land in the New Testament.[8] Thus most treatments are terse and superficial. When the land is discussed, four views predominate: (1) Paul abandons the land promises; (2) Paul replaces the land with the Spirit; (3) Paul replaces the land promises with salvation;[9] (4) Paul believes in the worldwide fulfillment of the land promises.

In what follows, I highlight the problems with the various proposals that Paul abandons the Abrahamic land promise. Previous affirmations of the worldwide fulfillment of the Abrahamic land promises rely upon flawed interpretations of the central section of Galatians. A fresh reading of Gal. 3:1–4:7 and 5:21, with a particular focus on Paul's interpretation of the land promise, will substantiate the claim that Paul looks to a worldwide fulfillment of the land promise through believers sharing in the Messiah's inheritance and kingdom.

1.3.1. Claims that Paul Abandons the Land Promise

F.C. Baur's *Paul, the Apostle of Jesus Christ* set out to explain the origins of Christianity.[10] He wants to show:

> how Christianity, instead of remaining a mere form of Judaism, and being ultimately absorbed in it, asserted itself as a separate, independent principle, broke loose from it and took its form as a new form of religious thought and life, essentially differing from Judaism, and freed from all its national exclusiveness.[11]

Although Baur does not address the issue of the land in Galatians directly, his claim that in order for Christianity to become universal it had to reject Judaism and its national expectations, including messianism and the land, set a trend for Pauline interpretation of the land promise.

---

8. See Davies 1979 and the canonical approach of Martin 2015.
9. These scholars usually do not outline the shape of this personal salvation and its relationship to the Abrahamic promises. This raises the question of where exactly this personal salvation occurs and the relationship of that location to the promises made to Abraham and David as interpreted by Paul in Galatians. See the discussion of Watson 2004 below.
10. Baur 1876: 2–3.
11. Ibid.: 3.

Hammer's work compares the inheritance theme in Ephesians (which he believes is non-Pauline) with the presentation of the inheritance in Paul's undisputed letters.[12] According to Hammer, Paul thinks that the believer received the inheritance in the past, while the author of Ephesians believes that inheritance will come in the future. In Hammer's reconstruction, Ephesians begins with Christ and ends at the eschaton.[13] Paul, by contrast, begins with Abraham and ends with Christ. Furthermore, according to Hammer, Christ is the content of the inheritance, the means by which believers inherit, and the heir to the inheritance.[14] For Hammer, this means that Jesus's death signals the end of the old age, and in the new age the believer inherits Christ. In addition, since Christ is the heir to the inheritance, Christ, in a sense, inherits himself.

Hammer's understanding of inheritance leads to a confusing account of συγκληρονόμος in Romans. He says that since Christ is the heir, the believer can be a co-heir with Christ. The believer, then, is saved in Christ and has Christ as the inheritance.[15] But since Christ is the inheritance and the believer is united to Christ, the believer too becomes the inheritance. He writes, "We may say that for Paul the *synklēronomoi Christou* become historically with Christ not only heirs but also the inheritance. That is, with Christ they become the means to and the content of the inheritance."[16] In this account, both Christ and the believers inherit themselves.

Hammer rightly focuses on the import of the inheritance language in Galatians, and he aptly highlights the fact that the believer derives his or her status as heir from Christ. Nonetheless, there are problems with his account. First, according to Hammer, Paul describes Christ as both heir and inheritance.[17] Paul never calls Christ the inheritance in Galatians. Second, Hammer removes all references to the inheritance that arise from what he deems to be pre-Pauline sources.[18] This means that all the kingdom language is excluded from consideration, including Gal. 5:21 and 1 Cor. 15:22-28. Hammer excludes these texts because he believes that if Paul derives a phrase from elsewhere that phrase does not reflect

---

12. Hammer 1960.
13. Ibid.: 269–70.
14. Ibid.: 271.
15. Ibid.
16. Ibid.: 272.
17. Ibid.: 271; see also Hammer 1992: 415–16, where he says, "Christ is the heir, but as the fulfilled promise of blessing to Abraham (Gal 3:14), he also is the inheritance."
18. Hammer 1960: 268 n. 13.

Paul's views.¹⁹ Since "kingdom" is pre-Pauline, a messianic understanding of the inheritance is ruled out a priori. This idea that messianism is Jewish and therefore, by definition, non-Pauline has its roots in Baur and the *Religionsgeschichtliche Schule*.²⁰ The *Religionsgeschichtliche Schule*, however, did not put forward that hypothesis on the basis of unbiased analysis of the Second Temple data, but rather as a result of a philosophy of history that places Christianity in its Western manifestation as the height of human achievement.²¹ Third, Hammer fails to explain the relationship between the believer's present status in Christ and the believer's future hope that arises from that status. For example, if the inheritance is *only* Christ, then Paul's concern for the resurrection of the body, the redemption of all creation, and the love that endures forever becomes difficult to explain (1 Cor. 13:8-13; 15:53-55; Rom. 8:20-21). Finally, to claim that believers and Christ are the means to and the content of the inheritance renders much of Paul's discussion of inheritance in Galatians and Romans difficult to comprehend.

The seminal book on the land in the New Testament is W.D. Davies' *The Gospel and the Land*.²² Davies begins this work by lamenting the dearth of research on the question of the land in biblical studies. He says that scholarship should not, "overlook one of the most persistent and passionately held doctrines with which the Early Church had to come to terms."²³ Davies then traces the land promises in the Old Testament before continuing on to consider the Second Temple period.

One element of his Old Testament and Second Temple examination is important for our discussion. In his review of the biblical literature, Davies acknowledges the connection between the Davidic king and the restoration to the land inheritance. In his interpretation of Isa. 9:1-6 Davies says, "the kingdom of the new David implies the restored land—restored in justice and righteousness, not in its sinful form."²⁴ Given this interpretation of Isa. 9:1-6, it is surprising that Davies does not consider the kingdom of the Davidic Messiah in his analysis of the land in Paul's thought.

Turning to Paul, Davies begins with 1 Cor. 15:3-8. He argues that the failure to mention the land shows that land is irrelevant. He says, "In

19. Ibid. On this see Denton 1982: 158.
20. See Wright 2015a: 12–16.
21. Ibid.
22. Davies 1979: 4.
23. Ibid.: 5.
24. Ibid.: 43.

this central recital there is no interest at all in geography."[25] This may be special pleading. 1 Corinthians 15:3-8 also fails to mention: baptism, the Lord's Supper, and the inclusion of Gentiles apart from the Law. Few would argue that these issues are unimportant to Paul.

Nonetheless, Davies is correct that Paul does not mention the land of Israel in 1 Cor. 15:3-8. This does not mean that Paul shows no interest in geography. In 1 Cor. 15:24 Paul claims that Christ will give the kingdom to the Father after he destroys every ruler and power. Then Paul says that Christ, "must reign until he has put all his enemies under his feet. The last enemy to be destroyed is death. For 'God has put all things in subjection under his feet' (1 Cor. 15:25-27)."[26] 1 Corinthians 15:25-27 contains an undisputed quotation of Ps. 8, which reads, "What are human beings that you are mindful of them, mortals that you care for them?… You have given them dominion over the works of your hands; you have put all things under their feet" (Ps. 8:4-6). Thus, the kingdom over which Jesus reigns in 1 Cor. 15:25–27 could be taken to include all creation. In 1 Cor. 15:50, Paul promises the believers that they will inherit that kingdom. Thus, Paul does show a concern for geography in 1 Cor. 15, the geography of the entire created order. It is important to examine Davies' handling of 1 Cor. 15 because he also fails to consider the explanatory power of a worldwide inheritance in Galatians and Romans.

During his analysis of Galatians and Romans, Davies says that Paul's doctrine of justification leads him to make three conclusions: salvation is "apart from the Law," "pan-ethnic," and rooted in the promise of faith.[27] For Davies, because the Law is for life in the land, the removal of the Law also signifies the unimportance of the land.[28] According to Davies, Paul replaces being in the land with being in Christ. Davies says, "Paul had made the living Lord rather than the Torah the centre in life and in death, once he had seen in Jesus his Torah, he had in principle broken with the land."[29] According to Davies, because the land of Israel is not important,

---

25. Davies 1979: 166. Davies also notes that Paul does not mention the land in his discussion of the gifts of Israel in Rom. 9:4. However, the adoption of 9:4 seems to refer to the Exodus event which chronicles a journey to the land. The worship mentioned on Rom. 9:4 takes place in Jerusalem, which is the focal point in the land. Finally, despite his argument to the contrary, one would assume that the land is among αἱ ἐπαγγελίαι in Rom. 9:4. In other words, most of the benefits assume Israel's presence in the land.

26. All biblical quotations are from the NRSV unless otherwise noted.

27. Davies 1979: 174–5.

28. Ibid.: 179.

29. Ibid.: 220.

Paul's interpretation of the inheritance is "a-territorial."[30] Davies believes that Paul's a-territorial view of the inheritance stands in contrast to the views of Paul's opponents who believe in an actual fulfillment of the land promise. Thus, Paul's silence about the land, "points not merely to the absence of a conscious concern with it, but to his deliberate rejection of it."[31] Davies' claim that Paul's doctrine of justification and his pan-ethnic understanding of salvation entails a break with the particularism of Judaism bears a remarkable similarity to the claims Baur made over a hundred years earlier.[32]

There are five problems with this account of the land promise in Paul. First, Davies draws a connection between justification, Torah, and the land promise that Paul never makes. In the two discussions of the Abrahamic promises, Paul says: (1) the seed of Abraham is promised the world (Rom. 4:13); (2) the inheritance does not come through the Law, but through the promise (Gal. 3:18). Paul does not say that justification by faith renders the inheritance null. Secondly, Davies assumes that Paul and his opponents hold different understandings of the land, but Paul never counters their interpretation. It is difficult to imagine that Paul and his opponents could disagree on an issue as central as the land and never discuss it. Third, he claims that being "in Christ" replaces the land as the territory of Christian redemption. Davies, similar to Hammer, does not explain the relationship between believers' present status "in Christ" and their future reception of life, the resurrection, the kingdom, or the new creation (1 Cor. 15:18-22; Gal. 5:21; 6:14-16). This brings us to a fourth and fundamental problem. Davies does not make a distinction between "a-territorial" and trans-territorial. Thus, none of his insights about the land in Paul actually address a potential worldwide understanding of the land promise. This is problematic given that Paul explicitly provides a worldwide interpretation of the promise in Rom. 4:13 and refers to inheriting the kingdom in Gal. 5:21, 1 Cor. 6:9, and 15:50. Furthermore, in Rom. 15:8-12 Paul ties the resurrection of the Messiah and his worldwide rule to God's faithfulness to his promises to Abraham, Isaac, and Jacob. Davies' failure to consider Rom. 15:8-12 is particularly interesting given his earlier claim that Davidic kingship and post-exilic restoration to land are linked in Isaiah.[33] Finally, Davies does not examine the portions of Galatians that might contain references to a worldwide inheritance. He does not consider what $\kappa\lambda\eta\rho\text{o}\nu\text{o}\mu\text{ί}\alpha$ the heir of Gal. 4:1-7, who is

30. Ibid.: 179.
31. Ibid.
32. Baur 1876: 3.
33. Davies 1979: 43.

called a κύριος πάντων, stands to receive. When Davies does discuss the κληρονομία of Gal. 3:18, he says that it refers to the "the divine blessing."[34] But Davies does not articulate what this divine blessing might entail. It is possible that the "divine blessing" includes, among other things, eternal life in the worldwide kingdom of the Messiah.[35] Davies also fails to examine the connection between the inheritance language of 3:1–4:11 and the kingdom of 5:21. In fact, Davies' work does not consider the kingdom in Paul in detail at all. He only says that Paul omits the discussion of the kingdom in Romans because of political sensitivities.[36]

1.3.2. *The Spirit Replaces the Land: Two Accounts*

The most popular interpretation of the land in Galatians is that the Spirit replaces the land.[37] Therefore, we will consider two attempts to explain how Paul comes to this conclusion.[38] Hans Dieter Betz bases his claim that the Spirit replaces the land on the two ἵνα clauses of Gal. 3:14 and their relationship to what many call Paul's argument from experience in Gal. 3:1-5.[39] Betz says that Paul, "arrives at this conclusion for these reasons: the Gentile Christians did receive the Spirit (3:2, 5), and they did so "through [the] faith" (διὰ τῆς πίστεως). If this is the fulfillment of the promise God made to Abraham (3:8), the blessing which is the content of the promise must be the gift of the Spirit."[40]

---

34. Ibid.: 175.
35. Davies (ibid.: 165) cites *m. Sanh.* 11:1. He thinks that this text represents the view of Abrahamic promises and salvation held by the majority of Jews of Paul's day. It says, "All Israelites have a share in the world to come, for it is written, 'Thy people also shall all be righteous, they shall inherit the land for ever…'" One would be hard pressed to prove that Paul has a different understanding of the locale of salvation or its relationship to the Abrahamic promises. He would simply claim that this share comes through one's relationship to the Messiah Jesus.
36. Davies 1979: 178. One might be tempted to wonder why Rom. 15:12 would not be politically dangerous. There Paul says of Jesus, "The root of Jesse shall come, *the one who rises to rule the Gentiles*; in him the Gentiles shall hope" (italics added); see Wright 2013: 1304.
37. Burton 1980 [1921]: 185; Witherington 2004: 245–6, 292; Das 2014: 390; Martyn 1997: 342–3; Williams 1997: 96–7; de Boer 2011: 185.
38. I will discuss other proposals about the Spirit and the land during the exegesis of Gal. 3:1-5 and 3:14.
39. Betz 1979: 153. A similar argument is made by de Boer 2011: 214–16. See the discussion in Chapter 4.
40. Betz 1979: 153.

Betz then goes on to consider the promises in Gal. 3:15-18. According to Betz, in Gal. 3:15-18, Paul is focused on "naming the recipients" of the promises.[41] Nonetheless, when Betz interprets "the promises" that Paul refers to in Gal. 3:16, Betz makes it clear that Paul has in mind the same promises that he discusses in Gal. 3:6-14. The claim that Paul has the same promises in mind as he moves on from Gal. 3:6-14 to 3:15-18 is important because Betz defines promises differently in Gal. 3:6-14 and 3:15-18.

In Gal. 3:15-18, Betz argues that Paul believes that the singular recipient of the promises is Christ, the singular seed.[42] Given that Betz equates the promised Spirit of 3:14 with the promises of 3:15-18, Betz should maintain that the Spirit (the inheritance) is not promised to Israel, but to the singular seed, Christ.[43] However, he does not make this argument. Instead, he offers a more expansive definition of κληρονομία in Gal. 3:18. In his interpretation of Gal. 3:18, Betz defines ἡ κληρονομία, as "all the benefits of God's work of salvation."[44] This interpretation requires Paul to define the promise (inheritance) in Gal. 3:14 as the Spirit and "all the benefits of God's work of salvation" in Gal. 3:15-18.[45]

There are problems with Betz's proposal about the Spirit replacing the land that will be explored in detail during the exegetical discussion of Gal. 3:1-18. For now we can say that Betz (and many others) unhelpfully collapse(s) the blessing that comes through Abraham to the Gentiles into the blessing of the land and people that God promises to Abraham and his seed. For Betz, the gift of the Spirit fulfills all three aspects of the Abrahamic promises. I will contend that Paul does not collapse these promises. Instead, I will show that the blessing of the Gentiles is their justification by faith in the Messiah. This justification by faith makes them a part of Abraham's family (seed). Now that they are joined to this family, they stand to receive the inheritance promised to Abraham and his seed (the Messiah) in the future. This is why Paul calls them heirs whose right to the inheritance comes through their relationship to the Son (Gal. 3:26-29). Thus, for Paul, the Abrahamic promises will be fulfilled through the Galatians' participation in the Messiah Jesus's inheritance of the whole earth as the seed of Abraham and David. If my reading of

---

41. Ibid.: 157.
42. Ibid.
43. Betz (ibid.: 156) says, "For the Apostle, the promises made to Abraham are identical with the blessing of Abraham discussed in 3:6-14."
44. Ibid.: 159.
45. Ibid.

inheritance is accurate, then Spirit is the beginning, not the fullness, of this shared inheritance.

Betz's own argument implies that the Spirit functions as a down payment. He says that the κληρονομία of 3:18 includes all the benefits of salvation.[46] But if the κληρονομία of 3:18 refers to the "benefits of salvation" then the full content of the promises cannot be reduced to the Spirit in Gal. 3:14.[47]

Williams' study of the promise and the Spirit in Galatians also examines the content of the Abrahamic promises. He begins by lamenting the fact that scholars tend to consider Paul's promise passages in Galatians in isolation without considering the impact the interpretation of one passage has on another.[48] For example, he says that if scholars claim that the Spirit is the content of the Abrahamic promises in Gal. 3:8-14, they must integrate that interpretation of the promises into Gal. 3:15-29. According to Williams, this need to carry forward the interpretation from Gal. 3:8-14 is especially important because Christ is deemed the heir in Gal. 3:16 and 3:19.[49] He says, "many writers...do not satisfactorily explain what is promised to Christ, what accrues to him as beneficiary."[50] This observation leads Williams to conclude that the content of the promises must be something that is promised to three parties: Abraham, Christ, and Christians.[51] He makes this observation because Paul states that the promises were made to Christ (Gal. 3:16), Abraham (3:16), and believers (3:26-29). This insight causes Williams to ask, "What is it that God has promised to Abraham and Christ, as well as to Christians?"[52]

Williams maintains that the Spirit meets his criteria and endeavors to explain how Paul could say God promised the Spirit to Abraham, Christ, and believers. According to Williams, God promised the Spirit to Abraham when God said that he would give him numerous descendants. Numerous descendants implies the gift of the Spirit because the Spirit creates the children of Abraham.[53] He finds confirmation of this theory in Gal. 4:28-31, when Paul says that believers, like Isaac, are born of the

---

46. Ibid.: 159.
47. See again Betz's own understanding of the link between 3:14 and 3:15–18 in ibid.: 156.
48. Williams 1988: 710.
49. Ibid.
50. Ibid.: 710 n. 4.
51. Ibid.: 711.
52. Ibid.
53. Ibid.: 714.

Spirit.[54] According to Williams, the Spirit is also promised to the believer because the Spirit makes them sons and heirs.[55] Finally, Williams wonders how the Spirit could be promised to Christ. To explain the link between Christ and the Spirit, he highlights the fact that God promises Christ the world. He finds evidence for the belief that God promises Christ the world in Gal. 3:16. When interpreting Gal. 3:16, Williams says that Paul interprets Gen. 17:8 to refer to God's promise of the world to Christ, the seed of Abraham. But, for Williams, this promise of the world is a promise of the Spirit. Williams says, "as Paul reads the Abraham story, God promised the world to Abraham and to his single seed, Christ; and this promise of the world is nothing other than the promise of the Spirit."[56]

Williams then explains how God could give the dead Abraham and current believers the world through their reception of the Spirit.[57] Williams argues that in the ancient world the descendants and the progenitor were identical. Therefore, Abraham receives the world through his offspring.[58] Believers, on the other hand, receive the world because they are free from the Law or nonhuman powers that used to rule over them. In this reading, the believer is currently a lord of all through the Spirit (Gal. 4:1-2).[59]

In the final section, Williams explains that Christ receives the world and the Spirit through the conversion of the Gentiles. He says:

> I am suggesting that what God promised to Christ, the seed of Abraham, was the Spirit—not in the sense that Christ was filled with the Spirit (an emphasis of Luke), nor, probably, in the sense that it was by His Spirit that God raised Jesus from the dead. Paul does not affirm that God "supplied" the Spirit to Christ. But implicit in the argument of Galatians 3 and 4 is the apostle's conviction that the world is becoming Christ's domain because the peoples of the earth, by the miraculous power of God's Spirit, are being begotten as children of God.[60]

Williams' study of the Spirit gets some things right. First, he rightly points out that the inheritance must be something possessed in the present or future by Christ, Abraham, and believers in fulfillment of the Abrahamic

---

54. Ibid.
55. Ibid.: 716.
56. Ibid.: 717.
57. Ibid.
58. Ibid.
59. Ibid.: 718.
60. Ibid.: 719. Martyn (1997: 342–3) comes close to this when he says, "In a word, the inheritance is the church-creating Spirit of Christ."

promises. Second, Williams acknowledges that Paul believes that God promised Christ the world. Third, Williams correctly says that the Spirit plays a role in validating the believer's status as an heir. But, again, his proposal has significant deficits. In Williams' account, Paul defines the promise as the Spirit but means three different things to three different parties. To Abraham the gift of the Spirit means that his descendants would receive the world through their experience of freedom from the Law and nonhuman powers. For believers, the promised Spirit is the means by which they become sons. For Christ, the Spirit is the world that he receives as the number of converts increases. To say that Paul has so malleable a definition of promised Spirit is improbable. In addition, Paul does not claim that the world becomes Christ's domain through converts. For Paul, Christ rules over the world as the result of the resurrection (Rom. 1:3-4). Finally, Williams' claim that the believer already reigns over the world over realizes Paul's eschatology (1 Cor. 4:8; Rom. 8:17). Rather than adopting the threefold definition of the promised Spirit proposed by Williams, it is much simpler to allow "world" to refer to the worldwide inheritance of the Messiah; but a full discussion of this claim must await the exegesis of Gal. 3:1–4:7.

1.3.3. *The Land Inheritance as Salvation*

In *Paul and the Hermeneutics of Faith*, Francis Watson discusses the relationship between the land inheritance in Genesis and Paul's argument in Galatians. According to Watson, the Genesis narrative does not focus on the blessing of the Gentiles. Instead, Genesis highlights the land promised to Abraham and his seed.[61] Paul, by contrast, focuses on the Gentile blessing. Watson suggests that for Paul, rather than containing a promise of the land, Gen. 15 "confirms the gospel claim that in Christ and his Spirit God has assumed total responsibility for human salvation."[62] According to Watson, Paul uses Gen. 15:6 in Gal. 3:8-14 to argue that salvation is from beginning to end the work of God, not the Law. Therefore, the Law cannot play a role in salvation because doing the Law would involve human initiative. For Watson, faith is not a human activity. Instead, faith is humanity's means of receiving God's work on their behalf.[63]

In his interpretation of Gal. 3:15-18, Watson argues that when Paul speaks about the "promises" he is referring to the covenant promises outlined in Gen. 15:7-21. Watson acknowledges that these promises focus

---

61. Watson 2004: 193–4.
62. Ibid.: 196. See also Moo 2013: 23–31.
63. Watson 2004: 196.

on the land and offspring.[64] But when Paul refers to the inheritance and the promises, he does not mean Canaan or any physical space. Paul means salvation.[65]

Watson rightly recognizes that the Genesis texts, which form the basis of Paul's argument in Galatians, focus on the promises of the land. One would think that recognizing the focus on the land in Paul's source text would lead to an exploration of how Paul interprets the land promises. It does not. Instead, Watson maintains that all Paul cares about is human salvation. But what exactly Watson means by salvation as it relates to the argument of Galatians is not entirely clear. For example, the *TLNT* definition of salvation says that salvation (σωτηρία), "will not be complete and definitive until entrance into heaven: eternal life."[66] If Watson or others have this definition of salvation in mind, then life in heaven replaces the land promise. But Paul does not refer to a trip to heaven in his letters. Instead, Paul consistently depicts Jesus's resurrection as a rising to rule over the world as his kingdom (Rom. 1:3-4; 15:12; 1 Cor. 15:24-28; Phil. 2:6-11).[67]

The *ISBE*, by contrast, defines salvation in Pauline theology as "God's rescue of the individual from sin and judgment."[68] If Watson has this definition in mind, his proposal is still problematic because defining the inheritance as rescue from sin and judgment makes it very hard to understand how Paul could claim that the inheritance or the promises belong to Christ in Gal. 3:16 and 3:19. The statement that the promises belong to Christ is not a mere aside and must be taken seriously in the exegesis of the letter. It is precisely because the promises belong to Christ that the believer who is "in Christ" can expect to share in Christ's inheritance (Gal. 3:14, 16, 26-29). Therefore, defining the inheritance as salvation from sin and judgment requires us to say that the promise of deliverance from sin and judgment was made to Christ. But we lack evidence that Paul believes that Christ needed to be saved from sin or judgment.

---

64. Watson 2004: 197. According to Watson, it makes no difference if we choose Gen. 13:15 or Gen. 17:7-8 as the source text for Gal. 3:16.

65. Watson 2004: 202. See also Dunn 1993: 186.

66. Spicq, "σῴζω, σωτήρ, σωτηρία, σωτήριος," *TLNT* 3:350.

67. Kingdom does not occur in Rom. 1:3-4 and 15:12, but his allusion to Isa. 11:1 in Rom. 15:12 shows that Paul looks to the rise and reign of Jesus as the promised Son of David. Although Phil. 2:6-11 does not allude to a messianic text, it does highlight the universal sovereignty of the Messiah Jesus.

68. Liefeld, "Salvation," *ISBE* [revised edition] 4:293.

I agree that Paul believes that Christ's death rescues believers from sin and judgment. However, this rescue results in believers becoming heirs in Christ to the whole earth. It is believers' status as heirs because of their relationship to the heir (Christ) that stands at the center of Paul's argument (Gal. 3:16, 29; 4:7). Therefore, both salvation as life in heaven and salvation as rescue from sin is an inadequate definition of the inheritance in Galatians.

Finally, it is noteworthy that many claim that salvation is a central theme in Galatians even though Paul never refers to salvation in the letter. This demonstrates that scholars believe that a concept can be present in a letter even when the term is not. If it is possible to maintain that Paul's real intention is to speak about salvation, then we have no a priori reason to dispute the fact that Paul's inheritance language in Galatians is really about sharing in the Messiah's inheritance of the whole earth.

1.3.4. *The Affirmation of a Worldwide Land Promise*

James Hester is one of the first to dedicate an entire work to the concept of the inheritance in Paul.[69] He begins with a study of the inheritance in the Old Testament. He concludes that inheritance "is a possession, normally land, which is given to a person or persons solely because of the relationship in which they stand to the giver. Usually this relationship, legal or spiritual, is that of a child to his father."[70]

Hester then considers how Roman inheritance law might illuminate Paul's use of inheritance and heir language in Galatians and Romans. He thinks that Paul refers to the practice of naming one an "heir" through adrogatio, in which a Roman citizen, "came under the patria potestas of another Roman citizen."[71] This entitles them to inherit the entire estate. According to Hester, the estate could be divided, but the estate could not be split in regards to land and money. Instead, it could be divided into portions of the entire estate. Thus, in standard Roman practice, in a situation with multiple heirs each heir inherits a portion of the entire estate.[72]

Hester then examines the use of inheritance language in the Second Temple period. He believes that many in that period delayed the full possession of the land until the end of time.[73] He asserts that the New

---

69. Hester 1968.
70. Ibid.: 5.
71. Ibid.: 17.
72. Ibid.
73. Ibid.: 31.

Testament is unique in that the "possession of the inheritance depends on a relationship to the Heir. The inheritance to which he gives access is the Kingdom of God."[74] He notes that despite the fact that the inheritance became worldwide it did not lose its status as a physical place because, "God rules in a definite place."[75] According to Hester, the believer's sonship is linked to his or her heirship, which Christ shares with the believer. According to Hester, since Christ has the inheritance rights of the son, he can displace the inheritance of Israel.[76] He says, "all that Israel has claimed as theirs is his."[77]

Hester correctly links Paul's understanding of the inheritance to his interpretation of the Abrahamic land promise. He also rightly recognizes Paul's belief in the kingdom explains his interpretation of the Abrahamic land promise. In addition, he makes the much-neglected point that a worldwide inheritance does not make the inheritance spiritual. Finally, Hester correctly insists that the believer only inherits because of their relationship to Christ.

However, Hester's work contains various problems. First, Hester divides the sonship of Christ and the inheritance rights he has as Son from the inheritance promised to Abraham and Israel. Paul draws these together in his Davidic and Abrahamic interpretation of Gal. 3:16. Furthermore, in Galatians Paul does not present the people of Israel in possession of an inheritance which Christ then takes by displacing the nation. Instead, Paul claims that the nation is under the curse that precludes their reception of the inheritance until the death of Jesus redeems them from the curse. This redemption from the curse allows believing Jews and Gentiles to become heirs to the eschatological reception of the inheritance. Hester's failure to note Paul's identification of Jesus with the plight of Israel for the sake of Israel's redemption renders his account of the inheritance in Paul untenable.

Forman also considers the topic of the land inheritance with a focus on Romans (although he does include a chapter on Galatians). Forman rightly notes that most scholarship on inheritance in Paul unhelpfully identifies the heir with the inheritance itself.[78] Put differently, most assume that:

74. Ibid.: 36–7.
75. Ibid.: viii.
76. Ibid.: 37.
77. Ibid.: 38.
78. Forman 2011: 4.

> What was typically understood in biblical and post-biblical tradition to refer to the land of Israel and to the inheritors of the land is now transmuted by Paul into a reference to individual Christians and their relationship to Christ.[79]

Forman laments the faulty deduction "that since Paul's inheritance is non-territorial, inasmuch as it is not tied to one specific tract of terrain, it is therefore also necessarily non-material or spiritual in reference."[80] This assumption that non-territorial equals a spiritualization plagues scholarship on the inheritance in Galatians.

In his analysis of Galatians, Forman highlights the striking parallels between Rom. 4 and Gal. 3. According to him, both rely on Gen. 15, 17, and 18.[81] Both argue that God planned to bring about a worldwide family through faith, not Torah. Regarding the content of the inheritance, he says, "while Paul can refer to inheriting 'the world' in Rom. 4:13, the concept is never referred to in such this-worldly terms in Galatians."[82]

According to Forman, the absence of a "this-worldly" definition of the inheritance leads many to conclude that Paul does not care about the land promises. However, Forman again astutely notes that Galatians focuses on who the inheritors are and not what the inheritance is. According to Forman, Paul's focus on the identity of the heirs leads some to contend that Paul gave no thought to the content of the inheritance.[83]

Although Forman acknowledges that a worldwide inheritance is not the focus of Paul's argument, he believes that Paul displays a belief in a worldwide understanding of the inheritance in Gal. 4:1-7. Forman suggests that designating the heir of Gal. 4:1-2 as κύριος πάντων implies that Paul believes that the heir is entitled to the whole world.[84]

According to Forman, Paul comes to believe that the Christian would possess the world because of the numerous progeny promised to Abraham. For Forman, a large family entails a worldwide fulfillment of the Abrahamic land promise.[85] Put simply, Abraham's offspring would need the space.[86]

---

79. Ibid.
80. Ibid.: 6.
81. Ibid.: 172.
82. Ibid.: 174.
83. Ibid.
84. Ibid.: 180, following the argument of Scott 1992.
85. Forman 2011: 182.
86. Ibid.: 182.

Forman concludes his consideration of the land in Galatians with an analysis of Gal. 3:26-29. He argues that Paul negates the divisions present in Jewish and Greco-Romans society for those in Christ. Thus, the kingdom of Christ functions differently than the kingdom of Rome.[87]

Forman's work correctly points out Paul's worldwide understanding of the land inheritance and the importance of kingdom. This will be important for our later argument. But his basis for a worldwide understanding of the Abrahamic land promise is flawed. Forman bases his claim about the worldwide understanding of the land promise on the large number of children who would make up Abraham's family. I contend that in Galatians the worldwide understanding of the inheritance is rooted in the idea that God promised the Davidic Messiah the world as his inheritance. It is what Paul believes about the kingdom, not the number of converts, that leads to his worldwide interpretation of the land promise.

Rodrigo Morales argues that Old Testament prophetic literature, which connects the gift of the Spirit with the restoration of Israel to the land, helps explain the role of the Spirit in Galatians.[88] Morales' work is pertinent to Paul's understanding of the land promise because he highlights the importance of texts that predict the restoration of Israel to the land. Morales supports his claim that the Spirit is linked to the restoration by showing the various ways in which authors associate the Spirit with the restoration and transformation of the people of Israel in Old Testament and Second Temple documents.

Turning to Galatians, Morales argues that Gal. 3:10-14 focuses on the curses that befell Israel because of her disobedience to the covenant. Christ's death, then, redeems the nation from the covenant curses and enables the justification of Jews and Gentiles by faith. According to Morales, the gift of the Spirit by faith proves that those who believe are participating in the beginning of the restoration promised in Isaiah and Ezekiel without having to do the works of the Law.[89] Morales maintains that Paul differs from other Second Temple Jews in that, "he interprets this curse as more fundamentally about death than about exile, and restoration as resurrection and new creation rather than a nationalistic return of the tribes to the land of Israel."[90]

---

87. Ibid.: 189–91.
88. Morales 2010: 4.
89. Ibid.: 79.
90. Ibid.

By interpreting the curse of Gal. 3:10-14 as a reference to the national curses, Morales adopts and modifies the proposals of James Scott and N.T. Wright.[91] He agrees with both that the curse in Galatians refers to curses on the nation as a whole. He disagrees with Wright that the fundamental image of that curse is exile. Instead, he suggests that the central punishment of the Deuteronomic curses is death.

While a full analysis of Morale's argument will be undertaken in Chapter 4, this much can be said here: Morales's work is helpful because he argues for a national focus in Gal. 3:10-14. But my work goes beyond and modifies his proposals in the following ways: (1) I show that Second Temple texts that focus on the final realization of the land promises through royal figures are a better source of comparison with Paul's argument in Galatians than texts that simply refer to the restoration of Israel; (2) I demonstrate that attending to the messianic shape of Paul's argument suggests that Paul does not abandon the land inheritance; he expands it to include the peoples and territories of the world; (3) I argue that Morales' claim that, because Paul speaks about death and resurrection, he is not speaking about exile and restoration creates an unnecessary division between overlapping concepts.

Johnson Hodge differs from Morales in how she explains the relationship between the Holy Spirit and the Abrahamic promises. Nonetheless, she agrees that the inheritance has been expanded to include the whole earth. This expansion of the inheritance merits her consideration here.

In *If Sons, Then Heirs* she challenges the notion that the early Christians abandoned the ethnic particularity of Judaism for a more universal form of religion. Instead, she maintains that Paul's gospel announces that Gentiles can be included into the family of Abraham through baptism and Spirit reception. According to Johnson Hodge, Paul justifies his advocacy for Gentile inclusion by invoking the story of God's call to Abraham. She says that for Paul the claim that God would bless the Gentiles in Gen. 12:3 refers to their inclusion in the people of God. Therefore, rather than denying kinship, particularity, and ethnicity, these factors are key components of Paul's gospel.[92] Furthermore, Johnson Hodge counters the assertion that Paul's account of Gentile kinship is fictive. She argues that all kinship is socially constructed. This insight allows her to claim that Paul's account of Gentile inclusion is just as real for him as those who

---

91. Ibid.: 92. See Wright 1992a: 144–8 and more recently Wright 2013: 863–8; Scott 1993: 645–5.

92. Johnson Hodge 2007: 4–5.

laud their biological relationship to Abraham.[93] She supports her thesis by demonstrating that both Jewish and non-Jewish authors construct kinship relationships to legitimate individuals or groups.[94]

To explain how God adopts Gentiles into his family, Johnson Hodge highlights the role of the Spirit. Johnson Hodge argues that many Jewish and Greco Roman authors believed that the pneuma was a material substance. For Paul, then, the Spirit is the "binding agent which unites gentiles to Christ."[95] Furthermore, "the spirit serves as a version of 'shared blood' in that it provides a tangible organic connection between Christ and the Gentiles."[96] Finally, in her account of Spirit reception she also highlights the relevant biblical texts that might inform Paul's portrayal of the Spirit, including Isa. 11:2-3 and Ezek. 36:26-28.[97] According to Johnson Hodge, the Gentiles new-found status as sons and heirs of Abraham entitles them to the whole earth.[98] She says, "Paul interprets the promise of land to Abraham and his descendants or seed…as a promise of the whole world."[99]

As it pertains to the question of the inheritance, Johnson Hodge supports the worldwide interpretation of the Abrahamic inheritance. She also rightly recognizes the importance of Paul's adoption metaphor for interpreting the timing of the inheritance. She grants that Pauline adoption (especially in Galatians) refers to obtaining the status of heir, not the reception of the inheritance.

Despite these places of agreement, my interpretation of Galatians diverges from the one offered by Johnson Hodge at various points. First, Johnson Hodge does not highlight the role that the Deuteronomic curses play in the argument of the letter. I contend that the problem for Paul is not simply that Gentiles need to be adopted into Abraham's family to become heirs to the inheritance. The inheritance itself cannot be received until Christ removes the curses that stand in the way of Abraham's seed

---

93. Ibid.: 15–17.
94. Ibid.: 19–42.
95. Ibid.: 75.
96. Ibid.: 76.
97. Ibid.: 72–3. She also maintains that Paul may have been influenced by the Roman and Jewish belief that the pneuma consisted of physical matter. Paul, then, would be arguing that Christ's own material Spirit resides in Gentiles and makes them heirs. See ibid.: 73–6.
98. Ibid.: 70.
99. Ibid.: 70.

receiving the inheritance.¹⁰⁰ Secondly, Paul does not simply draw on a Jewish tradition of Abrahamic inheritance of the world. Instead, Paul speaks of the Messiah's inheritance of the world and sees that inheritance of the world as the fulfillment of the promises made to Abraham. It is the linking of the Davidic and Abrahamic traditions that allows Paul to put forward a worldwide interpretation of the inheritance in Galatians. Third, by claiming that Gentile reception of the Spirit materially links them to Abraham, it becomes unclear how the Spirit benefits those who can already claim such a relationship. Stated differently, why would Jewish converts who could already claim a relationship to Abraham need to receive the Spirit? Finally, this book highlights the role that royal and messianic figures play in the final realization of the land promises in Galatians and other Second Temple texts, a theme that does not figure prominently in her work.¹⁰¹

Matthew Theissen sets out to examine Paul's solution to the Gentile problem. However, similar to Johnson Hodge, he makes comments on the inheritance that are relevant to this volume. The Gentile problem, as he defines it, refers to the fact that the covenant limits its blessings to Abraham's seed. Since Gentiles are not Abraham's seed, they are excluded from sharing in the blessings that God promised to Abraham. According to Theissen, various Second Temple authors propose different methods by which Gentiles can share in what God promised to Abraham's seed.

Theissen argues that Paul finds fault with Gentiles for trying to solve the Gentile problem by keeping commandments that are not meant for them.¹⁰² He argues Paul believes that certain laws are for Jews and others are for Gentiles.¹⁰³ Thus, Paul does believe that Jews and Gentiles should keep the Law, but keeping the Law means different things to different groups. Thus, for Thiessen, Paul does not criticize Jewish obedience to the Law or Judaism more broadly.¹⁰⁴ Instead, Paul offers a fresh account of how Gentiles can be included within the story of Israel without keeping the laws reserved for the Jewish people.¹⁰⁵

---

100. See the discussion of Gal. 3:10-14 in Chapter 4. See also the discussion of Gal. 4:3 in Chapter 5, where I argue that Paul's reliance on Deut. 27–29 sheds important light on the στοιχεῖα τοῦ κόσμου.

101. Johnson Hodge does note that Paul interprets texts messianically in a few places. See, for example, Johnson Hodge 2007: 90.

102. Theissen 2016: 9–10.

103. Ibid.: 10.

104. Ibid.: 12.

105. Ibid.

Paul's opponents, by contrast, argue that Gentiles must be circumcised to become a part of Abraham's seed.[106] Theissen argues that Paul believes that it is impossible for Gentiles to become Jews because "Jewishness was inherent, genealogical, and impermeable to penetration by non-Jews."[107] Instead of making the Gentiles into Jews, circumcision and wider Torah obedience would make them like Ishmael. He was circumcised, but was still outside of the covenant.[108]

If keeping the Law cannot make the gentiles Abraham's seed, then what does Paul suggest that they do? Building on the work of Johnson Hodge, Theissen argues that the reception of the Spirit through faith suffices to make the Gentiles heirs of Abraham.[109] To explain how faith leads to Spirit reception he cites the example of Philo, who says that Abraham receives the Spirit because of his trust in God.[110] Therefore, Paul does not merely rely upon the experience of the Galatians in 3:1-5. He evokes a common Jewish tradition that links Spirit reception to faith. Theissen writes, "faith leads to the reception of Christ's pneuma. Having received the pneuma of Christ, gentiles are incorporated into Christ Jesus, who is the singular seed of Abraham. For Paul, the reception of the pneuma materially relates Gentiles to Abraham."[111] This material relationship to Abraham makes the gentiles heirs to the world.[112] This Spirit reception also involves a real transformation that deals with the problematic reality that Gentiles are Gentiles.[113]

This still leaves unresolved the question of how the Spirit relates to the Abrahamic promises because the Abrahamic promises do not specifically mention the Spirit. Theissen solves this problem by an intriguing reading of Gen. 15:1-5. He says that when Paul refers to Christ as the promised seed in Gal. 3:16, Paul alludes to the narrative recounted in Gen. 15:1-5. In Gen. 15, God tells Abraham that his seed will inherit. Paul then links Gen. 15:1-5 with 2 Sam. 7:12 and thereby gives a messianic reading of seed.[114] Therefore Christ is the seed who will inherit and those who are joined to Christ through sharing his spirit are co-heirs.

---

106. Ibid.: 26–7.
107. Ibid.: 100.
108. Ibid.: 88.
109. Ibid.: 105–6.
110. Ibid.: 109. See also his discussion of the much later Mekhilta de Rabbi Ishmael.
111. Theissen 2016: 15.
112. Ibid.: 16.
113. Ibid.: 118.
114. Ibid.: 125–6.

Next Theissen relates the pneuma of Christ to the Abrahamic promises by turning his attention to prediction that Abraham's offspring would be as numerous as the stars in Gen. 15 and 22. He makes three points. First, some Second Temple authors interpret the reference to stars in Gen. 15 and 22 as a description of the quality and not simply the number of Abrahamic offspring. Stated differently, Abraham's seed would be like stars, not only as numerous as stars. Second, people in Paul's day associated the stars with divine beings. Third, Paul can therefore claim that because the Abrahamic promises say that Abraham's seed will be like stars, it is possible to read this promise as a promise of the Spirit.[115] This gift of the Spirit divinizes the Gentiles and makes them rulers over the earth in fulfillment of the promises to Abraham.[116]

Theissen offers an intriguing reading of Galatians and Romans. The full examination of his work would go beyond our focus on the inheritance. Nevertheless, I will highlight areas of agreement, then I consider his account of Spirit reception in Paul's thought. I will conclude by examining his explanation of why Paul expands the inheritance to encompass the whole earth.

First, the points of agreement. I agree that Paul thinks that faith and Spirit reception make the Gentiles seeds and sons of Abraham. I also agree that this status as seed and son entitles the Galatians to the Abrahamic inheritance expanded to include the whole earth. Theissen and I concur that the scholarly consensus surrounding the inheritance is incorrect.

I begin my critique by looking at Theissen's explanation of the relationship between the Spirt and the Abrahamic promises. Theissen's account of the Spirit's role in Paul's interpretation of the Abrahamic promises is unconvincing. It is unconvincing because Theissen does not seriously consider the account of the Spirit's role in the restoration of Israel to the inheritance in biblical and Second Temple texts. Building upon the work of Morales and others, I argue that many Second Temple and biblical texts associate the reception of the Spirit with the restoration of the people to the inheritance after the covenant curses outlined in Deut. 27–29 are over.[117] Many of these texts associate the reception of the Spirit with the moral transformation of those being restored. Therefore, Paul could associate the reception of the Spirit with the Abrahamic promises because he believes that biblical texts say that God will pour his Spirit upon Abraham's descendants after the curses are over. Since the Galatians

---

115. Ibid.: 135.
116. Ibid.: 138–9.
117. See the discussion of Morales above and the fuller analysis in Chapter 4.

have received the Spirit they must be a part of Abraham's seed, otherwise their reception of the Spirit would be impossible to explain. This reading of the link between Spirit reception and the covenant curses has the advantage of linking Paul's interpretation of the death of Jesus in Gal. 3:10-14 (it dealt was the problem of the Deuteronomic curses) to Paul's account of eschatological Spirit reception.

Theissen's explanation of the expansion of the inheritance could also be improved. Theissen puts forward two explanations for the expansion of the inheritance to encompass the world. First, he says that Paul relies upon a Jewish tradition that expands the inheritance to the whole earth. Then he says that the likening of the Abrahamic seed to the stars suggests their sovereignty over creation. However, Paul's messianic interpretation of seed in Gal. 3:16 points to a different solution. Paul can claim that Jesus is the Abrahamic seed because he believes that, as the seed of David, the inheritance belongs to Jesus as Messiah. Therefore, both seed and inheritance must be understood messianically. I argue that, based upon Ps. 2:7-8 and other biblical texts, Paul believes that Christ is entitled to the peoples and territories of the earth as his kingdom.[118] Therefore, Paul expands the inheritance because believers stand to share in the messianic inheritance of Jesus the seed of David and Abraham.

Oren Martin studied the land theme throughout the Bible. After tracing this theme as it develops in the canon, he concludes that, "the land and its blessings find their fulfillment in the new heaven and new earth won by Christ."[119] Although his study of Paul was brief, he maintains that Paul's theology of the kingdom is similar to much of the rest of the New Testament. He claims that the New Testament as a whole argues that "God's kingdom has finally arrived in the person and finished work of Jesus, through whom blessings for the nations come. Yet the fulfilment takes place in a surprising way, for God's saving promises are inaugurated but not yet consummated."[120]

Martin claims that Paul's extension of the land promise arises from his reading of Gen. 26:3-4 and 22:17, which Paul believes points to the eschatological fulfillment of the Abrahamic promises.[121] Regarding Paul's inheritance language, Martin says, "an important link is forged, then, between inheritance, the Promised land, and the Kingdom of God."[122]

---

118. See the discussion in Chapter 5.
119. Martin 2015: 17.
120. Ibid.: 54.
121. Ibid.: 134–5.
122. Ibid.: 137.

Despite some basic points of agreement, there are three significant differences between my work and that of Martin. First, I highlight the importance of Jesus's removal of the national covenant curses that stood in the way of the final realization of the land promises. Second, I show that Paul's belief that Jesus is the Messiah strongly influences his worldwide interpretation of the land promise. Third, Martin bases his argument on a biblical theology of the land, not a close reading of Galatians.

Similar to Martin, Beale believes that Jesus's resurrection "establishes the inaugurated end-time new-creational kingdom."[123] According to Beale, Paul's claim that the believer has risen with the Messiah supports the idea that the believer is experiencing an anticipation of the new creation as kingdom.[124] Beale also observes a link between resurrection and inheritance in Galatians. He notes that Galatians is the only text that opens with a mention of a resurrection in the first verse.[125] He also discerns a reference to resurrection in the letter's concluding discussion of new creation. Therefore, according to Beale, Galatians opens and closes with the hope of the eschatological fulfillment of the land promise as new creation.

Beale also addresses the role of the Spirit in Galatians. According to Beale, the Spirit begins life in the new creation. Beale believes that Paul could link the Spirit to the new creation and the land because "the fruit of the Spirit" is "a general allusion to the OT promise that the Spirit will bring about abundant fertility in the coming new age."[126]

My research goes beyond Beale by linking the removal of the covenant curse through the death of Christ in Gal. 3:1-14 to the final realization of the inheritance as kingdom. Thus, my work links the central section of the letter to the question of land and kingdom. In addition, I show that enabling the final realization of the inheritance promise should be seen as a messianic act because Second Temple messianic figures are often associated with the final realization of the land promises.

1.3.5. *Paul and the Land in Galatians: Conclusion*

This review of the history of the land question in Galatians has revealed a few tendencies. First, scholars tend to assume that Paul's break with either Judaism or the Law renders the question of the land inheritance moot.

---

123. Beale 2011: 249.
124. Ibid.: 252.
125. Ibid.: 275. He also notes the mention of resurrection in Rom. 1:4. I do not think that the verse distinctions are relevant, but he is correct to observe that both these texts open with a mention of resurrection that establishes the importance of resurrection throughout the letter.
126. Ibid.: 305.

Second, even when there is evidence that a worldwide understanding of the land promise might be in view, scholars assert that Paul cannot mean what his words clearly indicate.[127] Instead, they assume that Paul spiritualizes the Abrahamic land promise. Third, advocates of the "Spirit replaces the land" view run into difficulty when they try to apply that view to the three groups promised an inheritance in Galatians: Abraham, Christ, and believers. Finally, advocates of a worldwide understanding of the land promise focus on Paul's kingdom and inheritance language in Galatians and elsewhere in the Pauline corpus. However, each of these proposals for a worldwide interpretation of the land promise suffers from reconstructions of Paul's argument that are flawed.

My work will provide fresh support for a worldwide understanding of the inheritance in Galatians by substantiating the following insights. By presenting the cross as the solution to the covenant curses Paul links the death of Jesus to the final realization of the Abrahamic land promise because the covenant curses alluded to in Galatians focus on the loss of the inheritance (Deut. 27–29).[128] To remove the curses, then, is to begin the final realization of the promised inheritance. This link between the curse and inheritance has not been a feature of previous discussions of Paul and the land. Therefore, it represents a step forward in our understanding of Paul's interpretation of the land promises. Second, this link between the death of Jesus and the final realization of the inheritance is significant because one of the main responsibilities of a Davidic Messiah in the Second Temple period is to enable the final realization of the land promises during the course of his reign.[129] Therefore, by arguing that Jesus's death deals with the problem of the covenant curses, and makes the Galatians heirs to the inheritance, Paul says that Jesus's death accomplishes what the reign of messiahs are supposed to achieve. Jesus's death enables the fulfillment of God's promises through participation in Jesus's messianic inheritance or kingdom. This insight is significant because it clarifies exactly what is messianic about the death of Jesus. For Paul, Jesus's death is royal because it brings about the inheritance or kingdom, which Christ shares with those who believe. Third, Paul's messianic reading of seed in Gal. 3:16 and 3:19 carries with it a messianic reading of the inheritance. In other words, Paul's statement that God promised the inheritance to Christ must be taken seriously. What is it that belongs to

---

127. See Davies 1979, who does not discuss Paul's kingdom language, his inheritance language in Galatians, or Rom. 4:13 during his analysis of the land promise.
128. See Chapter 4 for the defense of the link between the end of the curses and the final realization of the land promise.
129. On the link between the Messiah and the land, see Chapters 2 and 3.

Christ as the promised seed?[130] The best answer to that question is that the whole earth belongs to Christ as the promised seed and Son (Ps. 2:7-8). Fourth, Paul's heir and inheritance language in the latter portions of the letter suggests that he believes that the Spirit only partially realizes the promised inheritance. According to Paul, the inheritance will be experienced in full when the Galatians inherit the kingdom alongside their king (Gal. 3:26–4:11; 5:21).[131]

1.4. History of Research on Pauline Messianism and the Land Inheritance in Galatians

1.4.1. Davidic Messiahs, Royal Figures, and the Basis for Comparison

Our review of research on the Abrahamic land promises in Galatians revealed the tendency to claim that Paul spiritualizes or abandons the land promises. We also noted that a few scholars counter this prevailing view by asserting that the land promises will be fulfilled through participation in Jesus's kingdom. Given its potential explanatory power, why is the worldwide kingdom of the Davidic Messiah largely ignored as an answer to the question about the land? The kingdom is rarely evoked because the place of Davidic messianism in the argument of Galatians is itself contested. Stated differently, many do not believe that the worldwide kingdom of the Messiah is a viable interpretation of the Abrahamic land promise because they do not believe that messiahship is a significant element of Paul's thought in Galatians or elsewhere. In rebuttal, I contend that Paul's claims about Jesus and his worldwide inheritance reveals the messianic shape of his argument.

Pauline scholars who affirm messianism in Galatians believe that Galatians is messianic precisely because Paul believes that Jesus has enabled the believer to share in the Messiah's inheritance of the whole world as his kingdom. The consistency of this claim about the kingdom has been lost amidst assertions that Second Temple messianic portrayals are so diverse that there is no set script for a Messiah to follow.[132] However, Paul's claim (that Jesus has enabled the final realization of the land promises) represents the central point of agreement between Pauline

---

130. Williams 1988: 719 says that Gal. 3:19 "raises a question that no exegete should avoid: What, in Paul's view, was promised to Christ?"

131. For the analysis of Paul's heir and inheritance language, see Chapter 5.

132. For the claim that there is no script for the Messiah to follow, see Green 1987: 1–14. See also the recent review of the history of the question in Novenson 2012: 12–63.

and Second Temple depictions of royal figures.[133] This point of consensus is that a primary agenda item for a royal or messianic figure is to enable the final realization of the land promises. Therefore, while it is true that messianic portrayals in the Second Temple are diverse, it is also accurate to say that Paul and many Second Temple authors agreed that if a Messiah were to come that would mean that the land promises are finally being fulfilled through participation in the Messiah's kingdom.

When I use the language of "royal figures" I coin a phrase that may help us move beyond an impasse in current debates. A royal figure, as I use the phrase, refers to an individual described in a Second Temple text who assumes leadership over Israel. I also set two criteria for discerning whether a royal figure qualifies as a Davidic Messiah. To qualify as a Messiah: (1) the author who describes the individual must refer to a biblical text or motif that is linked to a descendant of David; (2) we must have some evidence that the author believes that the individual was a descendant of David. Thus, a Davidic Messiah is a subset of a larger group of royal figures whom authors present as potential leaders of Israel.

Why make such a distinction and how does it further our understanding of Paul, messianism, and the land in Galatians? Making the distinction between royal figures and messiahs is important because it allows us to observe that to designate someone a Messiah is in effect to call them a king or ruler. To make a claim about rule places "messiahs" alongside other claimants for the position of rule over Israel. These potential leaders, be they a Davidic Messiah or another royal figure, often restore Israel to the land as a part of their rule.

Furthermore, when we examine the depictions of royal figures it quickly becomes clear that Second Temple authors are more than willing to use biblical texts that refer to descendants of David even when the royal figure in question makes no claim to Davidic descent.[134] Nonetheless, authors present these royal figures as God's means of establishing his people in the land. Authors who appropriate these Davidic texts are claiming that what God promised to do through a descendant of David will in fact happen through someone else. This appropriation of Davidic texts does not negate the importance of Davidic messianism. It highlights the ongoing influence of these biblical texts when referring to potential leaders of Israel. Given these appropriations of Davidic texts, it is no surprise that Paul, who does believe Jesus is a descendant of David, would make similar claims about Jesus and the land as kingdom.

---

133. In Chapters 2 and 3, I show that we do have evidence that other Second Temple authors did associate royal figures with the realization of the land promise.

134. See the discussion of 1 Macc. 14:6-14.

This is not a claim that all Second Temple authors interpret these biblical texts in the same manner. It is a claim that in their accounts of royal figures (or messiahs) these royal figures usually restore Israel to the land. Our proposal about the relationship between royal figures and the final realization of the land promises can be presented visually as follows:

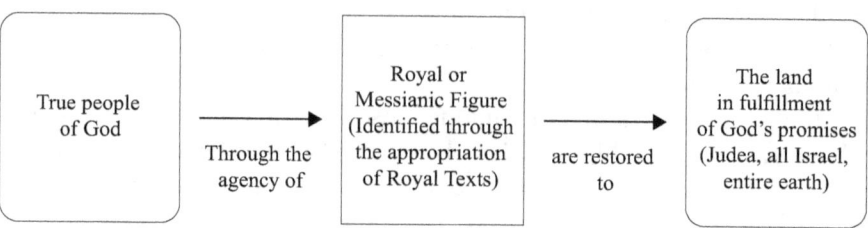

Fig. 1. *The Relationship Between Royal Figures and the Final Realization of the Land Promises*

We will see in later chapters that the scope of the land and the identity of those being restored could vary. Nonetheless, the link between royal figures and the final realization of the land promises is a stable feature of Second Temple discourse about royal and messianic figures. Therefore, the claim that Galatians is messianic because it looks to the final realization of the land promise as kingdom has good Second Temple support.

1.4.2. *Early Scholarship on Paul and Jewish Messianism in Galatians*

I begin our discussion of Paul, messianism, and the land by considering four scholars from the second half of the twentieth century: Rudolf Bultmann, W.D. Davies, Lucien Cerfaux, and Nils Dahl. I begin there because, before them, the influence of the *Religionsgeschichtliche Schule* led many to assume that land and messianism were Jewish ideas and therefore non-Pauline.[135] The work of Bultmann functions as a starting point because it contains an account of the lack of messianism in Paul that reflects the consensus of preceding era. I turn to Davies because his work represents a serious attempt to place Paul's thought within a recognizably Jewish context. Since this book also seeks to place Pauline messianism in the context of Second Temple messianism, his work is particularly pertinent. Lucien Cerfaux serves as an example of a scholar who affirms the link between messianism, kingdom, and the Abrahamic promises, but does so without sufficient exegetical rigor or serious engagement with Galatians. His work will highlight the need for a close

---

135. For a full discussion, see Novenson 2012: 13–19.

reading of Galatians that examines the link between Paul's messianism and his interpretation of the Abrahamic promises. We conclude this section with a discussion of Nils Dahl who has been rightly recognized as one of the most influential scholars of Pauline and Jewish messianism. During our analysis of Dahl we will observe that while many affirm his philological insights about Christ becoming a second name, few follow Dahl in claiming that messianism informs much of Paul's theology. Dahl's claim that Paul looks to the worldwide kingdom of the messiah provides supports the interpretation of the land promises offered in this volume. Dahl's work provides us with strong warrants for comparing Pauline and Jewish messianism. Following our discussion of this early generation of scholars, we will consider more recent work on Pauline messianism.

W.D. Davies. W.D. Davies attempts to locate Paul within the world of Rabbinic Judaism.[136] This leads him to consider a variety of Pauline themes in light of what he deems to be rabbinic parallels. This focus on rabbinic parallels enables him to conclude that Davidic messianism and the kingdom are central elements of Paul's theology.[137] To explain the lack of explicit mentions of the kingdom, Davies suggests that Paul abandons kingdom language because of political considerations. Although he believes that Paul avoids kingdom language, Davies argues that Paul keeps the theological substructure of Jewish messianism.[138] According to Davies, instead of the language of kingdom, Paul describes the kingdom as the new creation or new age. Davies says that by using new creation language, "Paul...was using terms familiar to Judaism."[139] Put differently, for a Jewish audience kingdom and new creation are two ways of describing the physical locale over which the Messiah would reign.

According to Davies, the experience of exile causes the Jewish people to look beyond the curses of the Deuteronomic covenant. Second Temple Jews realize that Israel's problem is not that they are disobedient to the covenant. Their problem is that they are in Adam.[140] Thus, the reversal of the covenant curses involves a new start to creation at the time of the messianic kingdom.[141] For Davies, to proclaim Jesus is the Messiah entails the belief that creation itself is being transformed. He suggests that Paul

136. Davies 1980 [1948]: 1–16.
137. Ibid.: 39.
138. Ibid.: 36–7.
139. Ibid.: 37.
140. Ibid.: 38–9.
141. Ibid.: 37–41.

adds Jesus's status as the second Adam to the Second Temple and early Christian belief in the new creation. Therefore, Christ enables the birth of the new people who would live in the new creation.[142]

Davies also ties the messianic age to the end of the Law. He says that Paul holds a view present in Rabbinic Judaism, which maintains that the coming of the Messiah would lead to a new Law.[143] Thus, Paul's belief about Jesus's status as the Messiah leads to Paul's belief about the Law.

Now for an assessment. Davies' reconstruction of Pauline messianism rightly takes Paul's claim that Jesus is the fulfillment of God's promises seriously. He also observes that even when Paul is not using the language of kingdom (for example in his discussion of new creation) the concept of the messianic kingdom can still be present. Furthermore, he aptly locates the ultimate problem with Deuteronomic curses in human sin. His work, however, has at least three major problems. First, it is strange that Davies affirms the importance of messianism and kingdom in his study of Paul and rabbinic Judaism, but not in his analysis of the gospel and the land.[144] Second, I am less confident than Davies that a majority of Jews reflected on the Deuteronomic curses and as a result came to believe in a Messiah whose coming would mean a new creation. Finally, his claim that the coming of the Messiah entails the end of the Law does not have support in contemporary primary texts. What scholars reject in Davies' account, then, is not the idea of a kingdom, but the assumption that the kingdom means the end of the Law.[145]

Lucien Cerfaux. Lucien Cerfaux also locates Paul within Second Temple Judaism. We can see the break with the *Religionsgeschichtliche Schule* when Cerfaux asserts that "the traditions of Jerusalem have molded his [Paul's] expression of faith."[146] According to Cerfaux, the resurrection begins the reign of Christ. His second coming will bring judgment and those who survive that judgment will enter the kingdom. Cerfaux's work links resurrection, παρουσία, and kingdom.[147] To support this union, he points to the royal connotations inherent in the idea of a παρουσία. Cerfaux maintains that authors associate παρουσία with the arrival of royal figures after triumphant battles.[148] Speaking of being with Christ at

---

142. Ibid.: 36–57.
143. Ibid.: 72–3. See also Bruce 1982: 176.
144. See the discussion above.
145. See Sanders 1977: 479–80.
146. Cerfaux 1962: 8.
147. Ibid.: 31–2.
148. Ibid.: 32–3.

his παρουσία, he says, "to be with Christ, to take part in his procession, to receive the honour of being made judges of men with him and his angels...obviously attaches some importance to the idea of reigning with Christ."[149] For Cerfaux, being with Christ in his kingdom is at the center of the community of faith. He says, "the followers of Jesus were the very men to whom the kingdom of God belonged."[150]

Turing to Galatians, Cerfaux ties justification to membership in Abraham's family. He says that believers are heirs to the promise made to Abraham and his seed, Christ.[151] According to Cerfaux, this heirship entitles the Galatians to the world.[152]

Cerfaux's work has its flaws. First, his analysis of Galatians is rather terse and superficial. Second, he does not tie Paul's understanding of the land promise to Davidic messianism or a worldwide kingdom. Nonetheless, the elements of a relationship between land and kingdom are present in his proposals about Pauline messianism. He maintains that Pauline messianism highlights Jesus's status as king and that believing Gentiles are heirs to the world.

Nils Dahl. The work of Nils Dahl had a tremendous impact on the study of Pauline messianism. Therefore, it warrants extended discussion. In an influential work on Pauline messianism, Dahl makes two seemingly contradictory claims. First, he says that, "Paul's Christology can be stated almost without referring to the messiahship of Jesus."[153] Then he claims that Jesus's messiahship is "crucial in the life of the one time persecutor and later apostle."[154] To substantiate these proposals, he examines these contradictions from three different angles: the philological, the historical, and the theological. His main point in the philological section is to prove that by Paul's time *Christos* has become a proper name.[155]

---

149. Ibid.: 44.
150. Ibid.: 67.
151. Ibid.: 213.
152. Ibid.: 214. He cites Rom. 4:13, which he believes is a development of Paul argument in Galatians. Cerfaux prefers Paul's argument in Romans because Paul makes his case "without the grammatical exegesis which is in any case not an integral part of his reasoning." I will argue the opposite. Paul's claim about the singular inheritance of the Messiah is crucial to his argument about Jesus's inheritance of the world as the seed of David and Abraham.
153. Dahl 1974: 37.
154. Ibid.
155. Ibid. Novenson 2012 answers the philological claims in a way that many find decisive. See the discussion below.

His philological analysis leads to his historical insights. For Dahl, Paul represents a "strikingly advanced stage in the evolution that transformed *Christos* from a messianic designation to Jesus' proper name."[156] Thus, in Paul's letters Christ does not mean Messiah. Dahl, however, makes a further historical point that is rarely appreciated. He says, "we must reckon with the probability that the messiahship of Jesus had for Paul a greater significance than emerges directly from the usage of the name 'Christ' in his epistles."[157] Thus, for Dahl, the importance of the title *Christos* and the significance of messianism in Paul's thought are separate questions. Most scholarship on *Christos* follows Dahl in dismissing the importance of *Christos*, but many do not follow him in arguing that messianic ideas play a significant role in Paul's theology.

A further clarification of Dahl's language is needed. When Dahl refers to Paul's belief in the messiahship of Jesus, he is not speaking about Jewish messianic expectations. Instead, he believes that, "what provides the content of the word Christ in Paul is…the pre-Pauline Christology of the church."[158] Therefore, according to Dahl, Paul's messianism is not Jewish because it is a form of Christian messianism. His distinction between Jewish and Christian messianism will be considered below.

After considering the philological and historical questions, Dahl turns to Paul's theology. It is in his analysis of theology that Pauline messianism surfaces. He maintains that Paul's theological understanding

> is complicated because Jesus' messiahship is not a dogmatic element which can be isolated from Paul's total Christology. To say that Christ is 'God's Son' is to say much more than 'Jesus is the Messiah.' Nevertheless, Jesus' divine sonship includes his messianic office.[159]

According to Dahl, Jesus's messianic office is actually contained within the designation *kyrios* which, when read in light of Ps. 110, "implies that he is the messianic sovereign at God's right hand."[160] Therefore when Paul calls Jesus "Lord" he has in mind the same thing that the early Jewish Christians have in mind when they call him "Christ." He says that *kyrios* is "an appropriate rendering of 'Messiah' because 'Christos' had no special connotations in Greek."[161] According to Dahl, then, it is precisely

---

156. Dahl 1974: 41.
157. Ibid.
158. Ibid.: 42 (italics added).
159. Ibid.: 43.
160. Ibid.: 44.
161. Ibid.

at the point of Jesus's universal sovereignty over creation that the Jewish and Hellenistic Christianity meet in agreement.[162] Thus, despite the fact that Paul does not use *Christos* to denote Jesus's status as Messiah, the messiahship of Jesus informs all of Paul's theology, including the fact that "the ones who believe in him are the 'saints' of the end of time, the ekklesia of God, the true children of Abraham, and therefore the Israel of God."[163] This status as children of Abraham makes them heirs of the whole earth. Dahl says, "Paul endorses an exegetical tradition from Jewish eschatology. But unlike his Jewish predecessors, Paul does not hope for political power in an earthly kingdom. For Paul, the promise guarantees participation in Christ's universal sovereignty."[164] This claim is partially correct. Paul does expand the inheritance to include the whole earth, but I fail to see how sharing in Jesus's sovereignty over creation is not earthly or political. What else is Jesus sovereign over other than the earth? The exercise of sovereignty is a political act, especially when Paul says that Jesus sovereignty replaces powers that previously exercised a detrimental rule over the earth (1 Cor. 15:24-26). Thus, Paul does look to a coming worldwide kingdom over which Jesus exercises a real authority.

So what are we to make of Dahl's philological, historical, and theological analysis? First, Novenson's recent critique of the philological aspect of Dahl argument seems persuasive.[165] He has shown that Paul's use of *Christos* should be understood as an honorific along the lines of Caesar Augustus.[166] Thus, Dahl's dismissal of the continuing lexical importance of *Christos* is mistaken. Second, in Pauline scholarship many of the theological and historical claims that Dahl made have been neglected. Various scholars follow Dahl in maintaining that *Christos* became a proper name. Few follow Dahl in asserting that Jesus's messiahship informs all of Paul's theologizing. Third, Dahl's claim that Jewish and Hellenistic forms of Christianity agree about the kingdom negates the assertion that messianism is not an important feature of Paul's theology.

This shared emphasis on kingdom in the so-called Hellenistic and Jewish strands of early Christianity leads to a series of a crucial insights. First, Dahl correctly says that Hellenistic and Jewish Christians affirm Jesus's status as the messianic sovereign who rules over the world. Second, he rightly notes that this same messiahship leads to Christians being called the children of Abraham who will inherit the kingdom.

162. Ibid.
163. Ibid.: 45.
164. Dahl 1977: 130.
165. Novenson 2012: 98–137.
166. See the discussion of Novenson 2012 below.

Therefore, we can compare Paul's claim about the kingdom of the Messiah Jesus to other kingdoms brought about by royal and messianic figures in Second Temple literature. Thus, Dahl is incorrect when he claims that Paul's understanding of messiahship is completely determined by Christian messianism because the early Christians are not unique in their affirmations of messianic kingdoms. Instead, kingdom is a point of contact between Jewish, Pauline, and early Christian messianism.

1.4.3. *Recent Scholarship on Paul and Jewish Messianism in Galatians*

This section reviews recent scholarship in messianism in Pauline scholarship with particular attention to Galatians. Examining all the research on Pauline messianism would be impossible in the space provided. Instead of a comprehensive review, I chose the following scholars because their work provides us with a basic introduction to the state of the discussion.

I include N.T. Wright because he has consistently argued that messianism is a central feature of Pauline theology. Although I do not follow him in arguing that all (or most) Second Temple Jews work within a similar narrative of Israel's history, I do maintain that we can compare the accomplishments of other Second Temple royal figures to Paul's presentation of the accomplishments of Jesus in Galatians. I review Richard Horsley because his work reflects an attempt to interpret Paul's affirmation of Jesus's messianic identity in light of the propaganda of Roman Empire. He maintains that Pauline messianism and its proclamation about a worldwide kingdom of the Messiah counters the worldwide vision put forward by Caesar and his supporters. The import of this proposal for our interpretation of the inheritance in Galatians should be clear. James Scott's work merits consideration because he argues that Paul's adoption metaphor in Gal. 4:1-7 relies upon a messianic interpretation of 2 Sam. 7:12-14 that was prominent in Paul's day. This interpretation said that God would adopt Israel and its Messiah at the time of the second Exodus to the land. Although I differ with him at numerous points, his proposal about the importance of the Davidic covenant to the argument of Galatians justifies its inclusion. Matthew Novenson presents a strong argument that *Christos* functions as an honorific and not a mere second name in Pauline texts. His challenge to the scholarly consensus about the importance of messianism in Pauline thought contains insights that bolster the proposal in this book. Richard Hays' interest in Paul as an interpreter of Scripture led to an increased appreciation of the importance of Jewish messianism in Pauline theology. Joshua Jipp's recent work on the influence of royal concepts in Pauline theology warrants his inclusion. I conclude with J.L. Martyn because his account of Pauline apocalyptic theology disputes the presence of messianic ideas in Galatians. Instead, he believes that Paul's opponents include messianism as a significant element of *their* theology.

N.T. Wright. N.T. Wright has long claimed that Paul's theology remains in basic continuity with Jewish and early Christian messianism.[167] Wright proposes two central theses about messiahship in Paul. First, he suggests that Χριστός referred to Jesus's status as the Messiah.[168] Second, he asserts that Jesus's messiahship is central to Paul's thought.[169] While it may seem that these two statements are identical, they are not. It is possible to claim that Χριστός became a second name for Jesus and that his status as Israel's Messiah is nonetheless central to his theology. Nils Dahl takes just this position.[170] My concern is not the philological question of whether Χριστός denotes messiahship.[171] Instead, I am examining the role that Jesus's status as Messiah plays in Paul's understanding of the land inheritance as the worldwide kingdom. On the topic of kingdom, Wright has had plenty to say.

According to Wright, Paul believes that Jesus is the figure described in the Royal Psalms as the Davidic ruler and inheritor of the ends of the earth (Pss. 2; 8; 89; 110; 2 Sam. 7:12-14).[172] According to Wright, this messiahship of Jesus is incorporative. When he describes Jesus's messiahship as incorporative, he means two things. First, incorporative refers to the fact that "the people of God and the Messiah of God" are so inextricably linked that "what was true of the one was true of the other."[173] Second, it means that "those who believed the Gospel, whether Jew or Greek, were likewise to be seen as incorporated into him and thus defined by him, specifically again by his death and resurrection."[174]

He maintains that Paul comes to these conclusions about the incorporative nature of Jesus's messiahship after a fresh reading of Israel's Scripture in light of Jesus's death and resurrection. This rereading allows

---

167. For other recent affirmations of Pauline messianism, see Collins and Collins 2008; Willitts 2012a; Jipp 2015.

168. Wright 1992b: 407–9; Wright 2013: 817–51, and most recently in Wright 2015b: 1–20.

169. See Wright 2013: 817–51.

170. Dahl 1974: 37. See also Dahl 1992: 392.

171. However, recent scholarship has shown that Wright is correct on this point. See Novenson 2012 and more recently Jipp 2015.

172. Wright 2013: 817–20.

173. Ibid.: 826.

174. Ibid.

Paul to discern the hints of incorporation in the stories of Abraham and Adam.[175] Wright points to the incorporative idea in royal depictions in Israel's Scriptures. He puts forward the representative role of the king in fighting on behalf of Israel's enemies in the David versus Goliath narrative. Then he looks to the concept of Israel having an inheritance in David (2 Sam. 20:1).[176] Wright no longer claims that Paul's understanding of corporate messiahship arises from these texts. Instead, these texts testify to the close relationship between the fate of the people and the fate of the king in biblical texts.[177]

More fundamental to Wright's understanding of Jewish messianism are what he describes as Second Temple retellings of Israel's story.[178] According to Wright, despite the diversity of these retellings, there are some elements of Israel's scriptural story that reappear. One feature of these retellings is the appearance of a Messiah figure who would bring Israel's history to its long-awaited climax.[179] Wright says that this is the role that Jesus plays in the theology of the Apostle Paul.[180]

Wright's proposal about Pauline messianism contains the kingdom motif that we have highlighted throughout. For Wright, Jesus is the Messiah in part because he rules over the world in fulfillment of texts such as Ps. 2:7-8. He also makes a claim about the Second Temple narrations of Israel's story that can be proven or disproven by recourse to the texts themselves. Are there coherent Second Temple tellings of Israel's story that seem similar to the story Paul tells about Jesus?

Scholars usually offer two responses to his claim about the role of Israel's story in Paul: (1) Wright assumes a universal reading of the Jewish story that ignores the diversity of thought indicative of the period;[181] (2) these Second Temple narrations of Israel's stories exist, but Paul does not tell the story of Israel in a coherent way in his letters.[182] One way to improve upon Wright's claim is by not focusing on the retelling of Israel's story, but on Second Temple accounts of the accomplishments of royal figures themselves. Whether or not we deem Galatians to be a story that

---

175. Ibid.: 828.
176. Wright 1992a: 46–7.
177. Wright 2013: 829–30.
178. Ibid.: 121–39.
179. Ibid.: 138.
180. Ibid.
181. See Barclay 2015a: 238. Wright, however, acknowledges the diversity of thought that characterized this period. See Wright 2013: 140–79.
182. See the various proposals on narrative in Pauline Theology in Longenecker 2002.

we can compare with other Second Temple stories, we can compare the accomplishments of Jesus in Galatians with other Second Temple depictions of the accomplishments of royal figures.

Richard Horsley. Horsley considers messianism from a different angle. He argues that while the historical Jesus was a leader of a renewal movement in Israel,[183] Paul led a counter-imperial movement that lauded the Lord Jesus as the world's true ruler and savior, not Caesar.[184] Horsley, in making this claim, places Jesus at the climax of Israel's history. He says, "Paul is asserting that history has been working not primarily through Rome, but through Israel, and the fulfilment of history has now come about in the fulfilment of the promise to Abraham."[185] Thus, according to Horsley, when Paul talks about the fulfillment of the Abrahamic promises he is positing Jesus as the worldwide king whose kingdom opposes the Roman Empire. Horsley believes that Paul travelled around forming egalitarian societies which await the return of the lord and the establishment of his worldwide rule.[186] This rule would prove the emptiness of the imperial promises.

James Scott. James Scott addresses the question of messianism when he discusses how Paul uses the adoption metaphor in Galatians and Romans.[187] According to Scott, Paul's adoption metaphor draws on a tradition evident in biblical and Second Temple texts. This tradition says that God will adopt Israel at the time of the second Exodus. Scott maintains that this divine adoption nationalizes the covenant God made with David in 2 Sam. 7:14.[188] This interpretation of the adoption metaphor is related to the relationship between the inheritance and Davidic Messianism because it makes Jesus's identity as the Davidic king central to a key image (adoption) in Galatians. According to Scott, if Jesus's status as the Davidic son makes Christ the heir, and the believers derive their sonship from Christ, then the inheritance given and shared is the inheritance that belongs to the king.

183. Horsley 1997: 1.
184. Ibid.: 6–7. See also the collection of essays in Horsley 2000. These essays focus on anti-imperial resonances in Paul's letters. However, in the course of calling attention to these resonances these essays often affirm the importance of messianism in Paul's writings. For example, see Elliott 2000: 22–3.
185. Horsley 1997: 7.
186. Ibid.: 8.
187. Scott 1992.
188. Ibid.: 96–117.

Scott is broadly correct about the link between Jesus's status as Messiah and the believer's hope to inherit alongside him. My work goes beyond and differs from Scott in that (1) I offer a different reading of Gal. 4:1-7; (2) his work focuses on the theme of adoption in Gal. 4:1-7 and only secondarily considers the link between messiahship and inheritance; (3) I demonstrate the link between Jesus's messiahship and inheritance throughout Gal. 3:1–4:7.[189]

Matthew Novenson. In his work on Pauline and Second Temple messianism, Novenson discerns a contradiction. On the one hand, scholars assert that Messiah does not have a particular meaning in the Second Temple period, and on the other, many insist that Messiah "cannot have meant whatever it is that 'messiah' did not mean."[190] To explain how this contradiction arose, he reviews the history of scholarship on Pauline messianism. He shows that scholars are right to be suspicious of a broadly agreed upon and excessively scripted form of Second Temple messianism. According to Novenson, this insight does not disprove the existence of Jewish messianism. Novenson says that these scholars believe that they proved, "that ancient messiah language was entirely indeterminate; it did not mean anything. What they have in fact shown is that the extant messiah texts from the period do not warrant any form of the older idealist paradigm of the messianic idea in Judaism."[191]

He believes that much of the confusion arises because many do not distinguish between "messiah language," that is, words used to describe a Messiah, "messianic hope," which he uses to refer to the widespread hope for a Messiah, and "social messianic movements," a label he uses to denote groups organized around a messianic figure.[192] According to Novenson, "it does not matter how many Jews were looking for the coming of the messiah; what matters is that members of the linguistic community were able to understand what was meant when someone talked about a messiah."[193] He concludes, "messiah language could be used meaningfully in antiquity because it was deployed in the context of a linguistic community whose members shared a stock of common linguistic resources."[194]

---

189. See also the more extensive interaction with Scott in Chapter 5.
190. Novenson 2012: 2. On the denials of a coherent Second Temple messianism, see Neusner 1987 and Oegema 1998a.
191. Novenson 2012: 41.
192. Ibid.: 43.
193. Ibid.: 43–4.
194. Ibid.: 47.

One of these linguistic resources was the Jewish Scriptures.[195] Although he argues that there are no messiahs in the Old Testament, "some Jewish authors of the Hellenistic and Roman periods evidently thought there were."[196] When these Jewish writers turn to biblical texts to describe the Messiah, they do not limit themselves to texts that contain the word Messiah. Instead, they prefer texts that "promise, either in oracular or in visionary form…an indigenous ruler for the Jewish people."[197] These authors use these biblical texts to protest the political realities of their day.[198] Novenson relies on the diversity of Jewish portrayals to argue that Paul's messianism is one among many portrayals of the Messiah in the Second Temple period.

Next Novenson shows that Paul's letters should be viewed as a manifestation of Second Temple messianism. He does this by considering the philological arguments used to suggest that by the time Paul began writing his letters Χριστός has become a second name. He disproves the second name theory by demonstrating that, for Paul, Χριστός functions as an honorific similar to those given to Hellenistic kings such as Augustus Caesar.[199] Then he disputes the assumption that the importance of Paul's use of Messiah language can be determined by examining the meaning of individual phrases such as "In Christ," "the Lord Jesus Christ," or "Christ Jesus."[200] Here he quotes Barr who says, "the linguistic bearer of the theological statement is usually the sentence and the still larger literary complex and not the word or the morphological and syntactical mechanisms."[201] Thus, discerning the importance of Messiah language is impossible apart from a wider analysis of the major themes and arguments in a given piece of writing.

What are we to make of Novenson's argument? His work helpfully demonstrates that Paul's use of Messiah language relies upon Jewish Scriptures and should be seen as a manifestation of Second Temple messianism. He is also correct to claim that there is not a single form of Jewish messianism shared by all Jews of the period. Nonetheless, his assertions about the diversity of messianic portrayals do not sufficiently explore areas of agreement. Although there is nothing about a Messiah that one had to say, there are certain features of messianic portrayals that

195. Ibid.: 47–8.
196. Ibid.: 52–3.
197. Ibid.: 58.
198. Ibid.: 61.
199. Ibid.: 87–96.
200. Ibid.: 98–136.
201. Novenson 2012: 135, quoting Barr 1961: 279.

figure prominently. One of those prominent features of Second Temple messianism, a feature which advocates of Pauline messianism have pointed to again and again, is the belief that the Messiah would rule over a kingdom. Although the size of this kingdom and its place in the scheme of eschatological events varied, participation in the kingdom brought into being through the Messiah's agency is a regular feature of Second Temple messianism.

Richard Hays. Richard Hays does not set out to explore Jewish messianism. In his *Echoes of Scripture in the Letters of Paul,* he is attempting to reinvigorate interest in Paul as an interpreter of Israel's Scripture. His emphasis on Paul as an interpreter of Jewish Scriptures is important to the study of Pauline messianism because his emphasis on the Jewish Scriptures raises the following question:

> How does the story of Jesus fit into the wider story of Israel, the story of election and promise told in the Old Testament? This question is of urgent importance for the interpretation of Galatians, a letter in which Paul was engaged in fervent debate with Jewish Christian missionaries who places the Jesus story within the story of Israel in a way that Paul regarded as disastrous.[202]

According to Hays, Jesus plays the role of the Davidic Messiah. He says, "Paul finds in Scripture the story of Israel a prefiguration of the story of Jesus the Messiah and of the church that he brings into being, 'the Israel of God (Gal. 6:16).'"[203] This assumption of messianism by those who emphasize the importance of Paul's use of Scripture is commonplace.[204] For example, Keesmaat, speaking of Rom. 8:14-26, says, "the inheritance for which they wait is that which was promised to Israel; and the image to which they are to be conformed is that of Jesus, the messiah of Israel."[205] Ciampa, speaking of Paul's use of Father–Christ imagery in Galatians, says that both, "have their foundations in the Scriptures and biblical traditions of Israel. Both were eschatologically oriented concepts in Second Temple Judaism… Paul clearly expects his reference to 'Christ' to be understood in light of a whole series of Jewish-Christian

---

202. Hays 2002: xxxv.
203. Ibid.: xxxviii. This is a different understanding of the issue than the one he presents in Hays 1989: 84–6.
204. See Keesmaat 1999; Ciampa 1998; Scott 1992; Harmon 2010; Novakovic 2014. None of these works are about messianism, but at various points in their arguments they assume or rely upon messianic concepts.
205. Keesmaat 1999: 151.

interpretive traditions."[206] It is important that many of these authors did not set out to prove that Jesus is the Messiah. This conclusion arises from their comparison of Paul's use of Scripture with that of other Second Temple Jews. Their work highlights the fact that the extent to which we agree that Jewish messianism influences Paul's thought depends in part on the type of thinker we perceive Paul to be. Those who highlight his continuity with Second Temple Judaism, as it pertains to his use of the Jewish Scriptures, tend to highlight the importance of messianism. Those who believe that Paul's use of Scripture in Galatians is the result of his attempts to fight off the claims of his opponents, tend to downplay Jewish messianism.[207]

Joshua Jipp. Joshua Jipp examines how Paul "creatively transforms the responsibilities, traits, and titles commonly understood to belong to kings and applies them to Jesus."[208] When Jipp refers to the responsibilities of kings, he has in mind both Greco-Roman and Jewish conceptions.[209] According to Jipp, the kingship of Jesus is a mix of Jewish and Hellenistic ideas.[210] This claim that Paul mixes Hellenistic and Jewish conceptions of kingship is important because it challenges the common assumption that Paul's encounter with Hellenistic Christianity means that messiahship ceases to be a viable category of thought. A turn towards Hellenistic categories need not entail a turn away from kingship. His work follows Novenson in not positing a singular understanding of messiahship, but his aim is broader. He wants to show that Paul says the types of things about Jesus that were said about kings in Greco-Roman and Jewish sources.[211] Although my comparison focuses on Second Temple presentations of royal and messianic figures, there is some methodological overlap with the approach adopted by Jipp.[212] I do not claim that all Second Temple Royal figures enabled the final realization of the land promises as kingdom, but many did. Therefore, Paul's claim that Jesus has enabled the final realization of the Abrahamic land promise as a worldwide kingdom fits within the spectrum of the things one could say about a Messiah.

---

206. Ciampa 1998: 39. He goes on to suggest that this tradition includes a belief that Jesus restores believing Israel to its inheritance. See Ciampa 1998: 271–4.
207. Hays 2014: 203–4.
208. Jipp 2015: 7.
209. Ibid.: 9.
210. I grant that separating Jewish from Hellenistic ideas in the Second Temple period is anachronistic. Paul is a man of both worlds. See Wright 2013: Part I.
211. Jipp 2015: 9.
212. I adopted this approach before encountering his work.

One of the elements of "royal discourse" that Jipp discerns in Paul's letters is the kingdom. According to Jipp, Paul did not "develop or integrate the concept into his letters in a creative or rigorous way."[213] Nonetheless, he believes that kingdom is present. Jipp claims that the concept of kingdom is present in places where Paul says that the believer would share in Christ's rule.[214] Jipp also maintains that:

> the royal benefits…include: sharing in the Son's sonship, sharing in the πνεῦμα of Christ, sharing in the Messiah's resurrection and glorified state, sharing in the Messiah's worldwide inheritance, and reigning with the Messiah over god's enemies by sharing in his lordship.[215]

Jipp's affirmation of a worldwide and messianic inheritance is helpful. However, my work differs from Jipp's analysis in four ways. First, his claims about the worldwide kingdom of the Messiah focuses on Romans.[216] In fact, his section on kingship, kingdom, and inheritance contains no serious analysis of Galatians.[217] This neglect of Galatians is surprising given the themes he outlines above: (1) sharing in Christ's Sonship (4:4-7); (2) sharing in Christ's inheritance (3:16, 18, 26–29; 4:1-7); (3) kingdom (5:21); and (4) sharing in his Spirit (4:4-7) are all present in Galatians.[218] Second, Jipp does not consider Second Temple depictions of royal figures, who enable the final realization of the inheritance. This comparison is a central feature of my project. Third, Jipp does not link the end of the covenant curses, which stood in the way of the realization of the land promises, to the establishment of the Messiah's kingdom (Gal. 3:13).[219] Most importantly, Jipp does not appreciate the fact that Paul's interpretation of the inheritance in Galatians is shaped by his belief that Jesus is the seed of Abraham and David (Gal. 3:16). If Paul's interpretation of the inheritance is shaped by his messianic beliefs, then Jipp's assertion that Paul does not integrate the kingdom into his letters in a "creative or rigorous way" is mistaken.[220]

---

213. Jipp 2015: 139.

214. Jipp (ibid.: 140–8) locates the shared rule in 1 Cor. 3:21-23; 4:8-9; 6:2-3, 9-11; 15:20-28, 50-58; 2 Cor. 1:21-22; Col. 1:15-20; Phil. 2:6-11. See also Rom. 5:17, where believers share in the reign [βασιλεύω] of righteousness through Christ.

215. Ibid.: 149–50.

216. Ibid.: 167–96.

217. For example, he mentions Gal. 4:4-5 to affirm Christ's sonship in Jipp 2015: 170. His other uses of Galatians are equally terse. See ibid.: 140, 172, 188.

218. Ibid.: 149–50.

219. See the discussion of Gal. 3:10-14 in Chapter 4.

220. Jipp 2015: 139.

J.L. Martyn. Summing up all those who oppose Pauline Messianism in Galatians is difficult because messianism is not simply denied—it is largely ignored. Here again I will simply note the consensus that messianism had ceased to be important to Paul.[221] Martyn's work, however, provides an entry point for this denial of messianism because Jewish messianism figures prominently in his reconstruction of Paul's opponents' views.

Martyn's discussion of messianism differs from other approaches. Scholars usually trace how messianic ideas develop from their Jewish roots on through to the transformation of Jewish messianism by the early church. They conclude by looking at the remnant of Christian messianism in Paul's letters. According to Martyn, this method is flawed. Instead of tracing the development of ideas as we move from Jewish to Hellenistic Christianity, we must recognize that the "ruling polarity is rather the cosmic antinomy of God's apocalyptic act in Christ versus religion, and this gospel versus religious tradition."[222]

For Martyn, scholars have been wrong to look for particular reasons why Paul opposes the Jewish Law. Martyn believes Paul's problem with the Law is that it is a religion, an attempt to liberate oneself from the enslaving power of the cosmos.[223] Thus, when the apocalypse of Christ makes it plain to Paul that religion (in his case Judaism) could not save, Paul abandons Judaism to preach Christ crucified. This abandonment of Judaism includes rejecting messianism.

According to Martyn, Paul's opponents do not abandon messianism or the Law. Martyn says they present Jesus as:

> the Law-observant, Law-confirming Messiah whose death as a martyr was the event in which God set things right by forgiving all sins previously committed by God's people Israel. They could then invite Gentiles to enter this forgiven people, trusting that their future forgiveness would ensue from their faith in Jesus, the Messiah, and from their observance of the Law, as ratified by him.[224]

Although Martyn reconstructs Paul's theology differently than Baur, his assertion that Paul abandons messianism is rooted in the same reasoning. Martyn shows his similarity to Baur by saying that Paul rejects Torah and messianism when he renounces the religion of his youth.[225] Further-

221. Lee 2016: 375.
222. Martyn 1997: 37.
223. Ibid.: 38.
224. Ibid.: 89–90.
225. For Martyn 1997: 38, this rejection is not unique to Judaism, but religion as a means of approaching God.

more, Paul's rejection of Judaism becomes the basis of the universalism of his gospel. Finally, in both Baur and Martyn we can discern a form of mirror reading in which whatever is affirmed by Paul's opponents (in this case messianism) is rejected by Paul. Martyn's reading of Galatians, by its very nature, screens out life in the worldwide kingdom of the Messiah as the inheritance that awaits the believer because the "apocalypse" of Christ eliminates all forms of religion, including Jewish hopes for the worldwide kingdom of Messiah.

1.5. Conclusion of Chapter 1

Current trends in Pauline interpretation show that the influence of Jewish messianism on Paul's interpretation of the inheritance is still very much contested and in need of further research. Novenson's work helpfully points out that there is no form of messianism that could claim to be held everywhere by all, but such an observation does not render all claims concerning Pauline messianism void. Granting this diversity, it is still possible to maintain that Paul's theology contains elements of Jewish messianism that were held by other authors of his day, including Jewish-Christians. One of these shared beliefs is the idea that the Davidic Messiah would enable the final realization of the land inheritance through participation in his kingdom.

In Chapters 2 and 3, I show that there is nothing unique in Paul's adjustment of the land to encompass the world. The meaning of the "land" or "kingdom" is flexible. Thus, with the caveats about the perils of parallels in place, whether or not royal figures are associated with the establishment of the people of God in the land is an answerable question.[226] We can answer the question of whether royal and messianic figures restore Israel to the inheritance promised to them by comparing the claims Second Temple authors make about other royal and messianic figures to the claims Paul makes about Jesus in Galatians.

Space will preclude a discussion of all royal figures in the Second Temple period, but an examination of the eight texts included in this project should be sufficient to establish the fact that Paul's claim about the kingdom of the Messiah Jesus would have been understood in the Second Temple period.

---

226. See Sandmel 1962: 1–13.

Chapter 2

Royal Figures, Davidic Messiahs, and the Land as Kingdom in the Pseudepigrapha

2.1. *Introduction*

This chapter shows that Second Temple authors regularly associate royal and messianic figures with the final realization of the land promises. The connection between royal figures and the final realization of the land promises is demonstrated through the examination of portions of four texts: *Pss. Sol.* 17; *2 Bar.* 29–30; 35–40; 72–74; *4 Ezra* 11:37–12:1; 12:31-34; 13:3-13; 13:25-53; and 1 Macc. 2:49-70; 13:41; 14:4-14. Although the scope of the recovered territory varies (sometimes Judea, in other cases the whole earth), the link between royal figures and the final realization of the land promises is a stable feature of Second Temple discourse. Therefore, Paul's assertion that the Messiah Jesus has enabled believing Jews and Gentiles to share in his eschatological inheritance of the whole earth as Son and Messiah should be seen as a recognizably messianic or royal claim.

Again, in this project, when an author uses a biblical text that refers to a native ruler of Israel when describing a character in his composition, I refer to the individual so described as a "royal figure." In this project, a Davidic Messiah is a subset of this larger group. When an author implies that a royal figure is actually of Davidic descent, I refer to that person as a Davidic Messiah. For our purposes, it is important that both the larger category of royal figures and the smaller category of Davidic Messiahs are associated with the final realization of the land promises in Second Temple texts.

I should offer an additional clarification of the phrase, "the final realization of the land promises." I use this phrase to separate my discussion from the more common language of "restoration." Restoration often implies the recovery of what was lost. Since, in many cases, the "restoration" of Israel transcends the boundaries of the original land promise, it seems more accurate to describe the restoration as a final realization of the promises.

2.1.1. Method

For each text, I examine the historical context in which it was composed. Then I consider the biblical texts that are used in the depiction of the royal or messianic figure. I show that these authors use the Jewish scriptures to depict royal and messianic figures as God's means of bringing about the final realization of the land promises. In my consideration of the link between messianism and realization, I also count evocations of the new Exodus as evidence of the link between royal figures and the land inheritance. Evocations of the Exodus are important because the new Exodus often culminates in a new reception of inheritance. Therefore, evocations of the Exodus are another way of speaking about the final realization of the land promises. In each section I also ask whether the recovered territory encompasses the land of Israel or if the land is expanded to include the whole earth. Finally, I highlight occasions when the author directly links the final realization of the land promise to the Abrahamic promises. Direct mentions of Abraham in these texts are not necessary to establish the validity of my proposal. Nonetheless, pointing out allusions to the Abrahamic promises will support my proposal that linking the fulfillment of the Abrahamic promises to the agency of the Messiah, as Paul does in Galatians, would not be unique.

This book focuses on Second Temple and Pauline allusions to biblical texts. This is controversial because scholars continue to debate the import of allusions, citations, and echoes in Second Temple and Pauline writings.[1] Space precludes a full discussion of this controversy here, but a brief discussion and defense of my use of this feature of Pauline and Second Temple texts is in order.

Many contend that those who rely upon allusions to biblical texts to bolster exegetical insights on Pauline theology claim more than they can possibly substantiate to the satisfaction of the wider guild.[2] This criticism in some cases may be well founded.[3] However, other than noting

---

1. Foster (2015) argues that the scholars who identify subtle echoes and then claim that those echoes form the foundation of central Pauline themes usually lack sufficient lexical evidence to support their assertions. Stanley (1999: 124–44; 2004: 38–61) argues that Paul's Gentile audience would not have recognized allusions to biblical material because the low literacy rate of the congregation and a lack of knowledge of the biblical texts. For a response to the argument of Stanley, see Abasciano 2007. See the discussion of Foster below. It is interesting to note that there is much less criticism when locating allusions and citations in other Second Temple texts than Pauline texts.

2. Foster 2015. See also Das (2016) whose work focuses on Galatians.

3. See Foster 2015: 102–4.

the presence of allusions and citations, my approach is different from previous examinations of allusions in Second Temple texts. While I note the presence of allusions in Second Temple texts, my strongest evidence is not the presence of these allusions, but the direct words of the Second Temple authors. Therefore, the method adopted in this book is not same as those criticized by Foster and others.[4] For example, in *2 Bar.* 73:1-6, even if one doubts the influence of Isa. 9 and 11 on that text, the author's own words state that the anointed one will exercise a worldwide rule. I do not use Isa. 9 and 11 to prove that *2 Bar.* 73:1-6 believes in a worldwide rule for the Davidic king. The author says as much. Isaiah 9 and 11 explain why *2 Bar.* 73:1-6 makes the claim that it does and why *2 Baruch* uses the language that it does when it makes that claim. This is true of most of the Second Temple Texts under consideration. They say that Davidic and royal figures enable the final realization of the land promises. Their use of Scripture shows that they tend to draw on Davidic texts when they want to talk about royal figures. Therefore, when Paul makes similar assertions in Galatians while also drawing on similar texts, we have reason to believe that authors are drawing similar meanings from those texts. Finally, almost all the allusions to biblical texts under discussion in Gal. 3:1–4:7 are widely recognized. The question, for the most part, is not whether those texts are present in Galatians; the debate in Galatians focuses on the import of the texts Paul uses. Therefore, Gal. 3:1–4:7 demands that all exegetes give an account of Paul's use of Scripture in this section of the letter.

2.2. *Psalm of Solomon 17*

2.2.1. *Introduction*

The author of *Psalm of Solomon* 17 writes this work in response to Pompey's invasion and sack of Jerusalem in 63 BC.[5] A dispute between Hyrcanus II and his brother Aristobulus II over who would be high priest caused this invasion.[6] The author of *Pss. Sol.* 17 (hereafter called the Solomonic psalmist) opposes Hasmonean rule, but feels that Pompey brought excessive suffering upon the people (*Pss. Sol.* 17:11-18). This

---

4. Foster's main complaint seems to be the presence of echoes, not allusion and citation. None of my arguments about the link between Second Temple royal figures and the final realization of the Abrahamic land promises hinge on the recognition of an echo.
5. See Oegema 1998a: 105; Collins 2010: 53; Atkinson 2004: 135.
6. Sanders 1992: 28–33.

suffering leads the author to predict the coming of the Davidic Messiah who would liberate the people and the land. Many recognize that *Pss. Sol.* 17 is a pivotal text for understanding Second Temple Davidic messianism.[7] Pomykala states, "Pss. Sol. 17 provides the most extensive description of an expected Davidic king and his kingdom, and therefore merits detailed attention."[8]

2.2.2. The Messiah and the Land Inheritance in Psalm of Solomon 17

In this discussion of the connection between the land and the Davidic Messiah, I highlight three occasions in which the author ties Davidic messianism to the final realization of the land promises. First, the Solomonic author models his psalm on Ps. 43 [44 MT]. The reliance upon Ps. 43 is important because in Ps. 43 the biblical author calls upon God to be faithful to his covenant promises by rising up to save his people. In *Pss. Sol.* 17, however, the author calls upon God to be faithful to his covenant promises by raising up a descendant of David who would enable the final realization of the land promises. Second, the author uses Ezek. 47:21 to predict that the king would personally distribute the tribes in the land. Finally, the author alludes to Jer. 37:8 LXX when he claims that the Davidic Messiah would lead a new Exodus to the inheritance.

Psalm of Solomon 17 contains a variety of thematic and lexical links with Ps. 43 LXX that reveal the author's reliance on that psalm as a structuring device. This reliance upon Ps. 43 is evident from the beginning. The opening focus on the kingship of YHWH in *Pss. Sol.* 17 corresponds to the focus on kingship in Ps. 43:

Pss. Sol. 17:1	Κύριε, σὺ αὐτὸς βασιλεὺς ἡμῶν εἰς τὸν αἰῶνα καὶ ἔτι ὅτι ἐν σοί, ὁ θεός, καυχήσεται ἡ ψυχὴ ἡμῶν[9]
Ps. 43:5	σὺ εἶ αὐτὸς ὁ βασιλεύς μου καὶ ὁ θεός μου ὁ ἐντελλόμενος τὰς σωτηρίας Ιακωβ[10]

This lexical overlap is not the only link. An analysis of the thematic correspondences between the biblical psalm and *Pss. Sol.* 17 shows that the author of *Pss. Sol.* 17 takes the key themes of Ps. 43 and incorporates

---

7. Collins and Collins 2008: 45–6; Charlesworth 1987: 236. Duling (1973: 68) calls *Pss. Sol.* 17 "the locus classicus for Pre-Christian expectation of the Son of David."

8. Pomykala 1995: 159.

9. All LXX Greek citations come from Rahlfs and Hanhart 2006 unless otherwise noted.

10. Atkinson 2001: 329.

2. Royal Figures, Davidic Messiahs   51

them into his work. Again, this use of Ps. 43 is relevant to the question of the link between the Messiah and the land because both Ps. 43 and *Pss. Sol.* 17 climax with an expression of hope for the restoration to the land.

First, I will outline the major themes in Ps. 43 and then highlight the reappearance of those same themes in *Pss. Sol.* 17. Psalm 43 recalls God's role in Israel's conquest of the land. It reads:

> O God, we heard with our ears; our fathers reported to us a deed which you wrought in their days, in days of old: your hand destroyed nations, and them you planted [καταφυτεύειν]; you distressed peoples, and cast them out; for not by their own sword did they inherit land, and their own arm did not save them; rather, your right hand and your arm, and the illumination of your countenance, because you delighted in them. (Ps. 43:1-3 LXX)[11]

Psalm 43 lauds God's planting [καταφυτεύειν] of the nation and the removal of her enemies. With God's help, Israel beats down those who rise up [τοὺς ἐπανιστανομένους] against them (Ps. 43:6).

The biblical psalmist follows his review of Israel's glorious past by recounting Israel's present suffering (Ps. 43:9-16). Despite this suffering, he claims that the people had remained faithful to the covenant (Ps. 43:17-22). Because of Israel's faithfulness, and for the sake of God's name, the biblical psalmist calls upon God to rise up [ἀνάστα] and redeem them (Ps. 43:26).

The Solomonic psalmist's own work repeats the major themes of Ps. 43. Both open with a declaration of God's kingship (*Pss. Sol.* 17:1; Ps. 43:4). Both chronicle the present suffering of their community (*Pss. Sol.* 17:4-20; Ps. 43:17-22). Both speak about how enemies have risen up [ἐπανιστάνω/ἐπανίστημι] against them (*Pss. Sol.* 17:5; Ps. 43:6). Finally, both call upon God to arise [ἀνίστημι] and deliver his people (*Pss. Sol.* 17:21; Ps. 43:26).[12]

The difference comes in the form of deliverance envisioned. The biblical psalmist asks God to arise and save his people. The Solomonic psalmist asks God to raise up a descendant of David to deliver his community. This king would remove sinners from the κληρονομία. Here are the words of the Solomonic psalmist again:

---

11. All translations of the LXX come from the New English Translation of the Septuagint unless otherwise noted. However, I have not retained its translations of biblical names. Instead, I adopt the more standard English renderings.

12. Willitts (2012b: 30) recognizes that many of these elements are part of the structure of *Pss. Sol.* 17, but he does not see the connection to Ps. 43.

> See, O Lord, and raise up for them their king, the son of David, at the time which you chose, O God, to rule over Israel your servant. And gird him with strength to shatter in pieces unrighteous rulers, to purify Jerusalem from nations that trample her down in destruction, in wisdom of righteousness, to drive out sinners from the inheritance [κληρονομία]. (*Pss. Sol.* 17:21-23)

Therefore, in *Pss. Sol.* 17 God's faithfulness to the covenant takes the form of raising up a Davidic king to restore Israel to its inheritance.

It appears, then, that a central feature of his role as the Davidic Messiah is the restoration of God's people to their inheritance in fulfillment of his covenant promises. When the Solomonic author refers to the inheritance, it is evident that he has the land in view. In the biblical material, inheritance language is used most often during God's encounters with Abraham:

> Abram said because you have not given me a seed a member of my household will inherit [κληρονομήσει] what is mine. And immediately a voice of the Lord happened to him saying, "he will not inherit [κληρονομήσει] what is yours, but one from your own body he will inherit [κληρονομήσει] what is yours…" And he said to him, "I am the God who brought you out of the country of the Chaldeans to give you this land to inherit [κληρονομῆσαι]." (Gen. 15:2-6, my translation)

Later κληρονομία is used as a shorthand to refer to the Promised Land (Num. 36:6-9; Deut. 3:18-20). We cannot be certain whether the Solomonic psalmist intends to refer to the Abrahamic or the Israelite use of inheritance language. Most likely, he relies upon the common assumption that the κληρονομία is the territory promised to Israel as the descendants of Abraham, Isaac, and Jacob.

A second connection between the Davidic Messiah and the land occurs in *Pss. Sol.* 17:28. It reads, "And he shall distribute them according to their tribes on the land, and no resident alien and foreigner shall live among them any longer."[13] His language in *Pss. Sol.* 17:28 comes from Ezek. 47:21.[14] Ezekiel predicted that when God acts to restore Israel, the people would receive the land by lots as Moses promised. According to the author of *Pss. Sol.* 17, the king would liberate the people and distribute the land. Thus, he is God's direct means of fulfilling the land promises.

---

13. My translation.
14. Atkinson 2001: 330.

2.2.3. *The Second Exodus to the Inheritance in Psalms of Solomon 17*

Another reference to the land comes via the use of new Exodus imagery and an allusion to Jer. 37:8 LXX. This allusion occurs when the author explains the need for a Davidic king. The king is needed because sinners (the Hasmoneans) usurped the throne promised to David and persecuted the author's community.[15] According to the Solomonic psalmist, God allows them to take power because of the nation's sinfulness (*Pss. Sol.* 17:5, 20). This is not the end of the story. According to the author, God punishes the Hasmoneans by raising up Pompey to remove the Hasmoneans from power (*Pss. Sol.* 17:7-9).[16] Pompey's invasion of Jerusalem, however, does not bring suffering upon the "sinners" alone; it causes hardship for all (*Pss. Sol.* 17:11).

The hardship surrounding the invasion and the sinfulness of the rest of the nation overwhelms the author's community. They decide to flee to the wilderness:

> Those who loved the congregations of the devout fled from them, as sparrows were scattered from their nest. They wandered in wildernesses that their souls be saved from evil, and their saved soul was precious in the eyes of those who sojourned abroad. They were scattered over the whole earth by lawless men. (*Pss. Sol.* 17:16-18)

The language of wandering in the wilderness evokes the Exodus journey. The scattering to the ends of the earth likens their situation to exile predicted in the Deuteronomic covenant.[17] Thus, the invasion of Pompey leads to a time of judgment that combines elements of Israel's sojourn in the wilderness and the Deuteronomic curses.

---

15. Winninge 1995: 99; Atkinson 2004: 136. Tromp 1993: 344–61 is virtually alone in claiming that the sinners here are Gentiles.

16. There has been some question concerning the interpretation of *Pss. Sol.* 17:7-9 because the Hasmoneans are not actually destroyed during Pompey's invasion. They retained the high priesthood, but lost their royal authority. Schwartz (1992: 42–53) argues that the main complaint against the Hasmoneans was that they combined the priestly and kingly offices. Therefore, according to Winninge (1995: 100), after they lost their kingly rights the author of this psalm was satisfied. Atkinson (2004: 137–8) solves this problem by proposing two periods of composition for the two halves of *Pss. Sol.* 17:1-20. The first half was written before the siege when the author expected the Hasmoneans to be destroyed. The second half was written in light of their mere loss of power. Neither interpretation of the historical situation impacts my claim about the relationship between the Messiah and the land.

17. See the use of διασκορπίζω in Deut. 30:1-3 in conjunction with the use of σκορπισμός in *Pss. Sol.* 17:16-18

In response to this trauma, the author asks God to raise up a descendant of David to rescue his scattered people. The author alludes to Jer. 37:8-9 LXX [30:8-9 MT] to make this claim:[18]

Jer. 37:8-9	ἐν τῇ ἡμέρᾳ ἐκείνῃ, εἶπεν κύριος, συντρίψω τὸν ζυγὸν ἀπὸ τοῦ τραχήλου αὐτῶν καὶ τοὺς δεσμοὺς αὐτῶν διαρρήξω, καὶ οὐκ ἐργῶνται αὐτοὶ ἔτι ἀλλοτρίοις· καὶ ἐργῶνται τῷ κυρίῳ θεῷ αὐτῶν, καὶ τὸν Δαυιδ βασιλέα αὐτῶν ἀναστήσω αὐτοῖς
Pss. Sol. 17:21	Ἰδέ, κύριε, καὶ ἀνάστησον αὐτοῖς τὸν βασιλέα αὐτῶν υἱὸν Δαυιδ εἰς τὸν καιρόν, ὃν εἵλου σύ, ὁ θεός, τοῦ βασιλεῦσαι ἐπὶ Ισραηλ παῖδά σου·

Jeremiah 37:8-9 looks to the breaking of the yoke and the end of slavery. After the yoke is broken, the people would serve God faithfully. Jeremiah's combination of the end of slavery and the beginning of service to the Lord is itself evocative of the Exodus narrative.[19] For Jeremiah, then, the end of foreign rule would be like another Exodus. A Davidic king, not a foreign nation, would rule the people of God. The rule of the Davidic king, then, is pivotal to Jeremiah's appropriation of the Exodus tradition. The author of *Pss. Sol.* 17 uses Jer. 37:8-9 to make a similar point. The rise of the Davidic king would be like another Exodus. He would break the yoke and regather the faithful to serve God in the land.

In the chronology of the Jeremiah text, God restores the people, defeats the Gentiles, and then provides a Davidic king to rule:

> On that day, said the Lord, I will shatter a yoke from off their neck, and I will burst their bonds, and they will no more work for foreigners. And they will work for the Lord, their God, and I will raise up David as their king for them. (Jer. 37:8-9, my translation)

For the Solomonic psalmist, God would accomplish those aims through the Davidic king. The king defeats the foreigners and regathers the people.[20] Then the people would live in the inheritance promised to them

---

18. Atkinson 2001: 330.

19. Keown, Scalise, and Smothers (1995: 94) say, "There is a subtle allusion to the Exodus from Egypt, when the LORD commanded the pharaoh who had subjugated Israel 'Let my people go that they may serve me'." See also Lundbom 2004: 389–90.

20. The use of Exodus imagery is intriguing given that the people are physically in the land. It shows that for some a mere return to the land did not fulfill the promises of Israel's restoration.

cleansed of enemies (*Pss. Sol.* 17:26-28). This change highlights the role of the Davidic king in bringing about the final realization of the land promises.

2.2.4. *Rule beyond the Borders of Israel in Psalms of Solomon 17*

The restoration in *Pss. Sol.* 17 is not limited to Israel. Instead, the author envisions a king whose rule would extend throughout the known world. The author says, "He shall judge peoples and nations in the wisdom of his righteousness... And he shall have the peoples of the nations to be subject to him under his yoke" (*Pss. Sol.* 17:29-30). There is no evidence that obedient nations suffer under his reign.[21] In fact, the author predicts that they would receive pity. Given the glowing description of the king, we could expect obedient nations to benefit from their submission to him:

> And he shall be a righteous king, taught by God, over them, and there shall be no injustice in his days in their midst, for all shall be holy, and their king the anointed of the Lord. For he shall not put his hope in horse and rider and bow, nor shall he multiply for himself gold and silver for war, nor shall he gather hopes from a multitude of people for the day of war. The Lord himself is his king, the hope of him who is strong through hope in God, and he shall have pity on all the nations before him in fear. (*Pss. Sol.* 17:32-34)

Commenting on this passage, Davenport says the king will "establish a just system of government, provide for a righteous society, redistribute the land, and extend his rule over the entire world, and see that righteousness reigns throughout the entire world."[22] Therefore, according to *Pss. Sol.* 17, the Davidic king would do more than restore Israel to the land promised to them. He would assume a worldwide rule that brings blessings to the world.

2.2.5. *Conclusion*

Psalm of Solomon 17 is a pivotal text for understanding the reign of a Davidic Messiah. According to the author, the coming king will restore Israel to the land and rule over the Gentiles. Furthermore, the Davidic Messiah will participate in a second Exodus that culminates in the

---

21. Embry (2002: 113) rightly recognizes that "the Messiah shows compassion to the nations who are reverent before him."
22. Davenport 1980: 74.

restored tribes dwelling safely in the land. Finally, *Pss. Sol.* 17 refers to the land as Israel's "inheritance," drawing on language with roots in the Abrahamic promises. Thus, it is an example of the Davidic Messiah bringing about the final realization of the Abrahamic promises in the context of a worldwide kingdom.

2.3. Second Baruch

2.3.1. Introduction

Second Baruch was composed at some point between AD 70 and 132.[23] The author drafts his document in response to the destruction of Jerusalem and the Temple in AD 70.[24] His work addresses the question of how God could allow such devastation to befall his chosen people.[25] Rather than deal with the events of AD 70 directly, the author uses Baruch and the catastrophic destruction of the First Temple to respond to the crisis of his day.

The first nine chapters establish the setting. According to the author, Baruch witnesses the destruction of Jerusalem. Instead of leaving Jerusalem with Jeremiah, God commands Baruch to remain and witness the desolation (*2 Bar.* 10:1-2). Chapters 10–77 consist of an ongoing dialogue between God and Baruch that contains laments, prayers, visions, and their interpretations.[26] Speaking of this middle section, Lied correctly observes that, "the dialogue between God and Baruch ensures Baruch's gradual acceptance of the current catastrophe and gives him a growing understanding of God's plan for the redemption of Israel… [T]he crisis is part of God's master plan: the destruction of Jerusalem and its temple, and the dispersion of the wicked tribes signal that the end of the world is approaching."[27]

The final section of *2 Baruch* consists of a letter from Baruch to the nine half tribes currently in exile in Assyria (*2 Bar.* 78–87).[28] For the author of *2 Baruch*, the end of the world does not mean that God has

---

23. Lied 2008: 26. It is difficult to be more precise than this range. We can be sure that it was written after the events of AD 70. It also shows no awareness of the events of AD 132. See also Henze 2011: 26.
24. Docherty 2014: 147; Harrington 2003: 668.
25. Harrington 2003: 668.
26. Hobbins 1998: 47.
27. Lied 2008: 1.
28. Docherty 2014: 149. Some have questioned whether the letter was originally part of *2 Baruch* because the letter exists in the manuscript tradition independently of

forgotten the promises he made to Israel. The author claims that the promises would begin to be fulfilled in the messianic age. This messianic age would serve as a point of transition to the coming age.[29] In the coming age, the promises attained provisionally by the Messiah would become eternal.

Our focus will be on the three portions of *2 Baruch* that contain predictions of the Messiah: *2 Bar.* 29–30, 35–40, 72–74. The importance of *2 Baruch* for understanding Second Temple messianism is well known. Nonetheless, this analysis is unique in that: (1) I call attention to the role that the Davidic Messiah plays in bringing about the fulfillment of the Abrahamic promises. This feature of the presentation of the Messiah in *2 Baruch* is largely ignored and has implications for Paul's claim that the Messiah Jesus brings about the fulfillment of the Abrahamic promises; (2) I show that throughout the letter the author looks to the coming worldwide kingdom of the Messiah, a feature not always appreciated in secondary literature on *2 Baruch*.[30]

2.3.2. *The Davidic Messiah and the Land in 2 Baruch*

Three passages chronicle the rise and reign of the Messiah: 2 Bar. 29–30, 36–40, and 72–74. I begin by demonstrating the Messiah's role in securing the land in *2 Bar.* 36–40. This link between the Messiah and the land will be supported by a brief analysis of the description of the kingdom in *2 Bar.* 72–74. I conclude by showing that *2 Bar.* 29–30 asserts that the land promises made to Jacob will be fulfilled during the Messiah's rule.

The clearest description of the Messiah's role in securing the land inheritance comes during the vision of the forest, the cedar, the fountain, and the vine (*2 Bar.* 36–40). Baruch's lament over the fate of Jerusalem and its Temple precedes this vision. In *2 Bar.* 25:2–4 we read:

> O that my eyes were springs, and my eyelids, that they were a fountain of tears. For how shall I be sad over Zion, and lament over Jerusalem? For at the place where now I am prostrate, the high priests used to offer holy sacrifices, and placed thereon incense of fragrant spices. Now, however, that of which we are proud has become dust, and that which our soul desired is ashes.[31]

the main text. However, Whitters (2003) has shown that the letter is thematically and structurally connected to the rest of the document. See also Doering 2013: 151–74. This unified reading of *2 Baruch* is the view adopted by the majority of recent commentators. See Lied 2011: 241.

29. Doering 2013: 159.
30. See Lied 2008: 198–202.
31. All quotations of *2 Baruch* come from Klijn 1983: 615–53.

Following his period of mourning, Baruch falls asleep and has a vision. At the beginning of the vision, he sees a forest planted on a plain surrounded by high mountains. This forest eventually expands to cover the entire area. After the forest expands, the vine and fountain appear. Eventually the vine and the fountain overcome the forest, including the last remaining cedar:

> And that fountain came to the forest and changed into great waves, and those waves submerged the forest and suddenly uprooted the entire forest and overthrew all the mountains which surrounded it. And the height of the forest became low, and that top of the mountains became low. And that fountain became so strong that it left nothing of the great forest except one cedar. When it had also cast that one down, it destroyed the entire forest and uprooted it so that nothing was left of it, and its place was not even known anymore. Then that vine arrived with the fountain in peace and in great tranquility. (*2 Bar.* 36:4-6)

This vision depicts the rise of kingdoms. These kingdoms oppress, exile, and rule over Israel. In response, the vine and fountain (the Messiah and his dominion) arrive to defeat Israel's enemies and reestablish them in the land.[32] The Messiah's role in securing the land is made plain in the interpretation that was given to Baruch:

> And it will happen when the time of its fulfilment is approaching in which it will fall…the dominion of my Anointed One which is like the fountain and the vine, will be revealed. And when it has revealed itself, it will uproot the multitude of its host. And that which you have seen, namely the tall cedar, which remained of that forest, and with regard to the words which the vine said to it which you heard, this is the meaning. The last ruler who is left alive at that time will be bound, whereas the entire host will be destroyed. And they will carry him on Mount Zion, and my Anointed One will convict him of all his wicked deeds and will assemble and set before him all the works of his hosts. And after these things he will kill him and protect the rest of my people who will be found in the place that I have chosen. (*2 Bar.* 39:7–40:2)

Some scholars claim that *2 Baruch* displays no concern for the land in this section or in any of the other messianic predictions.[33] According to

---

32. Tamási 2013: 213.

33. Lied (2008: 198–202) argues for a more limited reference to Mount Zion or a portion of Israel in all three texts. Charles (1896: 51) argues for a reference to Palestine in *2 Bar.* 29:2. Hobbins (1998: 60) and Henze (2011: 295) see references to the restoration of the whole land.

Lied, in *2 Bar.* 40 the author is only concerned with Mount Zion, not the entire Promised Land.[34] Her reasons are as follows. First, *2 Bar.* 40:1-2 contains the clearest description of the land. In that passage, Mount Zion is the place of protection. Second, there is no mention of the restoration of all twelve tribes during the messianic age. Third, the return of the remnant to Zion includes only a small number. According to Lied, this means that there is no need for a restoration of the whole land.

In rebuttal, we note that the vine and fountain clears away the entire forest and the last remaining cedar. This last cedar refers to Rome and its empire. Since the vine and the fountain replace Rome and its Empire, it is evident that the author believes that the kingdom of the Messiah would replace the Roman empire. Therefore, the vision of the vine and the fountain does envision a recovery of territory, but his concern is not limited to Mount Zion or Israel. The author looks to the Messiah's reign over the whole earth.

This worldwide spread of the Messiah's kingdom is also present in the vision of the vine and the flowers. The relevant portion reads, "And after these things I saw that the cedar was burning and the vine growing, while it and all around it became a valley full of unfading flowers. And I awoke and arose" (*2 Bar.* 37:1). Here, the destruction of the cedar leads to the expansion of the vine and the flowers. This is yet another picture of the messianic kingdom replacing the Roman empire.

The description of the messianic rule in *2 Bar.* 73 supports the assertion that the worldwide rule of the Messiah is a central feature of *2 Baruch*:

> And it will happen that after he has brought down everything which is in the world, and has sat down in eternal peace on the throne of the kingdom, then joy will be revealed and rest will appear. And then health will descend in dew, and illness will vanish, and fear and tribulation and lamentation will pass away from among men, and joy will encompass the earth. And nobody will again die untimely, nor will any adversity take place suddenly… And the wild beasts will come from the wood and serve men, and the asps and dragons will come out of their holes to subject themselves to a child. (*2 Bar.* 73:1-6)

The throne of the kingdom, joy, the absence of fear, and the leadership of a child are drawn from Isa. 9:1-7 and 11:6-8.[35] These Isaianic passages describe the restoration of the nation during the reign of a Davidic king. In Isaiah the Davidic king's rule extends beyond Israel. He reigns over

---

34. Lied 2008: 198–9.
35. Bogaert (1969: 129) and Charles (1896: 116) note the allusion to Isa. 11:6-8.

the Gentiles. *2 Baruch* uses these Isaianic texts to make similar claims about the Davidic Messiah. According to *2 Bar.* 71:1-6, the reign of the Messiah that begins with Israel will extend to the entire world. God's promises to Israel, including the promise of the land, would be realized in and through the king and his kingdom.

A final passage is relevant to our discussion. It does not contain a prediction of the messianic acquisition of the land, but it does point to the fulfillment of the Abrahamic promises regarding the land's fertility during the messianic age. Speaking of this messianic age, *2 Bar.* 29:2-6 says:

> For at that time I shall only protect those found in this land at that time. And it will happen that when all that which should come to pass in these parts has been accomplished, the Anointed One will begin to be revealed… The earth will also yield fruits ten thousandfold. And on one vine will be a thousand branches, and one branch will produce a thousand clusters, and one cluster will produce a thousand grapes, and one grape will produce a cor of wine. And those who are hungry will enjoy themselves and they will, moreover, see marvels every day.

Bogaert, building on the insights of Harris, claims that the ten thousand-fold production of earth is based upon a mistranslation of Gen. 27:28. He says, "Le chiffre 10,000 est une mauvaise traduction du mot רב dans la bénédiction de Jacob par Isaac (Gen. 27:28) qui aura été lu רבוא."[36] Genesis 27:28-29, the text alluded to in *2 Bar.* 29:2-6, records the blessing that Isaac gives to Jacob. It reads:

> May God give you of the dew of heaven, and of the fatness of the earth, and plenty of grain and wine. Let peoples serve you, and nations bow down to you. Be lord over your brothers, and may your mother's sons bow down to you. Cursed be everyone who curses you, and blessed be everyone who blesses you! (Gen. 27:28-29)

Genesis 27:28-29 is a reaffirmation and extension of the promises made to Abraham in Gen. 12:1-3. According to *2 Bar.* 29:2-6, then, the productivity of the land during the messianic age will realize the promise given to Jacob that he would receive a fruitful and prosperous land. This fertility of the land presupposes the fulfillment of the land promise. But this fruitfulness is not limited to the land of Israel. It is a fruitfulness of

---

36. Bogaert 1969: 63. For the source of this insight, see Harris 1895: 448–55. See also Klausner 1955: 342–4; Charles 1896: 55.

the entire earth. Therefore, *2 Bar*. 29–30 makes an explicit reference to the realization of the Abrahamic land promise expanded to encompasses the whole world during the messianic age.

2.3.3. *The Worldwide Rule of the Messiah in 2 Baruch*

2 Baruch pictures a rule of the Messiah that would extend beyond the borders of Israel. This is most definitively stated during the apocalypse of the cloud and the waters (*2 Bar*. 53–74). The first portion of this apocalypse divides biblical history into twelve periods. Beginning with Adam, it recounts the history of Israel up to the author's time. The author portrays his time as the beginning of the end.[37] Following a final period of confusion, 2 Baruch predicts the coming of the anointed one. His reign would be a time of judgment and the end of oppression:

> Now, hear also about the bright waters which come at the end after these black ones. This is the word. After the signs have come of which I have spoken to you before, when the nations are moved and the time of my Anointed One comes, he will call all nations, and some of them he will spare, and others he will kill... Every nation which has not known Israel and which has not trodden down the seed of Jacob will live. (*2 Bar*. 72:1-4)

Following this judgment, the Messiah would rule over the world and establish justice:

> And it will happen that after he has brought down everything which is in the world, and has sat down in eternal peace on the throne of the kingdom, then joy will be revealed and rest will appear. And then health will descend in dew, and illness will vanish, and fear and tribulation and lamentation will pass away from among men, and joy will encompass the earth... And the wild beasts will come from the wood and serve men, and the asps and dragons will come out of their holes to subject themselves to a child. (*2 Bar*. 73:1-6)

We have already noted the influence of Isa. 9:1-6 and 11:6-8 on this passage.[38] Here we will simply observe that *2 Bar*. 73:1-6 pictures a restored Davidic king reigning over the nations as a part of his kingdom.

The messianic age described in *2 Bar*. 73 would serve as a point of transition. It would end the old age and begin the new (*2 Bar*. 74:1-2).[39]

---

37. Henze 2011: 274.
38. Charles 1896: 116.
39. Lied 2008: 193.

This new age would begin with the resurrection and result in Israel receiving all that God promised them. This new age, however, cannot be separated from the fulfillment of those same promises in the messianic age. The new age's main distinction from the messianic age is the defeat of death:

> And it will happen after these things when the time of the appearance of the Anointed One has been fulfilled and he returns with glory, that then all who sleep in hope of him will rise. And it will happen at that time that those treasuries will be opened in which the number of the souls of the righteous were kept, and they will go out and the multitudes of the souls will appear together, in one assemblage, of one mind. And the first ones will enjoy themselves and the last ones will not be sad. (*2 Bar.* 30:1-2)

As Hobbins argues, the new age would be a reaffirmation, not a devaluation, of Israel's history and God's promises to them:

> A world beyond death is clearly an essential element in 2 Baruch's cosmology, but continuity, not just discontinuity, is posited between life now and life in the hereafter. 2 Baruch exhibits a profound concern for the process of history, for the rise and fall of nations and the exercise of world dominion. The work foresees a geopolitical transformation involving an ingathering of the diaspora Jews, a surpassing restoration of Zion, and the reestablishment of the land as a safe haven for the people. The messianic era on earth is a key component of 2 Baruch's expectations of consummation. The book's future hope lies within history, not just beyond it.[40]

There are a few connections that tie the events outlined in Baruch's visions to the Abrahamic promises that deserve attention. When describing the time of Abraham in his apocalypse, the author says:

> And after these you saw the bright waters; that is the fountain of Abraham and his generation, and the coming of his son, and the son of his son, and of those who are like them. For at that time…belief in the coming judgment was brought about, and the hope of the world which will be renewed was built at that time, and the promise of the life that will come later was planted. Those are the bright waters which you have seen. (*2 Bar.* 57:1-3)

The emphasis on Abraham's age as the birth of eschatology is noteworthy. The author asserts that Abraham believes in the renewal of the

---

40. Hobbins 1998: 71.

world, the resurrection of the dead, and the life to come.[41] Therefore, Abraham hopes for the very eschatological scenario that closes the apocalypse of the cloud. This means that the messianic age and the age to come recounted in those visions would realize the hopes of Abraham.

Further confirmation of the importance of the Abrahamic promises occurs during the letter that closes *2 Baruch*. Speaking to the nine half tribes in exile, in *2 Bar.* 78:3-6 he says:

> Are we not all, the twelve tribes, bound by one captivity as we also descend from one father… Therefore, if you think about the things you have suffered now for your good so that you may not be condemned at the end and be tormented, you shall receive hope which lasts forever and ever.

What unites the tribes is their common descent from Abraham. His descendants had experienced exile and now hope for restoration. The author comforts and reassures the exiles by evoking the memory of their common origin in the Abrahamic promises.

In addition, Lied and others have observed that the location from which Baruch receives his visions and writes his letter recalls the Abrahamic promises.[42] Establishing this connection to Abraham requires a brief setting of the scene. *2 Baruch* 47:1 recounts Baruch's move to Hebron. While in Hebron, Baruch receives his vision of the apocalypse of the cloud, "under a tree to rest in the shadow of its branches" (*2 Bar.* 55:1). Baruch also composes his letter to the exiles, "under the oak in the shadow of the branches" (*2 Bar.* 78:18). This tree and oak mentioned in *2 Bar.* 78:28 probably refers to the same location in Hebron mentioned in *2 Bar.* 47:1.[43] From this we can surmise that Baruch receives his vision and writes his letter under an oak in Hebron. This mention of oak and trees near Hebron suggests that the author of *2 Baruch* intends to allude to the oaks of Mamre.[44] The oaks of Mamre are important because the Abrahamic promises are reaffirmed there. The relevant section, Gen, 13:14-18, reads:

---

41. Henze 2011: 277.
42. Lied 2008: 154–62; Bogaert 1969: 137. See also Doering (2013: 162), who is more cautious in affirming a link to the Oaks of Mamre.
43. Lied (2008: 155) says, "Although only 77:18 says explicitly that the tree is an oak, the clear resemblance between the two descriptions of the trees and the identical location of the two at Hebron, makes it likely that both passages bring the same tree to mind."
44. Bogaert 1969: 137.

> The LORD said to Abram… "Raise your eyes now, and look from the place where you are, northward and southward and eastward and westward; for all the land that you see I will give to you and to your offspring forever… So Abram moved his tent, and came and settled by the oaks of Mamre, which are at Hebron; and there he built an altar to the LORD.

Abraham still resides at Hebron when God appears to him and establishes the covenant (Gen. 15:1-21).[45] Therefore, God gives Baruch a vision that reaffirms his covenant promises at the same location in which God first established his covenant with Abraham.

2.3.4. Conclusion of 2 Baruch

2 Baruch contains three distinct but complementary pictures of the messianic age (*2 Bar.* 29–30; 35–40; 72–74). In the course of these descriptions, the author predicts that the coming king will destroy Israel's enemies and recover the Promised Land during the course of his reign. The Messiah's kingdom, however, would not be limited to the geographic boundaries of Israel. His kingdom and rule would encompass the entire world. In addition, the entire world would take on the fruitfulness of the Promised Land. This fruitfulness of the entire world testifies to the expansion of the Abrahamic land promise to include the whole earth. Finally, in the concluding letter and throughout *2 Baruch*, the author reminds his readers that they can be sure that God will keep his promises made to Abraham.

2.4. *4 Ezra*

2.4.1. Introduction

4 Ezra was written toward the end of the first century in response to the destruction of the Second Temple.[46] The original text consisted of chs. 3–14, but it has been redacted to include a Christian expansion which precedes (chs. 1–2) and follows (chs. 15–16) the Jewish material.[47]

Within the fictive narrative of the book, *4 Ezra* is set in the aftermath of the destruction of the First Temple and the exile of the people of Israel to Babylon.[48] It consists of a series of dialogues between Ezra and Uriel

---

45. Lied 2008: 155. See also Gen. 18:1.
46. Bachmann 2014: 3.
47. Metzger 1993: 517.
48. Harrington 2003: 665.

as well as visions given to Ezra. Through these visions and dialogues Ezra explores the theological issues raised by the destruction of Jerusalem. Hogan sums up the central question of the book in the following manner:

> What does God plan to do about his covenant promises to Israel? The visions demonstrate to Ezra that these promises have not been forgotten—that the end of the age will bring vindication to Israel as well as universal judgment.[49]

Although *4 Ezra* is set during the first destruction of the Temple, the author writes to address the problem of the destruction of the Second Temple. The question, then, for the author of *4 Ezra* is, "How will God be faithful to his covenant promises given the massive pain and destruction inflicted upon the people of Judea and Jerusalem by the Romans?"

The author's answers to the question of God's faithfulness to his covenant promises are rich and varied and cannot be explored in full here. Our focus will be on the role played by the Davidic Messiah in his narrative. The author discusses the Messiah in 7:28-32; 11:37–12:1; 12:31-34; 13:3-13, 25-53; 14:9.[50] The presentation of the Messiah in these passages is not uniform. Nonetheless, we will see that, in various places, the author of *4 Ezra* argues that the Messiah will liberate those in the land, restore the lost tribes, and establish his worldwide kingdom. This link between the Messiah and kingdom, evident in *4 Ezra*, supports our claim that enabling the final realization of the land promises through participation in the Messiah's kingdom is a stable feature of Second Temple presentations of royal and messianic figures.

2.4.2. *The Passive Messiah and the Revelation of the Land in 4 Ezra 7:26-34*

The first major discussion of the Messiah occurs during Ezra's third dialogue with Uriel. The first dialogue asks why God would punish Israel through Babylon, a nation more sinful than them (3:1–5:20).[51] The second dialogue explores Israel's status as God's chosen people (5:21–6:43). The third dialogue considers the "theological issues arising from the aftermath of the destruction of Jerusalem."[52]

---

49. Hogan 2008: 173.
50. Stone 1987: 210. Since *4 Ezra* 4:9 merely mentions the Messiah, it will not be considered below.
51. Harrington 2003: 665.
52. Ibid.: 666.

In the third dialogue, the author argues that the solution to the problem of Israel's suffering would be the revelation of the land and the Messiah at the appointed time:

> For behold, the time will come, when the signs which I have foretold to you will come to pass; the city which now is not seen shall appear, and the land which now is hidden shall be disclosed. And everyone who has been delivered from the evils that I have foretold shall see my wonders. For my son the Messiah shall be revealed with those who are with him, and those who remain shall rejoice four hundred years. (*4 Ezra* 7:26-28)[53]

Most scholars agree that the unseen city and land refer to a preexistent heavenly Jerusalem that would be revealed in the last days. Alongside the revelation of the pre-existent land, the author also predicts the revelation of the pre-existent Messiah.

In *4 Ezra* 7:26-34, however, the Messiah does not play a role in bringing about the coming age or the final realization of the land promises. We are only told that he will bring joy to those who remain with him for four hundred years.[54] After this four hundred-year period ends, the Messiah and all those with him will die. Then creation will return to its primeval silence for seven days (*4 Ezra* 7:30). Following this seven days, the resurrection will take place and the elect will experience eternal bliss while the rest of humanity experiences torment (*4 Ezra* 7:47).

Despite the fact that the Messiah is passive in this brief account, there are three elements of this portrayal that are relevant to my proposal. First, the revelation of the Messiah is linked to the revelation of the land. This means that the author associates the land with the Messiah. Given that in the later visions the Messiah plays a more active role, I am justified in saying that *4 Ezra*, taken as a whole, gives the Messiah an active role in the final realization of the land promises. Second, although the Messiah dies after four hundred years, the people, once in the land, do not return to exile. Stated differently, the revelation of the Messiah and the land represent a definitive turning point in Israel's history such that the land and kingdom are never lost again.[55] That the messianic age gives way to something greater does not make it insignificant. Finally, the Messiah is

---

53. All citations of *4 Ezra* are from Metzger 1983.
54. Moo 2011: 48; Stone 1990: 209.
55. Ibid.: 127 says, "Even if the author consistently understands it to be an interregnum (something that is not always made clear), the messianic age is never portrayed as thereby insignificant, and it remains of central importance for the realization of God's justice."

described as God's Son. As we will see later, Ezra's sonship language is taken from Ps. 2:7-9, where God promises the Davidic descendant an inheritance of the entire earth and the defeat of his enemies.[56] Thus, *4 Ezra* is an example of the use of son language to describe an individual who brings about a worldwide kingdom in fulfillment of God's covenant promises.

2.4.3. *The Messiah, the Land, and the Worldwide Kingdom in the Eagle Vision of 4 Ezra 11:1–12:34*

The next major discussion of the Messiah in *4 Ezra* occurs during the eagle vision and its interpretation (*4 Ezra* 11:1–12:34). In this vision, the eagle represents the Roman empire and its rulers.[57] The author claims that this eagle would have a rule that spans the whole earth (*4 Ezra* 11:1, 15, 32).[58] This reign would last until the rise of the lion, who would rebuke the rulers for their unjust behavior and announce the end of their reign (*4 Ezra* 11:36-42). *4 Ezra* says that the final kingdom would be destroyed, "so that the whole earth, freed from your violence, may be refreshed and relieved, and may hope for the judgment and mercy of him who made it" (*4 Ezra* 11:46).

The interpretation of the vision states that the lion is the Davidic Messiah (*4 Ezra* 12:32). According to the interpretation, the Messiah would set up his judgment seat, pass sentence on the wicked rulers, and deliver the remnant of Israel that lives within the boundaries of the Promised Land (*4 Ezra* 11:34). Similar to the portrayal in *4 Ezra* 7:28-29, the Messiah brings joy to the people until the end of the age.

Various elements of the vision and interpretation speak to the link between the Messiah and the land as worldwide kingdom. First, the author plainly states that the Messiah would liberate the faithful remnant that remained in the Promised Land. This liberation results in their participation in the final realization of the land promises in the context of the worldwide rule of the Messiah. Second, in this vision the Messiah is portrayed as a lion. Genesis 49:10, a text that figures prominently in many Second Temple messianic texts, is the most likely source of the lion imagery.[59] Third, the whole earth benefits from the removal of the Roman empire. This suggests that the kingdom set up by the Messiah covers the

---

56. Stone (1990: 209) argues that the Messiah is the servant Messiah, not the Son. See the discussion in the next section.
57. Hogan 2008: 179.
58. Longenecker 1991: 113.
59. See the discussion of 4Q252 in Chapter 3 and Gal. 3:19 in Chapter 5.

whole earth and not just the liberated land of Israel. Fourth, by announcing their destruction and passing judgment, the Messiah plays an active role in liberating those in the land and establishing a worldwide kingdom.[60] This more active role stands in contrast to *4 Ezra* 7:28-29, where he does nothing to effect the liberation of the faithful remnant or the world.[61]

Stone argues that the figure portrayed in *4 Ezra* 12 is not royal.[62] According to Stone, rather than focusing on kingship, *4 Ezra* 12 highlights the Messiah's preexistence and cosmic function.[63] Bringing joy to one's subjects, however, should be seen as a royal act (*4 Ezra* 12:34). In addition, the judgment of one's enemies who oppress the people of God should also be seen as kingly actions (*4 Ezra* 12:33). Finally, this volume has shown that establishing a kingdom is itself a "royal" activity.

2.4.4. *The Messiah, the Land, and the Man from the Sea in 4 Ezra 13:1-50*

The account of the man from the sea is a reinterpretation of the figure from Dan. 7.[64] In *4 Ezra* 13, the man rises from the sea and rides on the clouds of heaven. This stands in contrast to Dan. 7:2-4, where the beasts rise from the sea. After his rise in *4 Ezra*, the man from the sea uses his voice to destroy those whom he encounters (*4 Ezra* 13:1-4). Following this a group gathers to fight against the man, only to be destroyed by the word of his mouth (*4 Ezra* 13:5-11). After defeating his enemies, the man from the sea gathers a multitude of peaceable people (*4 Ezra* 13:12-13).

Stone has persuasively argued that the differences between the vision and the interpretation make it likely that the vision consisted of previously written material that the author appropriates for his own purposes.[65] Therefore, the interpretation of the vision will be our focus. According to *4 Ezra* the man from the sea is the one, "the Most High has been keeping for many ages, who will himself deliver his creation; and he will direct those who are left" (*4 Ezra* 13:32). By describing him as the one kept for many ages, the author associates the man from the sea with the Messiah described in *4 Ezra* 12:32. The link to the Messiah of *4 Ezra* 12 means that, regardless of the intentions of the original author of the man from the sea narrative, for the author of *4 Ezra* the man from the sea is the Messiah. Therefore, his liberating activity is an example of the link between the Messiah and the land in Second Temple Judaism.

60. Chester 2007: 346.
61. Ibid.
62. Stone 1987: 210.
63. Ibid.
64. Collins 1992: 448; Knibb 1995: 170.
65. Stone 1987: 213; Collins 1992: 461–2.

According to the interpretation, in the last days a multitude will gather against the man from the sea, whom the author describes as God's Son (*4 Ezra* 13:37).[66] This son will reprove the hostile nations and destroy them with the Torah (*4 Ezra* 13:38). Collins argues that the placement of the king on Mount Zion and his destruction of the hostile nations shows that the author of *4 Ezra* draws upon Ps. 2:5-7.[67] Psalm 2:5-7 reads:

> Then he will speak to them in his wrath, and terrify them in his fury, saying, "I have set my king on Zion, my holy hill." I will tell of the decree of the LORD: He said to me, "You are my son; today I have begotten you." (Ps. 2:5-7)

This is very similar to the presentation of the man from the sea in *4 Ezra*:

> And an innumerable multitude shall be gathered together, as you saw, desiring to come and conquer him. But he will stand on the top of Mount Zion. And Zion will come and be made manifest to all people, prepared and built, as you saw the mountain carved out without hands. And he, my Son, will reprove the assembled nations for their ungodliness. (*4 Ezra* 13:34-37)

The setting on Mount Zion and the rebuke of foreign nations makes Stone's argument that the original version described the man from the sea as the Isaianic servant and not the son from Ps. 2:5-7 unlikely.[68]

The author's account of the destruction of the hostile nations gives way to the prediction of the return of the ten tribes that had been exiled and the deliverance of those who are still in the land (13:40-48).[69] This restoration of the twelve tribes to the land is a clear indication that the Messiah of *4 Ezra* brings about the final realization of the land promises. His destruction of foreign armies suggests that the rule of the man from the sea extends beyond the Promised Land.

2.4.5. *Conclusion of 4 Ezra*

The author of *4 Ezra* discusses the Messiah extensively on three occasions. The portrayals of the Messiah in these accounts have elements of continuity and discontinuity.[70] In all three, his reign begins the transition from

---

66. Ferch 1977: 145.
67. Collins 1992: 462–3.
68. Stone 1990: 207.
69. Ferch 1977: 145.
70. Stewart (2013: 386) rightly recognizes that we should not be overly concerned with the differences.

the first age to the age to come. In all three, the author associates him with the final realization of the land promises. In *4 Ezra* 7:28-29, however, he is largely passive and merely associated with the salvation of the remnant and the revelation of the preexistent land. In the latter visions, the Messiah is an active agent who destroys the Roman Empire and assumes a sovereignty over the world.[71] According to *4 Ezra*, this destruction of Rome will lead to peace for the world and joy for those whom the Messiah rules. In the final account, the author even claims that the faithful among all twelve tribes will experience a restoration to the land.

Three biblical texts stand out in the author's presentation of the Messiah in *4 Ezra*. First, the vision of the man from the sea relies upon the Son of Man from Dan. 7:1-14. Daniel 7:1-14 is important because in Dan. 7:13-14 the Son of Man receives a worldwide kingdom. Regardless of the original meaning of Dan. 7:1-14, for the author of *4 Ezra* it speaks about the Messiah. Second, the account of the Messiah's destruction of his enemies, his placement on Mount Zion, and his designation as son, reveals a dependence on Ps. 2 (*4 Ezra* 13:31-38). Psalm 2:1-8 is a text that describes the peoples and the territories of the earth as the inheritance of the Davidic monarch who is called the Son of God. Finally, the author describes the Messiah as a lion. This is drawn from Gen. 49:9-10. Taken together, these texts show that the author draws upon a variety of texts that describe native rulers of Israel to claim that the Messiah would liberate the faithful remnant and enable the final realization of the land promises as a part of his worldwide rule.

2.5. *1 Maccabees 13–14*

2.5.1. *Introduction*

1 Maccabees chronicles the rise of the Hasmonean leadership over Israel.[72] It reviews the exploits of Mattathias, Judas, Jonathan, Simon, and John Hyrcanus. The author of 1 Maccabees writes to justify the Hasmonean dynasty.[73] The climax of 1 Maccabees occurs when Simon removes the "yoke of the nations" from Israel (1 Macc. 13:41-42).[74] Simon's reception of the high priesthood marks the formal beginning of the Hasmonean era (1 Macc. 14:16-49).

---

71. Klein 1972: 514–15.
72. Harrington 2012: 5; Babota 2014: 9–10.
73. Goldstein 1976: 4–12; Hieke 2007: 74; Egger-Wenzel 2006: 141–9.
74. Doran 1996: 165.

1 Maccabees is important because the author links the actions of Simon to the post-exilic realization of the land promises.⁷⁵ Furthermore, the author alludes to Davidic biblical texts during the course of his description of Simon's rule. This use of Davidic biblical texts shows that the author wants to liken the rule of Simon to the highpoint of Israel's history. Finally, there is the little-noticed fact that the author of 1 Macc. 2:49-70 skips over the return under Nehemiah so that he could claim that the post-exilic restoration of Israel was accomplished by the Hasmoneans. Simon, not Nehemiah's generation, breaks the foreign yoke and establishes Israel in the land.

The description of Simon is not usually considered to be a form of messianism because Simon does not claim Davidic descent. But our focus is not limited to those who claim an explicit connection to David. Like the texts considered thus far, 1 Maccabees is an example of a Second Temple document that links the activities of a royal figure to the final realization of the land promises.

2.5.2. *The Land Inheritance and the Rule of Simon in 1 Maccabees 13–14*

We begin with the last words of Mattathias. His final speech retells Israel's history and highlights exemplary characters (1 Macc. 2:49-70). In his retelling of Israel's history, Mattathias focuses on biblical characters who display attributes that the Maccabeans would also manifest during their battle for Israel's independence. According to the author, since the Maccabeans have similar attributes to the biblical characters, they deserve similar rewards.⁷⁶ The author believes that the zeal and faithfulness to the covenant that won honor in the past would also be rewarded in their day.⁷⁷ For the Maccabees, their reward is the high priesthood and rule over Israel.

---

75. 1 Maccabees' concern for the land is disputed. See the discussion below.

76. Benson (1996: 200) says, "1 Maccabees developed the characteristics of leadership from the biblical descriptions of David and tried to apply them to the early Hasmoneans. Mattathias, Judah and Simon are all presented with varying degrees of fortitude, piety and justice, and 1 Macc describes all but Jonathan as divinely chosen leaders. Each of these traits reflects or alludes to biblical parallels, mostly from the life of David."

77. Wright (2013: 121–2) is correct to consider this a retelling of Israel's story and not a mere catalogue of exemplars. This is in contrast to Goldstein (1976: 7), who calls this a "series of examples." Goldstein's description neglects the fact that this series moves through the great events in Israel's history leading up to the author's day.

Matthathias's narrative moves chronologically, including characters from the key periods of Israel's history. It starts with Abraham and goes on to recount faithfulness in Egypt (Joseph), the wilderness (Phineas), the conquest (Joshua and Caleb), the monarchy (David and Elijah), and exile (Hananiah, Azariah, Mishael, Daniel).

Interestingly, this speech does not include any figures involved in Israel's restoration (Nehemiah, Ezra). Instead, the text moves from the events in Babylon to the time of the Maccabees. This is the author's way of implying that Israel's post-exilic restoration is occurring through the Hasmonean's activities. Matthathias's last words are important for our argument about the link between royal figures and the land because the structure of Matthathias's narrative implies that his generation would experience the restoration to the land.

When considered in light of the programmatic material found in 1 Macc. 2:49-70, the claim that Simon removes the yoke of the Gentiles in 1 Macc. 13:41-42 should be linked to the post-exilic realization of the land promises first made to Abraham. Speaking of the reign of Simon, the author says:

> In the one hundred seventieth year the yoke of the Gentiles was removed from Israel, and the people began to write in their documents and contracts, "In the first year of Simon the great high priest and commander and leader of the Jews." (1 Macc. 13:41-42)

The "yoke of the Gentiles" appears in a variety of prophetic passages that predict Israel's post-exilic restoration to the land:[78]

> The LORD of hosts will wield a whip against them, as when he struck Midian at the rock of Oreb; his staff will be over the sea, and he will lift it as he did in Egypt. On that day his burden will be removed from your shoulder, and his yoke will be destroyed from your neck. (Isa. 10:25-27)

> For the yoke of their burden, and the bar across their shoulders, the rod of their oppressor, you have broken as on the day of Midian. (Isa. 9:4)

> On that day, says the LORD of hosts, I will break the yoke from off his neck, and I will burst his bonds, and strangers shall no more make a servant of him. But they shall serve the LORD their God and David their king, whom I will raise up for them. (Jer. 30:8-9)

---

78. Doran 1996: 155.

The removal of the yoke in 1 Macc. 13:41-42 and the absence of Nehemiah's generation in 1 Macc. 2:49-70 makes the author's thesis clear: Israel's restoration was not accomplished in Nehemiah's day; the final realization of God's promises is the result of Simon's activity. For our purposes, it does not matter that Simon does not recover all of the land of Israel. What matters is that the author wants to present Simon's removal of the yoke as the realization of God's promises.

We have seen that the activities of Simon are associated with the final realization of the land promises, but do we have evidence that the author wanted to depict Simon as a royal figure? There are two reasons to suggest that Simon qualifies as a royal figure. First, in many of the "removal of the yoke" passages, the removal of foreign domination often coincides with the rise of a Davidic king.[79] In the biblical texts when an individual removes the yoke, that individual is usually a descendant of David. Second, the author's description of Simon's rule in 1 Macc. 14:4-14 makes the Davidic resonances explicit. For example, in 1 Macc. 14:11-12 the author says that, "he established peace in the land, and Israel rejoiced with great joy. All the people sat under their own vines and fig trees, and there was none to make them afraid." These references to peace in the land and Israel dwelling under their own vine and fig tree intentionally tie the rule of Simon to Israel's golden age under Solomon.[80] 1 Kings 4:24-25 describes this golden age in the following way:

> For he had dominion over all the region west of the Euphrates from Tiphsah to Gaza, over all the kings west of the Euphrates; and he had peace on all sides. During Solomon's lifetime Judah and Israel lived in safety, from Dan even to Beer-sheba, all of them under their vines and fig trees.[81]

Finally, the fact that Simon cares for the humble (1 Macc. 14:14) matches the idealized depiction of the Davidic king in Ps. 72:1-4.[82] Speaking of the overall impact of this ode to Simon, Donaldson says:

---

79. See Ezek. 34:24-27; Isa. 9:4-7; Jer. 30:8-9.

80. The fact that Solomon ruled over all of Israel and Simon only liberated portions of Judea does not seem to bother the author. This shows that the scope of the "land" could vary from author to author. In 2 Baruch the restoration spread to encompass the whole earth. In 1 Macc. 14:4-14 it was limited to Judea. Nonetheless, both claim that their royal figure made it possible for the people of God to dwell in the place promised to them.

81. Doran (1996: 159) says, "Just as Solomon brought safety to the land (1 Kgs 4:25), so too does Simon (v. 11)." See also Donaldson (1981: 194). Goldstein (1976: 490) observes an allusion to Solomon's kingdom in 1 Macc. 14:4-6.

82. Goldstein 1976: 491.

Simon subdues foreign kings (vv 5-7, 13), shows concern for the poor, defends the Law and establishes righteousness (v 14), glorifies the Temple (v 15) and enjoys a worldwide reputation (v 10). All of this is strongly reminiscent of the OT messianic ideal, not only in its broad contours but also in its details.[83]

Whether all these elements could be associated with messianic ideals is beyond the scope of this investigation. However, it is clear that 1 Macc. 14:4-14 uses Davidic texts to describe Simon, a royal figure who restores Israel to the land. Thus, 1 Macc. 14:4-14 supports the wider assertion of this chapter that authors associate Second Temple royal figures with the final realization of the land promises.

Berthelot disagrees with our claim about the realization of the land promises in 1 Maccabees. She says:

> Simon's explicit aim is to defend the people, the laws and the sanctuary, not to reconquer a so-called promised land. Moreover, it should be underlined that whereas references to the gift of the land by God frequently appear in biblical prayers before battles against invaders, no such reference is to be found in the numerous prayers or speeches contained in 1 Maccabees.[84]

In response I contend that this argument drives a wedge between Temple, Torah, and land that may be anachronistic. I say this because during this period land and Torah are linked. As evidence, I note that there are no significant armed Jewish rebellions outside the Promised Land. We simply do not see diaspora Israelites gathering an army to fight for Torah in Egypt, Assyria, or Babylon.[85] The battle for Torah happens in the land because the land and the Torah are linked. For the author of 1 Maccabees, faithfulness to the Torah demands that the people be liberated from foreign rule. This is the purpose of the battle for liberation described throughout the book. Finally, although 1 Maccabees does not include prayers for the land, it does allude to biblical texts, which envision the post-exilic restoration to the land during its depictions of Simon's rule.

---

83. Donaldson 1981: 197.
84. Berthelot 2007: 54.
85. The first major insurrection outside the Promised Land seems to be the War of Kitos from AD 115–117. See Fuks 1961: 98–104 and Barclay 1996: 78–81.

2.5.3. *Conclusion of 1 Maccabees*

The last words of Mattathias set the stage for what was to come in the rest of the book. Just as God had rewarded faithful Israelites in the past, he would reward the faithful Maccabeans. The reward that the Maccabees receive is to rule over a restored Israel. In 1 Maccabees, this restoration brought about by the Hasmoneans (not Nehemiah's generation) is likened to Israel's golden age under Solomon. This Solomonic age was a time when the king gained full control over the land promised to Abraham. Although Simon does not recover all the Promised Land, the author of 1 Macc. 14 uses biblical texts to depict the reign of Simon as the age of the fulfillment of the land promises.

2.6. *Conclusion of Chapter 2*

The authors of the *Psalms of Solomon*, 2 Baruch, *4 Ezra*, and 1 Maccabees articulate distinctive theological concerns and visions for the present and future of Israel. Nonetheless, they are united on this: they present their royal or Messianic figures as the means by which God would be faithful to his promise of a place for his people. According to the Solomonic psalmist, God would prove himself faithful to his covenant promises by raising up a Davidic Messiah to restore Israel to the land. This Davidic Messiah would assume a rule that transcends the boundaries of the original land promises to include the known world. Those Gentiles who obey him would be blessed by his righteous leadership. The author of *2 Baruch*, writing in the aftermath of the destruction of the Temple, also looks to the coming of an anointed one whose kingdom would encompass the whole earth. This kingdom would serve as a transition point to the coming age in which God's blessings would be enjoyed forever. The author of *4 Ezra* also believes that the Davidic Messiah's kingdom would serve as the point of transition to the age to come. Finally, 1 Macc. 13–14 looks back on the reign of Simon. According to the author of 1 Macc. 14, what God had promised to do through the king (restore Israel to the land) happened in and through the activities of Simon. In the texts discussed in this chapter, the scope of the land obtained by the king varied. The author could limit his concerns to portions of Judea, all of Israel, or the whole earth. Nonetheless, the link between royal figures and the final realization of the land promises in the present age or the age to come is a stable feature of their otherwise varied discourse on Second Temple royal figures.

Chapter 3

DAVIDIC MESSIAHS AND THE LAND IN THE DEAD SEA SCROLLS

3.1. *Introduction*

In the previous chapter, we showed that various Second Temple pseudepigraphal texts claim that royal figures would enable the final realization of the land inheritance. In some cases the royal figure's rule is limited to Judea or Israel; in others the royal figure's rule extends to the known world. Despite diversity of presentations, it is clear that restoring the people to the land is a stable feature of Second Temple portrayals of royal figures. This supports our proposal that Paul's claim that Jesus has given the believer the right to share in his messianic inheritance of the entire earth as his kingdom is a manifestation of Second Temple messianism.

This chapter will further support this claim by examining four texts from Qumran: 4Q174 (4QFlorilegium), 4Q252 (4QPatriarchicalBlessings), 4Q161 (4QIsaiah Pesher[a]), and 1QSb (Blessings). We will see that these documents also link the rise of the Davidic Messiah to the final realization of the land promises. This claim about the link between David Messiahs and the final realization of the land promises need not imply that all Qumran documents articulate the same vision. Lichtenberger's words about Messiah figures at Qumran speaks to this diversity. He maintains that, "a relatively closed group like the Qumran community knew of a plurality of latter-day (saviour) figures but was also able to imagine a time of salvation without saviour figures."[1] With that diversity being acknowledged, it is still true that these four texts support the claims put forward in Chapter 2. When an author did decide to talk about a Messiah figure, that figure usually enables the final realization of the land promises.

---

1. Lichtenberger 1998: 14.

3.1.1. *The Origins of the Qumran Community and Their Exegetical Methods*

Before beginning an analysis of each text, it is important to clarify what I mean by the Dead Sea Scrolls and the Qumran Community.[2] The Dead Sea Scrolls can accurately be described as a "library" consisting of biblical texts, pseudepigraphical works, and writings composed or collected by the community.[3] The group that gathered this material operated from the latter half of the second century BC until around AD 70.[4]

Theories on the origin of the Qumran community abound. They have been associated with the Pharisees, Sadducees, Zealots, Jewish Christians, Essenes, Enochic Judaism, and Karaite Judaism of the Medieval period.[5] Others have posited that there was no Qumran community. What we call the Dead Sea Scrolls is merely a collection of texts hidden before the first insurgency against Rome.[6]

A detailed engagement with these theories is beyond the scope of this project. The three most prominent views acknowledge that the Qumranites can be accurately described as Second Temple readers and interpreters of the Hebrew Scriptures.[7] In addition, proponents of the Essene, Enochic, and Gröningen hypotheses all agree that the texts under consideration in this chapter (4Q174; 4Q161; 4Q252; 1QSb) reflect the views of the community at Qumran.[8] Therefore, I am justified in describing these texts as Qumranic. Finally, my central thesis maintains that a variety of groups reading the Jewish scriptures make similar claims about royal figures. Thus, a precise identification of the Qumran Community is not required.

---

2. Very little of what follows is controversial or groundbreaking. Nonetheless it is important to set the stage for the analysis of the four texts considered in this chapter.

3. Dimant 2000: 170–2; Campbell 2004: 10; Lange 2002: 21.

4. Callaway (1988: 49) says, "The material culture of the caves and the Qumran complex dates approximately from the late second century BCE to c. 70 CE. Thus, one infers that the people that placed the scrolls in the caves lived at Qumran during this time." See also Dimant 1984: 484.

5. For an initial bibliography, see Vermès 1981: 19. For a more updated review of the various theories as well as a bibliography, see Campbell 2004: 10–11, 18–19.

6. Golb 1995.

7. This should not be regarded as a claim that the Qumranites had a strictly defined canon identical to what we would find in Judaism and early Christianity. As Vermès (1989b: 502) says, "the Bible – however this entity was defined – wielded a unique authority within the Community." See also Fishbane 1988: 339–78.

8. Boccaccini 1998: 150; Charlesworth 2002: 5–6; García Martínez and Tigchelaar 1995: 159–86. On the sectarian origins of 1QSb, see Xeravits 2003: 28.

Since this book highlights the use of Scripture in Second Temple depictions of royal and messianic figures, a discussion of Qumranic biblical interpretation is necessary. Dead Sea Scroll scholars devote considerable attention to the method of biblical interpretation in the documents known as the Pesharim.[9] The scholarly disagreement surrounding these texts focuses on the question of hermeneutics. Do the authors at Qumran believe that they are interpreting Scripture, or are they using scriptural texts to make coded assertions about current events? Maier's summary of Pesher interpretation serves as a good presentation of the latter view:

> Characteristic for most Pesher texts are consequently references to current events, introducing frequently typological interpretations of earlier historical events, all in light of the imminent 'end of days.' A Pesher passage displays in many cases already in the form of the citation a pre-existence interpretation. The authors looked for text passages and ('atomizing' the text) even for rather small parts of them, to find the passage or word fit to serve as a vehicle for the message to be presented as a result of Pesher interpretation... The respective actual situation of the community, on the verge of the 'end of days' provided the criteria for this apparently arbitrary treatment of the prophetic texts.[10]

This definition circumscribes the importance of the biblical text. According to Maier, neither the main nor the evoked text are important to the author. Instead, biblical texts are merely useful tools for discussing ideas derived independently of the texts themselves.

This claim of atomization and lack of concern for context does not consider all the data presented to us in the Dead Sea Scrolls. Close readings of individual Pesharim reveal that the authors do not always atomize the text. In some cases, they produce contextually aware interpretations that are influenced by the text before them.[11] Vermès helpfully notes that Qumranic Pesharim contain: (1) "Cryptic-historical" exegesis that gives the characters in the prophecies sobriquets; (2) "Plain historical" exegesis that decodes a prophecy and gives it a past fulfillment; (3) "Theological" exegesis that justifies a Qumranic teaching; (4) "Neutral, non-specific interpretations" that simply interpret the text.[12] This variety shows that

---

9. See Brooke 2006: 289–300.
10. Maier 1996: 127.
11. Berrin 2005: 126–30. See also Brooke's interpretation of 1QbHap 12:14–13:4 in Brooke 2006: 313–14.
12. Vermès 1989a: 188–90. His summary focuses on continuous Pesharim (4Q161). However, he says that thematic texts such as 4Q174 contain Pesher-like interpretations. For a similar defense of engagement with the biblical text in the thematic Qumran texts, see Brooke 2005: 134–57.

each use of Scripture in the Dead Sea Scrolls must be examined in its own right to discern whether the author's use of Scripture takes the context into consideration.

In conclusion, there is a difference between a biased and an arbitrary reading of biblical texts. Qumranic exegesis shows evidence of bias more often than mere arbitrariness. This biased, but nonetheless contextually aware exegesis causes some to refer to Qumranic interpretation as "fulfilment hermeneutics"[13] or "inspired exegesis."[14] Describing the exegesis as "inspired" allows us to account for the influence of the text on the author as well as the author on the text. Therefore, we will be open to the possibility that when authors use biblical material that refer to royal and messianic figures, they do so with some awareness of the contexts of the biblical material that they use.

3.2. *4Q174 (4QFlorilegium)*

3.2.1. *Introduction*

4QFlorilegium (hereafter 4Q174) is a "pesher-like"[15] document that interprets an array of biblical texts.[16] The central passages in the extant portion of 4Q174 are 2 Sam. 7:10-14, Ps. 1:1 and Ps. 2:1.[17] The portion directly relevant to this book is the interpretation of 2 Sam. 7:10-14. It will become clear that the author believes that the Davidic Branch will enable the final realization of the land promises. Again, we will ask the following questions of the text: Does the author link the coming of the royal figure to the final realization of the land promises? Does the royal figure rule over Israel or the entire earth? Does the author use Exodus imagery to describe the journey to the inheritance?

---

13. Charlesworth, 2002: 6. For similar thoughts, see Brooke 2006: 293–4 and Vermès 1989a: 189.

14. Berrin 2005: 130.

15. Dimant (1984: 504–5) names three types of Pesharim: continuous, thematic, and isolated (imbedded within larger works). 4Q174 is called "Pesher-like" because it deviates from standard Pesharim methodology. For example, some of its interpretations of biblical material do not begin with the word "pesher."

16. Zimmermann (1998: 99) claims, "Die Schriften ist früherodianisch, 4Q174 wurde im letzten Drittel des 1 Jh. V. Chr. geschrieben." See also Steudel 1994: 7.

17. Zimmermann (1998: 107) interestingly notes, "Die Abfolge der Grundtexte (Dtn 33; 2Sam 7; Psalmen) entspricht der Abfolge Tora, Propheten, Schriften im hebräischen Kanon des AT."

3.2.2. *The Branch of David and the Land as Kingdom in 4Q174*

The 4Q174 interpretation of 2 Sam. 7:12-14 reads:

> ['And] YHWH tells you that he will build a house for you, I shall set up [קום] your seed after you and I shall establish his royal throne [for eve]r. I shall be to him as a father, and he will be to me as a son'. He is 'the Shoot [צמח] of David' who will arise with the Interpreter of the Law, who [...] in Zi[on] in the last days; as it is written, 'And I shall raise up [קום] the tabernacle of David that is fallen.' That is the tabernacle of David that is fal][len' is he] who will arise to save Israel. (4Q174 I 10-13)[18]

4Q174 describes the coming Davidic king as the Branch [צמח]. Many note that צמח alludes to a figure described in Jer. 23:5; 33:15 and Zech. 3:8-10; 6:12.[19] We can be sure that the author alludes to the figure described in these texts because they are the only ones that use צמח in a titular fashion. Using the language of Tooman, צמח is unique to Jeremiah apart from its reuse in Zechariah.[20] We can be more precise. Although Zechariah refers to a coming ruler as צמח, only the two Jeremiah texts explicitly refer to him as the צמח of David. Thus, these texts are the source of the author's allusion. The author links the Jeremiah texts to 2 Sam. 7:12 because both use קום to describe the coming Davidic offspring:

2 Sam. 7:12	When your days are fulfilled and you lie down with your ancestors, I will raise up [קום] your offspring after you, who shall come forth from your body, and I will establish his kingdom.
Jer. 23:5a	The days are surely coming, says the LORD, when I will raise up [קום] for David a righteous Branch.
Jer. 33:15a	In those days and at that time I will cause a righteous Branch to spring up [קום] for David.

In all three biblical texts, the rise of the Davidic descendant coincides with Israel's post-exilic safety in the land (Jer. 23:5; 33:15) or the establishment of this descendant's kingdom (2 Sam. 7:12). Thus, in these texts the king's rise carries with it the establishment of his kingdom.

By alluding to Jer. 23:5 and 33:15 during his interpretation of 2 Sam. 7:12, the author of 4Q174 asserts that the prophecy about the establishment of the son of David's kingdom does not refer to Solomon. Instead, 2 Sam. 7:12 predicts the rise of a future Davidic offspring. Brooke says:

---

18. All quotations of the scrolls come from García Martínez and Tigchelaar 1997 unless otherwise noted.
19. Collins 2010: 64; Oegema 1998b: 77.
20. Tooman 2011: 27–30.

The clear reference to David's immediate heir is dropped so that the commentary speaks only of an undesignated son whose throne God will establish. As the commentary makes clear, there is no reference to the house of David established by Solomon, but rather a way of introducing the shoot of David, the replacement of the old dynasty that has fallen by the new growth who will arise with the interpreter of the Law to save Israel.[21]

The author of 4Q174 supports this prediction of the coming Branch by quoting Amos 9:11, which also contains קום and David. Amos 9:11 reads, "On that day I will raise up (קום) the booth of David that is fallen, and repair its breaches, and raise up its ruins, and rebuild it as in the days of old." Although Amos 9:11 envisions the restoration of the nation, the author of 4Q174 interprets it as a reference to the restoration of the Davidic monarchy.

4Q174 refers to this Branch's role in the final realization of the land promises when it predicts that the Branch will save [ישע] Israel. Only one other Qumran text describes the king as the one who saves the nation. 1QM 11:1-3 says:

> For the battle is yours! With the might of your hand their corpses have been torn to pieces with no-one to bury them. Goliath from Gath, gallant giant you delivered into the hands of David, your servant, for he trusted in your powerful names and not in sword or spear... By the hand of our kings, besides, you have saved us many times. (1QM 11:1-3)

Even though it speaks of the king's activity, 1QM 11:1-3 ultimately credits God with bringing about Israel's salvation. 4Q174 stands alone in claiming that the king himself will save Israel.[22]

This unique focus on salvation in 4Q174 can be explained. The Qumran author refers to the salvation of Israel because Jer. 23:3-6 speaks about salvation. It reads:

> Then I myself will gather the remnant of my flock out of all the lands where I have driven them, and I will bring them back to their fold, and they shall be fruitful and multiply... The days are surely coming, says the LORD, when I will raise up for David a righteous Branch, and he shall reign as king and deal wisely, and shall execute justice and righteousness in the land. *In his days Judah will be saved [ישע] and Israel will live in safety.*[23]

21. Brooke 2005: 145.
22. Brooke (1985: 198) says that apart from 4Q174, "There is not a single use of the verb ישע that is specifically eschatological."
23. Italics added. See also Jer. 33:14–26, which mentions the salvation of Judah and Jerusalem.

As we can see from the text, the salvation of Israel and Judah consists in their return from exile to the land. However, there is a crucial difference between Jer. 23:3-6 and 4Q174. In Jer. 23:3-6, YHWH restores Israel to the land and the time of the king is characterized by salvation. The author of 4Q174 says that the king will bring salvation. This salvation of Israel in 4Q174, similar to Jer. 23:3-6, consists in the people dwelling safely in the land under his just rule. Therefore, in 4Q174 the Davidic Branch brings about the final realization of the land promises through his post-exilic reign as king.

3.2.3. *The Second Exodus to the Inheritance in 4Q174*

Two elements of 4Q174 allude to the Exodus and the final realization of the land promises. First, the author believes that his generation will experience the completion of the Exodus when God finally fulfills his promise to build the eschatological temple. Second, the author contends that God's promise that he would plant Israel in the land (Exod. 15:17) will be fulfilled when he raises up the Davidic Branch and establishes his kingdom.

To observe the first Exodus motif, we must turn our attention to the author's prediction that God would build an eschatological temple. This prediction of the eschatological temple occurs during his interpretation of 2 Sam. 7:10-11a. The biblical text reads:

> And I will appoint a place for my people Israel and will plant them, so that they may live in their own place, and be disturbed no more; and evildoers shall afflict them no more, as formerly, from the time that I appointed judges over my people Israel; and I will give you rest from all your enemies. (2 Sam. 7:10-11a)

For the author of 4Q174 the promise that YHWH would provide a place for Israel refers to the house [בית] that YHWH will build for Israel in the last days:

> [Not] [will] an enemy [strike him any]more [nor will] a son of iniquity [afflict] him [aga]in as in the past. From the day on which [I appointed judges] over my people Israel. This (refers to) the house [בית] which he will establish for [him] in the last days, as is written in the book of Moses, the Temple of YHWH your hands will est[a]blish. YHWH will reign for ever and ever. (4Q174 1:1-4)

According to 4Q174, God's promise to build a temple in 2 Sam. 7:10-11 is a reaffirmation of the promise God made to Moses at the Red Sea:

> You brought them in and planted them on the mountain of your own possession, the place, O LORD, that you made your abode, the sanctuary, O LORD, that your hands have established. (Exod. 15:17)

For the author, then, the first conquest did not complete the Exodus because it did not result in the building of the eschatological temple. Instead, the Exodus will be completed in the last days. Until God builds his final temple, his promise that he would provide a place for his people remains unfilled.

Temple building is not the only concept present in Exod. 15:17-18 and 2 Sam. 7:10-11. Both Exod. 15:17-18 and 2 Sam. 7:10-11 also look forward to Israel's planting in the land:

> You brought them in and planted them on the mountain of your own possession. (Exod. 15:17a)

> And I will appoint a place for my people Israel and will plant them, so that they may live in their own place. (2 Sam. 7:10a)

We know that this mutual discussion of planting is not a coincidence because a third text cited in 4Q174 (Amos 9:11) also looks forward to Israel's planting in the land:

> On that day I will raise up the booth of David that is fallen, and repair its breaches, and raise up its ruins… I will restore the fortunes of my people Israel, and they shall rebuild the ruined cities and inhabit them… I will plant [נטע] them upon their land, and they shall never again be plucked up out of the land that I have given them, says the LORD your God. (Amos 9:11-15)

The author believes that the fallen booth of David of Amos 9:11 is the Branch who will save Israel (4Q174 1.10-13). We can see then that, for the author, the restoration of the Davidic monarchy would also be the time of Israel's planting in the land as foretold in 2 Sam. 7:10-14, Exod. 15:17, and Amos 9:11-14. This planting, brought about by the saving work of the Branch of David, would complete the Exodus.

Therefore, although 4Q174 highlights the building of the eschatological temple, temple building itself is tied to Israel's planting in the land. This peaceful establishment in the land would complete the Exodus and signal the final realization of the land promises.

3.2.4. Conclusion

In 4Q174 the author argues that 2 Sam. 7:12-14 predicts the coming of the Davidic Branch described in Jer. 23:5 and 33:15. According to 4Q174, his coming would mean the salvation of Israel. This salvation would take the form of the Qumranites, the faithful remnant of Israel, dwelling safely in the land promised to them. Furthermore, the rise of the Branch and the building of the eschatological temple would mean that the conquest of the Promised Land is finally complete.

What cannot be missed in all of the varied texts that 4Q174 draws together is the starting point of all his reflections, namely 2 Sam. 7:10-14. 2 Samuel 7:10-14 is about a descendant of David and the establishment of his kingdom. The use of 2 Sam. 7:10-14 to predict that a coming king who would establish Israel in the land and complete the Exodus shows a thoroughgoing link between the rise of the Davidic Messiah and the final realization of the land promises in 4Q174.

3.3. 4Q252 (4QcommGen^a)

3.3.1. Introduction

4Q252 interprets and retells certain events from the book of Genesis. These events are the flood, Canaan's punishment, Abram's entry into the land, the covenant of the pieces, the destruction of Sodom and Gomorrah, the binding of Isaac, the annihilation of the Amalekites, and the blessing of the sons of Jacob. Some of the material, such as the account of the flood, can be loosely categorized as "rewritten bible" or "exegetical paraphrase" (4Q252 1:1–2:7).[24] The relevant section of this text for our purposes is the interpretation of Gen. 49:10. Therefore, it will be our focus. We will see that the author of 4Q252 believes Gen. 49:10 predicts the rise of the Davidic Branch who will restore Israel to the land and complete the Exodus.

3.3.2. The Land Inheritance and the Branch of David in 4Q252

The clearest reference to the land promises in 4Q252 comes during its allusions to the Branch prophecies found in Jeremiah. While 4Q174 focuses on Jer. 23, 4Q252 betrays a greater dependence on Jer. 33:14-26. The 4Q252 interpretation of Gen. 49:10 reads:

---

24. Saukkonen 2009: 64–5; see also Brooke 1994: 122.

3. Davidic Messiahs and the Land in the Dead Sea Scrolls

> The scepter shall [n]ot depart from the tribe [משבט] of Judah. While Israel[25] has the dominion, [there will not] be cut off someone who occupies the throne of David. For the "staff" is the covenant of royalty, the [thousa]nds of Israel are "the standards." Until the coming of the messiah of righteousness, the shoot of David. For to him and his seed has been given the covenant of kingship of his people for everlasting generations. (4Q252 5:1-4)

The statement that, "there will not be one who is cut off from the throne of David" appears in numerous texts. The greatest lexical overlap, however, is Jer. 33:17:

4Q252 5:2	לוא יכרת יושב כסא לדויד
Jer. 33:17	לא יכרת לדוד איש ישב על כסא בית ישראל

Jeremiah 33:17 is a part of a larger section that predicts the restoration of monarchy after the exile:

> The days are surely coming, says the LORD, when I will fulfill the promise I made to the house of Israel and the house of Judah. In those days and at that time I will cause a righteous Branch to spring up for David; and he shall execute justice and righteousness in the land. In those days Judah will be saved and Jerusalem will live in safety... For thus says the LORD: David shall never lack a man to sit on the throne of the house of Israel. (Jer. 33:14-17)

According to Jer. 33:14-17, the rise of the Branch would coincide with the restoration of Israel and their reception of the inheritance. Jeremiah 33:25-26 describes people restored to the land as the offspring of Abraham, Isaac, and Jacob. This mention of Abraham, Isaac, and Jacob connects the restoration to the land in Jer. 33:17-25 to the Abrahamic promises. According to 4Q252, this restoration would occur when Israel has the dominion.

---

25. Schwartz (1981: 257–66) claims that Israel stands for either a Herodian or Hasmonean king. He argues that the text says that the scepter (the Davidic lineage) would not depart from Judah (the Qumran community) during the time that Israel (the illegitimate king) has dominion. This assumes an association of Israel with the Herodians and an identification of the Qumran community with Judah that cannot be established in this context. Secondly, it assumes that the text speaks about present realities rather than the future restoration of Israel. On the future orientation of this prophecy, see Zimmermann 1998: 115–16. In addition, the Davidic figure is spoken of using the language of Jer. 33:15. The wider context of Jeremiah speaks about the restoration of Judah and Israel.

The dominion predicted in 4Q252 refers to the reestablishment of Israelite supremacy in the land and beyond. According to 4Q252, when Israel achieves this dominion, it will be led by a Davidic monarch because God gave him the covenant of royalty. Here the author evokes the covenant God established with David, which promises his offspring a kingdom (2 Sam. 7:12). Therefore, the restoration of Israelite dominion cannot precede the arrival of the Branch because the royal covenant ties Israel's safety in the land to the kingdom of the Davidic monarch. Therefore, for the author of 4Q252, the final realization of the land promises cannot be achieved without an offspring of David.

3.3.3. *The Second Exodus to the Inheritance in 4Q252*

One aspect of the 4Q252 interpretation of Gen. 49:10 evokes the Exodus. This occurs during the description of the Qumranites. It reads:

> The scepter shall [n]ot depart from the tribe of Judah. While Israel has the dominion, [there will not] be cut off someone who occupies the throne of David. For the "staff" is the covenant of royalty, the [thousa]nds of Israel (ואל[פי ישראל]) are "the standards." Until the coming of the messiah of righteousness, the shoot of David. For to him and his seed has been given the covenant of kingship of his people for everlasting generations. (4Q252 5:1-4)

In the 4Q252 interpretation, the feet [רגלים] of Gen. 49:10 are the "thousands of Israel." Pomykala astutely recognizes that:

> אלפי ישראל referred to the organizational structure of an ideal Israel, modeled on the Pentateuchal accounts of ancient Israel's wilderness journey and now represented in the Qumran community itself, for whom 'אלפים' designated both social units and military units.[26]

According to 4Q252, then, the elect of Israel will be organized and prepared for a second Exodus when the Davidic Messiah arrives. The author of 4Q252 says that they would remain organized, "until the coming of the messiah of righteousness, the shoot of David" (4Q252 5:3). Since they are waiting for his arrival, it stands to reason that when he comes he will lead them in a second conquest of the land.

---

26. Pomykala 1995: 185; Eisenman 1992: 84; cf. Exod. 18:21, 25; Num. 31:4, 48.

3.3.4. *The Branch's Eschatological Rule Beyond the Borders of Israel*

4Q252 implies that the Davidic king's rule would extend beyond the borders of Israel. The author references his rule beyond Israel when he says that the Davidic king would rule when Israel has dominion [ממשל]. Dominion could merely signify Israel's independence from foreign rule. However, other Qumran texts use ממשל to refer to Israel's rule over the nations and creation:

> He sends everlasting aid to the lot of his [co]venant by the power of the majestic angel for the sway of Michael in everlasting light, to illuminate with joy the covenant of Israel...to exalt the sway of Michael over all gods, and the dominion [ממשל] of Israel over all flesh. (1QM 17:6-8)[27]

The author of 1QM makes an analogy between Israel and the angel Michael. Just as Michael will be exalted above divine beings, Israel will have dominion over all other created beings. He makes a similar point earlier in the same text, which says:

> And this is a time of salvation for the nation and a period of rule [ממשל] for all the men of his lot, and of everlasting destruction for all the lot of Belial...and [the sons of jus]tice shall shine to all the edges of the earth. (1QM 1:5–8)

According to 1QM, the Qumran community are the sons of justice whose influence will spread throughout the earth when they defeat the sons of Belial and the Kittim. 4Q252 envisions a similar scenario. When Israel defeats her enemies and establishes her rule over the nations of the earth, there would be a Davidic king reigning on the throne.

4Q252 justifies the claim for universal dominion by asserting that God gave David the covenant of kingship:

> Until the coming of the messiah of righteousness, the shoot of David. For to him and his seed has been given the covenant of kingship of his people for everlasting generations. (4Q252 5:1-4)

The phrase ברית המלכות is not found in the Old Testament. Psalms 89:3-4, 20-29; 132:11-12, 2 Sam. 23:5, and Isa. 55:3 speak about a ברית with David.[28] Only Ps. 89:26-29 and Ps. 132:11-12 mention a covenant

---

27. Pomykala 1995: 184 n. 51.
28. Ibid.

and the establishment of David's throne. Of the two, Ps. 89:26-29 has the strongest claim to have influenced 4Q252 because it describes the covenant with David, mentions his throne, and lauds his rule over the kings of the earth:

> I will make him the firstborn, the highest of the kings of the earth. Forever I will keep my steadfast love for him, and my covenant with him will stand firm. I will establish his line forever, and his throne as long as the heavens endure. (Ps. 89:27-29)

The potential allusion to Ps. 89:27-29 further substantiates the claim that he foresees a worldwide reign for the Davidic king.

3.3.5. *Conclusion of 4Q252*

In the course of the author's interpretation of Gen. 49:10, he alludes to the Branch of David described in Jer. 33:14-26. In its original context, the Branch's rise coincides with the restoration of the offspring of Abraham, Isaac, and Jacob. By alluding to Jer. 33:14-26, the author of 4Q252 uses a text in his interpretation of Genesis that references the fulfillment of the Abrahamic promises during the reign of the Davidic king. This testifies to the link between Davidic messianism, the fulfillment of the Abrahamic promises, and the kingdom of the Messiah in some Second Temple texts.

4Q252 also predicts a second Exodus by placing the Davidic king at the head of thousands of Israelites organized and prepared for a final conquest of the land. This Davidic king would have a dominion that extends beyond the boundaries of Israel. This dominion properly belongs to the king because Ps. 89:26-29 states that God made a covenant with David that he would establish his throne high above all other rulers. Therefore, 4Q252 looks to the rise of the Davidic Branch as the time when the faithful remnant will experience the final realization of the land promises during the worldwide reign of the king.

3.4. *4Q161 (4QIsaiah Pesher^a)*

3.4.1. *Introduction*

4Q161 contains fragments of a continuous commentary on the book of Isaiah.[29] The decipherable portions comment on Isa. 10:20–11:5. The divisions in the extant portions of this commentary are self-evident:

---

29. Blenkinsopp 2006: 90.

3. Davidic Messiahs and the Land in the Dead Sea Scrolls

Isa. 10:20-21	4Q161 1:20-25
Isa. 10:22-23	4Q161 2:1-7
Isa. 10:24-27	4Q161 2:8-16
Isa. 10:28-32	4Q161 2:17-25
Isa. 10:33-34	4Q161 3:1-10
Isa. 11:1-5	4Q161 3:11-25

In our discussion of the land and royal figures in 4Q161, first I will highlight the allusions to the fulfillment of the land promises in the author's interpretation of Isa. 10:21-22. Next, I turn to the eschatological fulfillment of the land promises that will take place when God acts through the Prince of the Congregation to defeat the Kittim and establish Israel in the land. I conclude by examining the worldwide rule of the Davidic king as implied during the interpretation of Isa. 11:1-5.

3.4.2. *The Land Inheritance and the Davidic Messiah in 4Q161*

This first promise of a return to the land occurs during the author's interpretation of Isa 10:20-21. Isaiah 10:21-22 reads:

> A remnant will return, the remnant of Jacob, to the mighty God. For though your people Israel were like the sand of the sea, only a remnant of them will return. Destruction is decreed, overflowing with righteousness.

The author of 4Q161 believes that Isa. 10:21-22 pronounces judgment upon the majority Israel. He also thinks that Isa. 10:21-22 predicts the survival of a remnant. According to the Pesherist, the Isaianic prophecy does not speak to events of Isaiah's day. Instead, Isaiah looks to the author's day:

> [the remnant of I]srael is [the assembly of his chosen one...] [...] the men of his army and ...[and the remnant of Jacob is] [...] the priests [...] [Even if your people, Israel were like the sand of the sea, only a remnant will return; extermination is decreed]... [...its interpretation concerns] [...to des]troy on the da[y of slaugh]ter and many will per[ish]...but they will be saved, surely, by their planting in the land. (4Q161 1:23-25; 2:1, 5-7)

This text is fragmented, but its basic thrust is clear enough. The text contends that God decreed judgment and slaughter for the rest of Israel. By contrast, the Qumran community will be saved by their planting in the land.[30]

30. Jassen 2011: 66–9; Willitts 2006: 14.

The statement that even though Israel was like the "sand of the sea, only a remnant of them will return" could be a general reference to the loss of abundance.[31] However, this reference to "the sand of the sea" is probably an allusion to the Abrahamic promises recorded in Gen. 22:16-18.[32] In Gen. 22:16-18, God makes the following statement:

> I will indeed bless you, and I will make your offspring as numerous as the stars of heaven and as the sand that is on the seashore. And your offspring shall possess the gate of their enemies.

By using Gen. 22:16-18, Isa. 10:21-22 suggests that even though God blessed Israel by fulfilling his promise to make Abraham into a great nation, only a remnant of that multitude will survive. The description of the survivors as the "remnant of Jacob" in Isa. 10:21-22 makes the allusion to the Abrahamic promises clear. For our purposes it is important to recognize that the Qumranic author thinks that his community is this remnant of Jacob that will be restored to the land at the end.[33] This restoration to the land will realize God's promises to Abraham.

3.4.3. *The Second Exodus Led by the Prince of the Congregation*

In the 4Q161 interpretation of Isa. 10:24-27, the author says that his community will experience a second Exodus that will climax in a second conquest of the land. Isaiah 10:24-27 originally functioned as a word of comfort for the people of Israel. Isaiah consoles the people by telling them that the oppression of the Assyrians will only last a short time. After this brief period of Assyrian hegemony, YHWH will remove the Assyrian burden from Israel's neck in the same way that he rescued his people when the Egyptians oppressed them:

> Therefore thus says the Lord GOD of hosts: O my people, who live in Zion, do not be afraid of the Assyrians when they beat you with a rod and lift up their staff against you as the Egyptians did. For in a very little while my indignation will come to an end, and my anger will be directed to their

---

31. Gen. 41:49; Josh. 11:4; Judg. 7:12.
32. Blenkinsopp (2006: 115) says, "The people numerous as the sand of the sea is a fairly explicit allusion to the Abrahamic promise of progeny, 'the great nation' theme. It seems that both the Isaianic author and his Qumran interpreter have subjected this promise to drastic revision."
33. It is interesting to note that the Abrahamic promises are only made explicit for the purpose of negation. In other words, in Isaiah's day at least, some assumed that they would be saved because God made promises to Abraham. It becomes necessary to deny these promises to assure the people that the coming judgment is real.

destruction. The LORD of hosts will wield a whip against them...his staff will be over the sea, and he will lift it as he did in Egypt. On that day his burden will be removed from your shoulder, and his yoke will be destroyed from your neck. (Isa. 10:24-27)

Again, the author of 4Q161 interprets this text as a word for his own community. They will be the ones who will receive comfort. He writes, "The interpretation of the word concerns [...] when they return from the wilderness of the pe[ople]s [...] the Prince of the Congregation, and after it will be removed from them." As with other portions of 4Q161, only fragments remain. Nonetheless, we can make sense of the basic contours of his interpretation. According to the author, the community currently resides in the wilderness. The Prince of the Congregation will come, and the burden of their enemies will be removed.

The phrase "the wilderness of the peoples" [מדבר העמים] is important because it shows the Pesherist believes that his community will experience a second Exodus to the land. I make this claim because the "wilderness of the people" is a phrase unique to Ezek. 20:35:

> I will bring you out from the peoples and gather you out of the countries where you are scattered...and I will bring you into the wilderness of the peoples [מדבר העמים], and there I will enter into judgment with you face to face. As I entered into judgment with your ancestors in the wilderness of the land of Egypt... You shall know that I am the LORD, when I bring you into the land of Israel, the country that I swore to give to your ancestors. (Ezek. 20:33-37, 42)

Zimmerman, commenting on this passage, notes the connection to the Exodus when he says, "der Ort, an dem Gott Israel aus der Zerstreuung sammeln und über es Gericht halten wird; es handelt sich um das 'typologische Gegenbild' zur 'Wüste Ägyptens' nach dem Ersten Exodus."[34] Thus, for the author of 4Q161, the community's withdrawal to the desert prepares them for covenantal renewal and a return to the land.[35] Chronologically, the author thinks that his community is currently in the wilderness preparing for the return. They will return to the land at the time set by YHWH. When this second Exodus happens, the Prince of the Congregation will be in their midst. If the move to the wilderness prepares them for a second Exodus, then the battle he describes in the latter portions of 4Q161 is a second conquest of the land.

---

34. Zimmermann 1998: 66, quoting Zimmerli 1979: 456; cf. Blenkinsopp 2006: 117.

35. Zimmermann (1998: 66) mentions 1QM 1:1-7.

The role and identity of the Prince of the Congregation in 4Q161 2:14 is contested. Nonetheless, we have sound reasons for calling him a Davidic Messiah. First, CD 7:18-21 claims that the Prince of the Congregation is the scepter from the Balaam Oracle (Num. 24:17). Then in CD 7:18-21, the Interpreter of the Law is identified with the star. It reads, "And the star is the Interpreter of the Law who will come to Damascus, as is written: A star moves out of Jacob, and a sceptre arises out of Israel. The sceptre is the prince of the whole congregation and when he rises he will destroy all the sons of Seth" (CD 7:18-21). Given the fact that Num. 24:17 is a well-known messianic text, we have warrant for believing that in CD 7:18-21 and in 4Q161 the Prince of the Congregation is a Messiah figure. Secondly, in CD 7:18-21 the Prince of the Congregation engages in a battle with the community's enemies. Similarly, a messianic figure (the Branch) engages in battle with the community's enemies in 4Q161 3:11-25. The similarities to 4Q161 3:11-25 are important because that passage includes an interpretation of Isa. 11:1-5, a text that looks to the restoration of the Davidic Dynasty. Thus, similarities between the Prince of the Congregation in the earlier section of 4Q161 and the Branch in the latter portions of 4Q161 lead to the conclusion that both titles refer to the Davidic Messiah.[36]

The 4Q161 2:17-24 interpretation of Isa. 10:28-32 continues the presentation begun in 4Q161 2:8-16 by giving the royal figure a central role in the second land conquest. Originally Isa. 10:28-32 describes the march of the Assyrians to Jerusalem.[37] But in the hands of the Pesherist, Isa. 10:28-32 becomes a prediction of an eschatological battle.

Despite the agreement on the overall meaning of 4Q161 2:17-24, scholars dispute a few details in this section. The contested portion reads:

> The interpretation of this saying concerns the final days, when the [...] comes [...] [...] from his climb from the plain of Akko to do battle against Pales[tine...] [...] and there is none like her and in all the cities of the [...] and up to the boundary of Jerusalem. (4Q161 2:22-25)

Willitts believes that 4Q161 describes the march of the Messiah and the remnant to Jerusalem.[38] Once in Jerusalem, they will do battle with the Kittim and the wicked of Israel.[39] He claims:

---

36. Blenkinsopp 2006: 117.
37. Motyer 1993: 119–20.
38. Willitts 2006: 16.
39. Ibid.: 15; Bauckham 1995: 204; Blenkinsopp 2006: 118.

4Q161 is an account of the eschatological war of the sons of light led by the Messianic figure against both the Kittim and the wicked of God's people. The sons of Light comprise the remnant of Israel whom God has saved through their participation in the planting.[40]

As evidence, Willitts cites 1QM 1:1-7. 1QM 1:1-7 also mentions a return from the wilderness of the peoples and a battle against the Kittim and disobedient Israel.[41] Zimmerman disagrees. He believes that 4Q161 chronicles the march of the Kittim against Israel.[42] He says, "Wahrscheinlich word in der eschatologischen Interpretation darin Feldzug der Kittim und die von ihnen ausgehende Bedrohung gesehen, die 'bis zum Gebiet Jerusalems' (Z. 25 Auslegung zu Jes 10, 32) reicht."[43]

Since the author already said that community is in the wilderness, the view that they will accompany the Messiah to Jerusalem for the final battle best fits the context of 4Q161.[44] In either interpretation, the messianic figure and his armies act to liberate Israel from oppression. Therefore, he leads the second Exodus to the promised inheritance.

3.4.4. *The Branch's Rule Beyond the Borders of Israel in 4Q161*

The final extant interpretation of Isaiah focuses on Isa. 11:1-5. According to the Pesherist, this text foretells the coming worldwide rule of the Branch of David. In context, Isa. 11:1-5 predicts the restoration of the Davidic monarchy in the form of a king who will be empowered by the Spirit of YHWH to practice justice and righteousness:

> A shoot shall come out from the stump of Jesse, and a branch shall grow out of his roots. The spirit of the LORD shall rest on him, the spirit of wisdom and understanding… He shall not judge by what his eyes see, or decide by what his ears hear; but with righteousness he shall judge the poor, and decide with equity for the meek of the earth; he shall strike the earth with the rod of his mouth, and with the breath of his lips he shall kill the wicked. Righteousness shall be the belt around his waist, and faithfulness the belt around his loins. (Isa. 11:1-5)

---

40. Willitts 2006: 16.
41. Ibid.: 19.
42. Zimmermann 1998: 67.
43. Ibid.
44. Even if the interpretation of Zimmerman is adopted it would not change the role of the Davidic Branch. In his reading the Branch and the armies of Israel defeat the Kittim upon their arrival in Jerusalem. See ibid.: 71.

According to 4Q161, Isa. 11:1-5 describes the Branch of David who will arise in the last days. It says:

> [the interpretation of the word concerns the shoot] of David which will sprout in the final days, since] [with the breath of his lips he will execute] his ene[my] and God will support him with [the spirit of c]ourage…[… throne of glory], h[oly] crown and mutli-colour[ed] vestments […] his sword will judge all the peoples. (4Q161 3:18-21)

This reference to judgment of "all peoples" refers to the universal reign foretold in Isa. 11:1-5. According to the author of 4Q161, the restoration of Israel at the time of the second Exodus will lead to the worldwide sovereignty of the Branch of David.

3.4.5. Conclusion of 4Q161

The author of 4Q161 thinks that the Davidic Branch will participate in a second Exodus that will climax in the fulfillment of the land promises. When this happens the Davidic king will have a rule that extends beyond the borders of Israel. The author presents the coming accomplishments of the Davidic king as the fulfillment of the Abrahamic promises during his interpretation of Isa. 10:21-22. Isaiah 10:21-22 alludes to the Abrahamic promises when it says that only a remnant of the "sand of the sea" will survive the coming judgment. This sand of the sea language is best explained as an allusion to God's promise to Abraham that his offspring would become a great nation and inherit the land. According to the author of 4Q161, however, the vast majority of Israel had forfeited this right. His community, the remnant of Abraham and Jacob's people, will receive what the rest of Israel had lost. They will flourish under the reign of the Davidic king. Thus, 4Q161 is an example of a Second Temple document that says that God's promises to Abraham will be realized through the establishment of the worldwide kingdom of the Davidic Messiah.

3.5. *1QSb (Blessings)*

3.5.1. Introduction

1QSb consists of a series of blessings given to members of the Qumran community, including the high priest, the Zadokite priesthood, the community as a whole, and the Prince of the Congregation.[45] Our focus

---

45. Scholars debate how many groups were blessed in this document. Abegg (2003: 8) and Stegemann (1996: 496–9) argued for six. Charlesworth and Stuckenbruck

will be on the last of these, the blessing of the Prince of the Congregation. This blessing is directly relevant to my thesis because it concludes with a plea that the Prince of the Congregation establish the kingdom for the Qumranites. Thus, it is yet another example of the link between Davidic Messiahs and the final realization of the land promises as kingdom in Second Temple Judaism.

3.5.2. *The Prince of the Congregation and the Kingdom*

The pertinent section of 1QSb begins with a call for the Master, a prominent member of the Qumran community, to bless the Prince of the Congregation (1QSb 5:20).[46] The exact language of the opening is fragmented and hard to discern. Charlesworth and Stuckenbruck argue that 1QSb's blessing of the Prince of the Congregation begins with a call to renew the covenant with the Qumran community. In their reconstruction, 1QSb 5:21 says: וברית היחד יחדש.[47] However, Stegemann observes that, "the restoration of its gap in the editio princeps is disputable, as the word היחד needs one more broad letter than the available space allows. Instead, the restoration of the name דויד fits well with the space of the letters."[48] In this reading the author asks God to renew the covenant with David.[49] Thus, the reconstructed text should read: וברית דויד יחדש.[50] This reconstruction is relevant to our argument for two reasons. First, it shows that the author of 1QSb thinks that the Prince of the Congregation is a Messiah because the Davidic covenant will be renewed with him.[51] Second, it displays the link between Davidic messianism and the establishment of the kingdom that we have been arguing for throughout. According to 1QSb, the purpose of

---

(1994: 119) discerned eight. Xeravits (2003: 28) believed that identifying exactly who was blessed is impossible. Settling this debate is beyond the scope of this book. For our purposes, it is sufficient to note that most agreed that 1QSb 5:20-29 describes the blessing of the Prince of the Congregation.

46. Charlesworth and Stuckenbruck 1994: 120.

47. Ibid.: 128.

48. Stegemann 1996: 499. See also Xeravits 2003: 31 and Zimmerman 1998: 53–4.

49. Zimmerman (1998: 55) notes that the contextual evidence supports this reading even if the manuscript itself is less than clear. He says, "Die Rede von der Erneuerung des Davidbundes ist zwar nicht sicher, fügt sich aber gut in den Kontext des Segens."

50. Stegemann 1996: 499.

51. Xeravits (2003: 32) argues that the Davidic covenant language was influenced by Ps. 89:4. See our discussion of Ps. 89:4 and its potential influence on 4Q252 above.

renewing the covenant with the Prince is so that he will, "establish the kingdom of his people forever" (1QSb 5:21).[52]

According to 1QSb, establishing this kingdom will involve the Prince of the Congregation judging "the poor with justice" and entreating the humble to "walk in perfection" (1QSb 5:21-22). Here the author alludes to Isa. 11:2-5, which contains a prediction of the post-exilic restoration of the Davidic monarchy.[53] If the kingdom of 1QSb is the kingdom led by the Davidic king in Isa. 11:1-5, then the reign of the Messiah in 1QSb will not be limited to Israel. He will have dominion over the nations of the earth as predicted in Isa. 11.

1QSb further reveals a belief in the expansive and worldwide kingdom of the Prince of the Congregation on four occasions. First, the blessing says concerning the Prince of the Congregation, "with the power of your [mouth.] With your scepter may you lay waste the earth" (1QSb 5:24). Here the author again draws upon Isa. 11:4 to describe the rule of the Prince of the Congregation. Isaiah 11:4 can be identified as the source text because it says that the Davidic monarch will strike the earth with the rod of his mouth. But destruction is not the full extent of the Prince's rule. The author also uses Isa. 11:2 to describe the Prince's just rule (1QSb 5:25). Taken together it seems, then, that the author believes that the Prince of the Congregation will destroy Israel's enemies and rule righteously over the Qumranites, the faithful remnant of the people of God. The second reference to his worldwide authority comes when he says that the Prince will, "trample the nations like the mud of the streets" (1QSb 5:27). This again makes it quite clear that as a part of the renewal of the covenant, God will use the king to defeat Israel's enemies and establish the kingdom.

The final two mentions of the worldwide kingdom come in 1QSb 5:27-28. There the author claims that God will raise the sceptre for the Prince. Here the author draws upon Num. 24:17, another text that was read messianically in the Second Temple period.[54] Lastly, the author says that "all nations will serve" the Prince of the Congregation. Here the author is influenced by the prayer that all nations will serve the Davidic son in Ps. 72:11. This claim of an allusion to Ps. 72:11 can be strengthened by looking at the fragmented section of 1QSb 5:28. In the 1QSb manuscript, there is space for a missing phrase between the discussion of the rulers

---

52. Even if 1QSb 5:21 refers to the covenant with the community, the king is still tasked with restoring the kingdom for the people. Thus, in either interpretation, 1QSb looks to the final realization of the land promise through the establishment of the Messiah's kingdom.

53. Evans 2003: 92–3; Oegema 1998b: 59; Xeravits 2003: 31.

54. Pate 2000: 111.

3. Davidic Messiahs and the Land in the Dead Sea Scrolls

and before the proclamation that all nations will serve the Prince of the Congregation.[55] 1QSb 5:28 reads: למושלים לפניכ...וכול לאומים יעובדוכה. The New English Translation of the Dead Sea scrolls suggests that the missing phrase is a prayer that all peoples bow down [וישתחוו] to him.[56] If this reading is correct, then the author of 1QSb 5:28 would be following the parallelism of Ps. 72:11, which says, "May all kings fall down before him [וישתחוו], all nations give him service [יעבדוהו]."[57] The potential link to Ps. 72:11 is important because the call for the nations to serve and bow down to the Davidic king is explicitly tied to the expansion of the Abrahamic land promise to include the whole earth during the reign of the Davidic king (Ps. 72:8-11). Even if we cannot establish a direct link to Ps. 72:8-11, the fact remains that the author believes that the Prince of the Congregation will rule over the nations of the earth when he establishes his kingdom.

3.5.3. Conclusion of 1QSb

The blessing of the Prince of the Congregation is brief. Nonetheless, in the author's terse remarks, he fills his blessing with texts that are given messianic readings in the Second Temple period. He alludes to Isa. 11:1-5, Num. 24:17, Ps. 72:11, and Gen. 49:9-10.[58] He also makes it clear that the coming of the Prince of the Congregation means that the Qumran community will participate in the kingdom that he brings into being. This kingdom is not limited to the nation of Israel. All nations will serve him. Thus, this document displays the link between the Messiah and the final realization of the land promises as kingdom.

3.6. Conclusion of Chapter 3

This chapter considered four texts from Qumran: 4Q174, 2Q252, 1QSb, and 4Q161. In each text, the author uses a variety of biblical texts to predict the coming of a royal figure in the last days. In each of these Qumranic accounts, a central feature of his arrival and rule is the final realization of the land promises. In addition, all four use second Exodus

---

55. See Charlesworth and Stuckenbruck 1994: 130.
56. Wise, Abegg, and Cook 1996.
57. That Ps. 72 itself contains prayers for the king makes it likely that the author of 1QSb would turn to this text for inspiration.
58. In 1QSb 5:28 he describes the Prince of the Congregation as a "lion" over against his prey. This text, again, draws upon 49:10, a text that is given a messianic reading in 4Q252. On the use of Gen. 49:9, see Oegema 1998b: 59.

imagery to describe this final realization of the land promises. This link between the royal figure and the final realization of the land promises supports the claim that these authors associate the Davidic Messiah with the final fulfillment of the land promises. In 4Q174, the author focuses on the establishment of his community in Israel. In 4Q252, 1QSb, and 4Q161, the authors believe that the final realization of the land promises will occur alongside the worldwide sovereignty of the Davidic Messiah. Furthermore, the final two (possibly three) texts (4Q252, 4Q161, and 1QSb[?]) allude to the fulfillment of the Abrahamic promises through the establishment of the messianic figure's kingdom.

What does the preceding analysis of these Second Temple texts mean for the study of messianism and inheritance in Galatians? First, I contended in Chapter 1 that those who have argue for messianism in Galatians consistently maintain that what makes Galatians messianic is its focus on the inheritance as kingdom. Chapters 2 and 3 have shown that if Paul does argue that Jesus, as God's Son and Israel's Messiah, began the final realization of the land promises, such a claim is the type of claim that Second Temple authors make about royal figures. The kingdom, then, is a central point of contact between Pauline and Second Temple portrayals of royal and messianic figures. Furthermore, the universalization of the land promises in Galatians would not be without precedent. Other Second Temple Jews make similar claims.

It is the burden of the following chapters to show that sharing in the messianic son's inheritance of the whole earth is indeed a central feature of the argument of Galatians. But before turning to Galatians it is important to note the distinction between the means of enabling the final realization of the land promises in Galatians and the Second Temple texts considered thus far. Most of these Second Temple texts assume that the promises about the land will be achieved through an eschatological battle against the enemies of the people of God. These enemies are often Gentiles and other Israelite groups that the author deems unfaithful to the covenant. This theme of the destruction of the Gentiles is obviously absent in Galatians. Instead, we will see that Paul highlights the participation of Jews and Gentiles alike in the messianic son's inheritance of the whole earth, which Christ makes possible through his death that ends the curse. Paul is unique in his beliefs about the means of acquiring the inheritance. Secondly, in contrast to what we have seen so far, the ownership of the inheritance is radically personalized. Rather than focusing on the fact that the Messiah enables the faithful to participate in the inheritance promised to the nation, Galatians focuses on Jesus's right to the inheritance that belongs to him as king and Messiah (Gal. 3:16, 26-29). It is Paul's claim that the Messiah owns the inheritance that is unique in Second Temple Judaism. Nonetheless, this initial singular heirship of the Messiah Jesus forms the basis for a radical sharing of that same inheritance as an act of graciousness. It is precisely because the inheritance belongs to Christ that all those united to him by faith can hope to experience the final realization of God's promises to Abraham in Christ's worldwide kingdom. This is why at two climactic points in his argument Paul reminds the Galatians that they are heirs through their relationship to Christ, "And if you belong to Christ, then you are Abraham's offspring, heirs according to the promise... So you are no longer a slave but a child, and if a child then also an heir, through God" (Gal. 3:29; 4:7).

Chapter 4

THE END OF THE CURSE AND THE BEGINNING
OF THE INHERITANCE:
DAVIDIC MESSIANISM, THE SPIRIT,
AND THE ABRAHAMIC LAND PROMISE IN
GALATIANS 3:1–14

4.1. *Introduction*

In this chapter we turn our attention away from Second Temple depictions of royal figures to consider Paul's argument about the Messiah Jesus in Gal. 3:1–14. In previous chapters I showed that it was quite common to associate royal figures with the final realization of the land promises. In these portrayals the "land" could be limited to Judea or Israel. The royal or messianic figures in these accounts could also conquer and rule the whole earth. With this diversity of portrayals being granted, we can still affirm with confidence that the link between royal or messianic figures and final realization of the land promises is a stable feature of Second Temple discourse.

In this chapter (and the one that follows), I show that Paul portrays Jesus as the Messiah who enables believing Jews and Gentiles to share in his messianic inheritance of the renewed earth on the basis of faith apart from the works of the Law. I prove that, according to Paul, the inheritance of the whole earth belongs to Jesus because he is the messianic seed and son of God. Therefore, Paul's understanding of the inheritance is inseparable from his claim that Jesus is the Messiah.

In my analysis of Gal. 3:1-14, I support the claim that Paul has the believer's participation in the worldwide inheritance of the Messiah Jesus in mind by demonstrating that Paul presents the death of Jesus as the solution to the problem of the Deuteronomic curses. Establishing a focus on the Deuteronomic curses is important because these curses stand in the way of the final realization of the land inheritance (Deut. 28:64-68). Here my claim is simple. The covenant curses to a large extent focus on the loss of the land inheritance. Therefore, to posit Jesus's death as the means by which God removes the curse means that his death inaugurates the final realization of the land inheritance.

This link between the removal of the curse and the reception of the inheritance explains the transition from curse to heir and inheritance language as we move from Gal. 3:1-14 to Gal. 3:15–4:7. The fact that the area recovered (the whole earth) extends beyond the area lost (Israel) does not make Galatians any less about restoration than it would have been for the authors of *2 Baruch* or *4 Ezra*.[1] Furthermore, I argue that by alluding to Davidic texts in the midst of his argument in Gal. 3:1-14 (and 3:15–4:7), Paul demonstrates that he makes an indisputably messianic claim reformulated around the cross. According to Paul, it is precisely in and through his death and resurrection that Jesus reveals himself to be Israel's Messiah because his death ends the covenant curses. By ending the curses he enables those who believe to participate in the worldwide inheritance over which Christ reigns (Ps. 2:7-8; 2 Sam. 7:12; Gal. 3:16, 26-29).

This reading of Gal. 3:1-14 will posit two revisions of the scholarly consensus. First, I maintain that the blessing of Abraham alluded to in Gal. 3:8 and 3:14 refers to the justification that makes the Gentiles Abraham's seed. This reading stands in contrast with those who claim that the blessing of Abraham is the Spirit. This status as Abraham's seed makes the Galatians heirs in Christ to his inheritance of the whole earth.[2] Second, I contend that the gift of the Spirit described in Gal. 3:2-5 and 3:14b does not replace the land inheritance. Instead, the gift of the Spirit signals the believer's status as an heir and functions as the beginning of the inheritance.[3]

I divide my analysis of Gal. 3:1-14 in a way that should be non-controversial. I open with a consideration of 3:1-5 before turning to Gal. 3:6-9. I conclude with an analysis of 3:10-14. In each section, I summarize the major points of my argument first and then engage in a close reading of the text. Although there are innumerable contested issues surrounding Gal. 3:1-14, I will deal only with those that have direct bearing on the question of Davidic messianism and the inheritance. Finally, it is important to keep in mind that although Paul does not mention the inheritance directly in Gal. 3:1-14, this passage prepares the way for an extensive discussion of heirs and inheritance in 3:15–4:7. This justifies our consideration of this section of the letter.

1. See Chapter 2.
2. See the discussion of Christ's inheritance in Chapter 5.
3. See 2 Cor. 1:22; 5:5; Rom. 8:23; Eph. 1:14.

4.2. Galatians 3:1-5

4.2.1. Overview

Galatians 3:1-5 reflects Paul's belief that Jesus's death removes the curse and makes the Galatians heirs to the whole earth as their inheritance. I pursue two lines of evidence to support this interpretation. First, I adopt and expand upon Eastman's claim that Paul's use of βασκαίνω to describe his opponents' bewitching behavior likens them to the people who cast the evil eye in the context of the Deuteronomic curses (Deut. 28:53-61).[4] This allusion to the Deuteronomic curses bolsters the claim about the inheritance in Galatians because Paul asserts that his opponents remain under the covenant curses. In Gal. 3:1, then, Paul warns the Galatians that if they come under the spell of his adversaries, they too will come under the curse and alienate themselves from the community that stands to inherit. The evidence for the inheritance in Gal. 3:1, then, is indirect. The positive status of heirs to the inheritance can be seen by what Paul believes the Galatians will lose by coming under the Law. Later in 3:26-29 and 4:4-7 Paul affirms his central claim that those in Christ are heirs to the Messiah's inheritance. Second, I strengthen the argument for an allusion to the Deuteronomic curses in 3:1 by attending to Paul's so-called argument from experience in Gal. 3:2-5. While many highlight the "experience of the Spirit," scholars neglect the fact that the outpouring of the Spirit signals the end of the Deuteronomic curses and the beginning of the final realization of the land promises in the very prophetic texts that they themselves cite.[5]

One notable exception to this trend of ignoring the link between the Spirit and the end of the Deuteronomic curses will be Morales.[6] He argues that Spirit reception is linked to the restoration of Israel in biblical and Second Temple texts. I agree that Spirit reception is linked to the restoration to the land in the texts he analyses. However, Morales does not sufficiently highlight the fact that the best parallels to Paul's thought would be those accounts of restoration that center around the agency of the Messiah.[7] Stated differently, Galatians does not merely draw upon the motif of the Spirit and restoration; it draws upon the motif of restoration through the agency of the Messiah.

Recognizing the connection between the Spirit, the end of the curses, and the restoration to the inheritance explains why the Spirit functions as

---

4. Eastman 2001: 69–87.
5. On allusions to prophetic texts in Gal. 3:2-5, see Schreiner 2010: 184; Barclay 1988: 84; Dunn 1993: 153; Das 2014: 289.
6. See Morales 2010.
7. See his discussion of messianic restoration in Morales 2010: 15–17.

evidence that the Galatians are members of Abraham's family. The Spirit evinces family membership because many of Israel's prophetic texts predict that God will pour out the Spirit upon Abraham's family after the national curses outlined in Deut. 27–29 are over. Thus, the Spirit described in Gal. 3:2-5 and later 3:14 supports my claim that the "curse" referred to throughout this section refers to the national curses, which stand in the way of the final realization of the inheritance. According to Paul, Jesus's redemptive-restorative death ends this curse and enables believing Jews and Gentiles to become heirs to the inheritance that ultimately belonged to Jesus, the seed of David and Abraham (Gal. 3:16-19).

4.2.2. *The Evil Eye and the Covenant Curses in Galatians 3:1*

Paul opens by claiming that the foolish Galatians must be under the influence of the evil eye [βασκαίνω] if they want to come under the works of the Law after hearing Paul preach Christ crucified. Much of the discussion surrounding this text focuses on whether or not Paul's claim is metaphorical.[8] There are two reasons for suggesting that Paul has a literal interpretation in mind. First, in Paul's day casting the evil eye was quite common, and his audience would have probably taken his claim seriously.[9] Second, Oakes has shown that the examples of the metaphorical use of βασκαίνω put forward by Betz, Witherington, and de Boer are actually literal.[10] While the debate over how seriously to take Paul's wording is important, we are still left with the question of why Paul refers to the influence of the evil eye at all.

Eastman argues that Paul's use of βασκαίνω evokes the use of the evil eye in the context of the covenant curses outlined in Deut. 28:53-61.[11] The curses described in Deut. 28:53-61 foretell the results of national disobedience to the Law. This text predicts that, in the midst of a foreign army's siege, starving Israelites will, "cast the evil eye on their next of kin [βασκανεῖτῷ ὀφθαλμῷ]."[12] If Paul alludes to this text, then he is claiming that those of the works of the Law are under the Deuteronomic curses

---

8. On the metaphorical use of βασκαίνω, see Witherington 2004: 203; de Boer 2011: 170; Betz 1979: 131. For a reading that claims that Paul believes that his opponents did indeed "cast an evil eye," see Bruce 1982: 148; Martyn 1997: 282; Becker 1998: 46. Schlier (1965: 119) calls their influence "Bezauberung." Moo (2013: 181) takes a mediating position between the metaphorical and the literal reading.
9. Nanos 2003: 3–4.
10. See Oakes 2015: 101–2.
11. Eastman 2001: 69–87. See also Garlington 2007: 180; Wilson 2007: 54–5.
12. Eastman 2001: 70.

and for that reason are outside of community that stands to inherit. This interpretation of βασκαίνω has the benefit of linking the evil eye in 3:1 to the use of Deuteronomy in the latter portions of this section (Gal. 3:10, 13). Thus, the proposal warrants further consideration.

Wilson, who also adopts this reading, summarizes the major pieces of evidence: (1) βασκαίνω is a rare lexeme occurring only four times in the LXX. Two of these four uses occur in Deut. 28:53-61. (2) Paul quotes Deut. 28:58 in 3:10b. This shows that this section of Deuteronomy is a central feature of this portion of Galatians. (3) If Gal. 3:1 alludes to the covenant curses, then both 3:1 and 3:13 present the crucified Jesus as the antidote to the curse.[13]

Based on this evidence, I infer that Paul believes that, by virtue of their demand that the Galatians do the works of the Law, his opponents are acting from within the curse by casting an envious evil eye on the Galatians' freedom. Furthermore, their behavior is a threat to the Galatians because it could draw them into the same cursed state.[14] Eastman translates Gal. 3:1 as, "You foolish Galatians! Who has put you under the curse, you before whose eyes Jesus Christ was publicly portrayed as crucified?"[15]

In conclusion, Paul believes that his opponents remain under the covenant curses and, for this reason, they are in danger of not inheriting with the Messiah Jesus. The use of the language of the evil eye, then, has the rhetorical function of likening his opponents' behavior to the behavior of the generation that first experienced the covenant curses. Paul's rhetorical move at the opening of this section suggests that the national curses play a central role in his depiction of those defined by the "works of the Law."

4.2.3. *The Spirit and the Restoration from the Covenant Curses in Galatians 3:2-5*

In Gal. 3:2-5 Paul reminds the Galatians that they received the Spirit through believing what they heard and not by doing the works of the Law.[16] Many scholars consider Gal. 3:2-5 to be Paul's argument from experience, which he later substantiates through his exegesis of biblical

---

13. Wilson 2007: 54–5.
14. Eastman 2001: 72.
15. Ibid.: 72.
16. The meaning of ἀκοῆς πίστεως is contested. There are two options for interpreting ἀκοῆς. It can refer to the act of hearing or the message that one hears. Πίστεως can describe the act of believing or the message that is believed. The two options for interpreting each word generates four possible readings: (1) the Galatians received the Spirit by hearing with faith; (2) the Galatians received the Spirit by hearing about

material in Gal. 3:6-14.[17] They contend that Paul relies upon the vibrancy of the Galatians' experience to convince them that God accepted them by faith apart from the works of the Law.[18] Representing this view, Dunn says, "it cannot really be understood in other than experiential terms... [T]he appeal is clearly to an event which Paul could expect them vividly to remember."[19]

While the vibrancy of their experience should not be denied, an appeal to experience alone assumes that Paul's interpretation of the Galatians' experience does not itself rest on his interpretation of biblical texts. Rabens, in a study on the relationship between experience and interpretation, recognizes that, "Experiences are dependent on interpretation, because, alongside the sensory perceptions, a prestructuring cognitive interpretation is part of the experience."[20] He goes on to suggest that one of these "prestructured cognitive" influences on Paul is the Jewish Scriptures. He says, "The religious experiences of the early churches were interpreted against the backdrop of (biblical) prophecies and expectations."[21] Therefore, it is not sufficient to claim that Paul appeals to their experience. Instead, we must seek to understand why Paul concludes that their experience of the Spirit functions as evidence that God accepts the Galatians by faith without requiring the works of the Law.

the faith (the gospel message); (3) the Galatians received the Spirit by the message that leads to faith; (4) the Galatians received the Spirit by the message of the faith. Since Paul's impending discussion of Abraham will emphasize that faith is the sole requirement for covenant membership, it seems that in 3:2-5 he refers to the fact that the Galatians believed the message that they heard. Thus, Paul's meaning here is similar to Rom. 10:17. See Wright 2002: 668. For a more lengthy treatment of the exegetical issues involved, see Hays 2002: 124–32 and Schreiner 2010: 182–3. For an extensive defense of "believing what is heard" that considers Rom. 10:14-17 and an allusion to Isa. 53:1, see Harmon 2010: 125–33.

17. Witherington 2004: 200; Dunn 1993: 150; Betz 1979: 132; Mußner 1974: 208; Schlier 1965: 121.

18. Cosgrove (1998: 1–38) is correct to highlight the importance of the Spirit in the argument of Galatians. Nonetheless, he is incorrect to assert that Spirit, not justification was the driving issue in Galatians. In his proposal, he suggested that Gal. 3:1-5 should define the central theme of the letter because 3:1-5 contained Paul's first words that addressed the situation in Galatia. Galatians 1:1–2:21, however, set the parameters for much of what is discussed in the latter portions of the letter. See Lyons 1991: 173; Carson 1990: 241; and Barclay 2015b: 389 n. 2. See also the importance of letter openings in setting the stage for the central themes of Paul's letters as set forth in Jervis 1991.

19. Dunn 1993: 153; Moo 2013: 182.

20. Rabens 2012: 140 (emphasis added).

21. Ibid.: 154.

The prophetic texts that describe the outpouring of the Spirit on the other side of the Deuteronomic curses led Paul to interpret the gift of the Spirit as the sign that the Galatians are experiencing the beginning of the inheritance.[22] Many note that the gift of the Spirit is associated with the eschatological age: (1) Schreiner cites Isa. 32:15;[23] (2) Barclay points to Ezek. 37;[24] (3) Dunn suggests Isa. 32:15, Ezek. 37:4-14, and Joel 2:28-29.[25] Yet none of these authors connect Paul's reference to the Spirit in Gal. 3:2-5 and 3:14 to the question of whether Paul alludes to the national covenant curses outlined in Deut. 27–29 in Gal. 3:1 and later in Gal. 3:10-14. However, the prophetic texts cited above all depict the outpouring of the Spirit as an element of Israel's restoration to the inheritance on the other side of the national covenantal curses.[26] Thus, describing the gift of the Spirit solely in terms of the eschatological age clouds the relationship between the Spirit, the Deuteronomic curses, and the restoration to the inheritance in the prophetic texts cited above and in Galatians.[27]

I cite one of these texts as representative. Isaiah 32:14-16 reads:

> For the palace will be forsaken, the populous city deserted; the hill and the watchtower will become dens forever, the joy of wild asses, a pasture for flocks; until a spirit from on high is poured out on us, and the wilderness

---

22. Fung (1988: 134) comes close to this when he calls the Spirit, "the pledge of final salvation." But again, in Galatians the Spirit was the pledge of the final inheritance.

23. Schreiner 2010: 184.

24. Barclay 1988: 84. In his later work Barclay says that Paul's argument about the gift of the Spirit in 3:1-5 is similar to the argument we encounter in Acts. By this he means that the gift of Spirit shows that God has accepted the Gentiles into his family. If Paul is influenced by an idea similar to what find in Acts, my proposal would be unaffected because Acts interprets the gift of the Spirit in light of prophetic texts that envision Israel's restoration after the curses. For example, Acts 2:40 concludes with a call to σώθητε ἀπὸ τῆς γενεᾶς τῆς σκολιᾶς ταύτης. Many see this as a clear allusion to Deut. 32:5 where those who experienced the curses are called γενεὰ σκολιά. Thus, in Acts 2:40 conversion entails fleeing the generation under the covenant curses. On the allusion to Deut. 32:5 in Acts 2:40, see Wall 2002: 68 and Jervell 1998: 151. On the similarity between Acts and Galatians as it pertains to the gift of the Spirit, see Barclay 2015b: 391 and Schlier 1965: 121.

25. Dunn 1993: 153. On the allusion to Joel, see Das 2014: 289.

26. On the Spirit and the restoration in prophetic texts, see Morales 2010: 13–39.

27. Moo (2013: 182) says that the Spirit marks "the new age of salvation." This is true enough, but it clouds the relationship between the Spirit, the restoration, and the inheritance in Galatians. See the discussion of Watson 2004 and his focus on salvation below.

becomes a fruitful field, and the fruitful field is deemed a forest. Then justice will dwell in the wilderness, and righteousness abide in the fruitful field. (Isa. 32:14-16)

Isaiah 32:14 begins with the city in a state of ruin because of the nation's disobedience. These ruins are the visible manifestation of the covenant curses. The Spirit signals the end of those curses by transforming the people and the land, and by enabling the flourishing of a just society. According to Paul, if the Galatians have received this Spirit, then they are a part of the people being restored to the inheritance after the covenant curses are over. Speaking of Paul's so-called argument from experience, Jobes says:

> the argument appears at first to be a weak one because it seems to be based upon subjective human experience. To the contrary, Paul is grounding his argument not in the subjective experience of the Galatian churches, but in the canonical prophecy given by Isaiah, which identifies the seed who will inherit as those upon whom the Spirit rests.[28]

Crucial to this interpretation is the role that the Spirit plays in identifying the people being restored. Given that the Spirit helps identify those being restored, there is no reason to believe that the Spirit replaces the final realization of the inheritance. In fact, there is a clear sense in Isa. 32:15 and the other texts cited above that the Spirit will also transform creation.

In any case, the relationship between the gift of the Spirit and the end of the curses enables us to see how Paul could claim that the gift of the Spirit through faith in Christ proves that the Galatians are sons and heirs (3:6-9, 26-29; 4:1-11). If the Galatians have the Spirit, then they must be in Abraham's family. This need not imply that the Gentiles were under the Deuteronomic curses before they received the Spirit. Instead, Paul's argument suggests that they have been invited to join the people of God after those curses have ended.

Therefore, the Spirit does function experientially in Galatians. The Galatians' experience of the Spirit confirms they are the Spirit-filled people predicted in elements of Israel's prophetic tradition. Thus, it is a mistake to claim that the Spirit replaces the land inheritance. It does just the opposite. The Spirit allows the Galatians to begin a life of love and mutual sacrifice until the coming kingdom arrives (Gal. 5:16-21).[29]

28. Jobes (1993: 312) has a different portion of Isaiah in mind, but the statement is true of the prophetic depictions of the Spirit more broadly. See also Morales 2010: 85.
29. On Jesus's status as the Davidic Messiah, see the discussion of 3:6-9 below.

To summarize, in Gal. 3:1-5 Paul argues that those attempting to convince the Galatians that they should come under the works of the Law are operating from within the age defined by the covenant curses. Worse still, they are attempting to bring the Galatians under that curse. This bewitching behavior should be impossible because of Paul's preaching of the gospel and the Galatians' experience of the Spirit. This Spirit inaugurates the restoration predicted in some of Israel's prophetic texts. Those prophetic texts look to the restoration of a people transformed by the Spirit to a creation made new on the other side of the covenant curses.

4.3. Galatians 3:6-9

4.3.1. Overview

In Gal. 3:6-9 Paul uses Gen. 15:6 to prove that πίστις has always been the sole criterion for participation in the Abrahamic covenant. Therefore, those who believe are Abraham's offspring. This family membership entitles them to an inheritance that is only partially realized. I support the assertion that the inheritance will be fully realized in the kingdom of the Son by examining Paul's claim that Gen. 12:3 preached the gospel in advance [προευαγγελίζομαι]. Paul insists that Gen. 12:3 preached the gospel because he believes that the blessing of the Gentiles entails God accepting them as Gentiles and therefore looks to their inclusion in Abraham's family by faith after the death and resurrection of Christ. Paul has Jesus's death and resurrection as *Messiah* in view because he reads Gen. 12:3 in light of Ps. 71:17 LXX, which predicts that the Gentile participation in the worldwide kingdom of the Son of David will fulfill the Abrahamic promise to bless the nations. Thus, the good news of the death, resurrection, and kingdom of the Son undergirds Paul's discussion of justification and the Gentile blessing in Gal. 3:6-9.

4.3.2. Galatians 3:6-7: The Blessing of the Gentiles as Justification

Most believe that in Gal. 3:6-9 Paul begins his argument from Scripture, which follows on from his argument from experience.[30] However, we suggested that Gal. 3:1-5 itself relies on Paul's interpretation of Scripture. Nonetheless, in Gal. 3:6-9 Paul does attempt to show that his scriptural interpretation of the Galatians' experience is in accord with the terms of the Abrahamic covenant.

---

30. Witherington 2004: 216; Das 2014: 300.

To defend his claim that justification comes through faith, Paul alludes to Gen. 15:6, a text that recounts God's justification of Abraham and the installation of the Abrahamic covenant (Gen. 15:1-21). The events surrounding the installation of the covenant are important because Abraham had just rescued Lot and lamented the fact that he does not have an heir. Thus, the context of Gen. 15 fits the central question Paul seeks to answer in Galatians: Who are the heirs to the inheritance (Gal. 3:29)? Following Abraham's lament, God promises him a multitude of descendants who will inherit the land. Abraham's trust in God's promise leads to his justification. For Paul, Abraham's trust in God's promise reveals the requirements for covenant membership. Here Paul is probably responding to the teaching of his opponents who stress Abraham's obedience to Torah.[31]

For our purposes, it is crucial to recognize that Abraham does not receive the inheritance when God declares him δίκαιος. It leads to a promise of the inheritance for his descendants in the future. Δίκαιος in Gen. 15:6 speaks to Abraham's status vis-à-vis the covenant. In the same way, Paul claims that justification makes the Galatians sons of Abraham. This sonship entitles the Galatians to the inheritance promised to Abraham's seed.[32] Later Paul will claim that the Messiah Jesus is the promised seed, and the Galatians share in his inheritance (Gal. 3:16, 26-29). Thus, whatever it is that the Galatians stand to receive as a result of their justification, it must be something that can reasonably be described as Christ's inheritance that comes to him on the other side of the resurrection. As we will see below, justification entitles the Galatians to share the worldwide inheritance that belongs to Jesus as the Davidic and Abrahamic seed. This is why Martyn's translation of 3:6 is problematic. He writes, "He trusted God, and as the final act in the drama by which God set Abraham fully right, God recognized Abraham's faithful trust."[33] Martyn is correct that faith

---

31. Dunn 1993: 160–1; Burton 1980 [1921]: 153; Hays 2000: 255; Lee 2013: 36; Longenecker 1998: 132.

32. Trick (2016: 35–60) argues that in Gal. 3:7 Paul only has Jewish sonship by faith, not Gentile sonship in view. Here Trick is rightly countering those who claim that Abraham functions as an exemplar in Gal. 3:6-9. However, I do not argue that Abraham functions as a mere example. I claim that for Paul Gen. 15:6 lays out the terms for the participation in the covenant. Paul contends that since faith is all that God required of Abraham (and by extension Jews) for participation in the covenant, the same must be true of Gentiles. Therefore, I suggest that Paul does have Gentile and Jewish sonship through faith in mind in Gal. 3:7-9.

33. Martyn 1997: 297.

sets Abraham fully right, but the drama of Genesis and Galatians extends beyond justification to the question of the inheritance (Gen. 15:17-21; Gal. 3:26-29; 5:21).[34] Paul makes it clear that he thinks along similar lines as the Genesis narrative when he says that justification gives birth to a future hope (Gal. 5:5).

4.3.3. *Galatians 3:8-9: The Messianic Blessing of the Gentiles Foreseen in Genesis 12:3*

That this future hope contains elements of messianism can be seen in how Paul concludes this portion of his argument. In Gal. 3:8 he asserts that Gen. 12:3, foreseeing [προοράω] the justification of the Gentiles by faith, preached the gospel ahead of time [προευαγγελίζομαι] to Abraham. There are two strands of interpretation regarding Paul's use of προευαγγελίζομαι. The first view understands Paul's use of gospel in Gal. 3:8 to refer to God's decision to justify the Gentiles by faith. Moo states this most strongly when he says, "God's justification of the Gentiles, foreseen by Scripture, is the essential content of the gospel, a gospel that was 'announced ahead of time' to Abraham in the promise that 'all nations would be blessed in him.'"[35] A second view maintains that Paul believes that Gen. 12:3 foretells the death and resurrection of the Messiah.[36] In this reading, the Galatians appropriate the benefits of his death by faith and receive the blessing of justification.[37] Making a choice between these two options is relevant to my argument. It allows us to discern whether Paul believes that Gen. 12:3 focuses solely on the means of justification or if Paul believes that Gen. 12:3 foresees the justification of the Gentiles by faith after the death and resurrection of Christ, which marks the end of the curse and turning of the ages. The latter interpretation highlights the role of the Messiah Jesus in realizing the Abrahamic inheritance.

Paul's use of προοράω in Gal. 3:8 suggests that he believes that Gen. 12:3 looks to the coming of Christ. προοράω is the language of prophecy

---

34. See Watson (2004: 193–4) on the importance of the inheritance in Gal. 3:15–29.

35. Moo 2013: 198–9 (italics added). See also Das 2014: 307 and Betz 1979, 142–43.

36. Hunn (2016: 514) does not highlight the messianic shape of Paul's argument. However, she does say that, "Abraham's belief that one of his descendants would bring blessing to all nations (vv. 8, 16) is an incipient form of the gospel embraced later by Paul's converts."

37. Although Becker (1998: 49–50) does not emphasize the messianic aspect Paul's interpretation of Gen. 12:3, he does believe that Gen. 12:3 refers to Christ. See also Schreiner 2010: 194; Dunn 1993: 165; George 1994: 226.

and points to its fulfillment at a certain point in time.[38] προοράω is inescapably chronological. Paul's point throughout Galatians is that the death of Jesus removes the curse of Law and enables the justification of the Gentiles by faith (Gal. 3:10-14; 4:4-7). Therefore, this point in time is after Jesus's death and resurrection. Thus, interpretations that only stress the mode of justification as the content of the gospel neglect the prophetic and chronological language that Paul uses to make his point.[39] Genesis 12:3, then, can be described as a preaching of the gospel ahead of time because it looks to God's blessing of the Gentiles through their justification by faith after the curse-ending death of the Messiah.

For Paul, God's promise to Abraham necessitates the Gentiles being blessed as Gentiles. Thus, if the Gentiles must do the works of the Law to be blessed, then Gen. 12:3 cannot be fulfilled.[40] Therefore, his opponents' claim that one must effectively become Jewish through the works of the Law nullifies the promise. According to Paul, the blessing of the Gentiles on an equal basis with Jews points to a time when Torah no longer defines the people of God.[41] Thus, in Paul's reading of Israel's history, Gen. 12:3 looks to the death of Jesus as the event that marks the end of the age of the Torah.[42] In as much as Gen. 12:3 looks beyond the

---

38. See Acts 2:31-32. It says, "Since he [David] was a prophet, he knew that God had sworn with an oath to him that he would put one of his descendants on his throne. Foreseeing [προοράω] this, David spoke of the resurrection of the Messiah, saying, 'He was not abandoned to Hades, nor did his flesh experience corruption.'" Acts 2:31-32, then, uses προοράω to speak about a specific event in the future.

39. Wright (2002: 419), speaking about Rom. 1:2-4, says, "for Paul 'the gospel' is not a system of salvation, a message first and foremost about how human beings get saved. It is an announcement about Jesus, the Messiah, the Lord." The same seems to be true for Paul's reference to the gospel in Gal. 3:8.

40. Trick (2016: 94–7) comes close to this reading when he says that the blessing cannot be based upon doing the works of the Law because Gentiles by definition cannot do the works of the Law and remain Gentiles. However, his reading of Gal. 3:8 does not highlight Paul's prophetic and messianic reading of Gen. 12:3 that I posit here.

41. Dunn (1993: 165) says, "The promise which constituted Israel as heirs of the promise, seed of Abraham, also placed the blessing of the Gentiles to the forefront. Paul takes the 'all the nations' seriously – Gentiles as well as Jews, not Gentiles as distinct from Jews. The promise to Abraham's seed was incomplete without the Gentiles sharing in the same blessing." See more recently Trick 2016: 31.

42. Watson (2004: 187) says "the Genesis text is employed to explain the rationale and goal of Christ's death." He goes on to list four implications, one of which is the justification of the Gentiles by faith.

Torah, God's first words to Abraham preached the gospel about Christ in advance.[43]

But can we really contend that Paul believes that Gen. 12:3 foresaw the death and resurrection of Jesus as *Messiah*, and how does this claim touch on the question of the inheritance?[44] Genesis 12:3 could refer to the death, resurrection, and rule of the Davidic Messiah because Paul read Gen. 12:3 in light of Ps. 71:17 LXX. Psalm 71:17 states that the Abrahamic blessing of the Gentiles will be fulfilled through their participation in the worldwide kingdom of the Son of David.[45]

Before examining the lexical and thematic connections between Gen. 12:3 and Ps. 71:17 LXX, it is important to situate our claim about the messianic blessing of the Gentiles within the larger argument of the letter. First, we must consider the role that Jesus's death plays in Galatians. Although much of this is discussed below, let me anticipate it here: presenting the death of Jesus as the end of the covenant curses implies a narrative of curse and restoration to the inheritance (3:10-14). Second, Paul uses Son language during depictions of Jesus's redeeming death (Gal. 2:20; 4:4-7). This suggests, among other things, that Paul believes that Jesus is the messianic son of God. Third, Paul states that the promises and the κληρονομία belong to Christ (Gal. 3:16, 19). Christ's singular possession of the κληρονομία is important because Ps. 2:7-8, a text that Paul alludes to in Rom. 1:3-4, declares that the nations and their territory belong to the Son as his singular κληρονομία.[46] Thus, in Ps. 2:7-8, sonship,

---

43. Harmon (2010: 136–40) suggests that Paul interprets Gen. 12:3 through the lens of Isa. 51:1-18. Isaiah 51:1-8 is a text that relies upon the Abrahamic promises as the basis for the hope of the restoration of Israel. Harmon believes that Isa. 51:1-8 is important because it calls upon the nations to listen to the message of God's saving promise. However, it seems that Paul believes that the Genesis text itself preaches the gospel. See Watson 2004: 185–93.

44. See also *4 Ezra* 3:12-14 for the idea that God gave Abraham a vision of the eschatological age.

45. See also Scott 1995: 129–30. Collins (2003: 75–86) claims that Paul alludes to Gen. 22:18 in Gal. 3:8 and 3:16. According to Collins, in Gal. 3:16 Paul interprets Gen. 22:18 to refer to the Messiah of Ps. 71:17. Collins is correct to claim that in Gal. 3:16 Paul argues that the seed is the Messiah. Paul's point in Gal. 3:8, however, is that from the beginning of Abraham's story (Gen. 12:3), God planned to bring about the blessing of the nations through the Son of Ps. 71:17. Paul's argument in Gal. 3:16 is different. In Gal. 3:16, Paul claims that the Messiah is the rightful heir to the inheritance.

46. The origins of the creedal statement in Rom. 1:3-4 and its allusion to Ps. 2:7-8 are controversial. However, the conclusion of Romans should inform our

4. *The End of the Curse and the Beginning of the Inheritance*

a worldwide kingdom, and κληρονομία are all linked. Therefore, Paul's assertion about the singular κληρονομία of Christ (Gal. 3:16) is informed by his belief that Jesus is the anointed Son of Ps. 2:7-8. What is missing in this proposal is a link between Davidic messiahship, inheritance, and the Gentile blessing.

This brings us to the messianic reading of Gen. 12:3. The lexical and thematic connections between Gen. 12:3 and Ps. 71:17 LXX allowed Paul to link participation in the Son's κληρονομία to the Abrahamic blessing. Outside of the Genesis narrative, there is only one text that claims that God will bless the nations through an individual.[47] This individual is the Davidic Son of Ps. 71 LXX:

Gen. 12:3	ἐνευλογηθήσονται ἐν σοὶ πᾶσαι αἱ φυλαὶ τῆς γῆς
Gen. 18:18	ἐνευλογηθήσονται ἐν αὐτῷ πάντα τὰ ἔθνη τῆς γῆς
Gen. 22:18	καὶ ἐνευλογηθήσονται ἐν τῷ σπέρματί σου πάντα τὰ ἔθνη τῆς γῆς
Gen. 26:4	καὶ ἐνευλογηθήσονται ἐν τῷ σπέρματί σου πάντα τὰ ἔθνη τῆς γῆς
Gen. 26:14	καὶ ἐνευλογηθήσονται ἐν σοὶ πᾶσαι αἱ φυλαὶ τῆς γῆς
Ps. 71:17	καὶ εὐλογηθήσονται ἐν αὐτῷ πᾶσαι αἱ φυλαὶ τῆς γῆς

Although others have suggested that Paul alludes to Ps. 71:17 LXX, few note that Ps. 71 LXX also reworks Gen. 15:18.[48] Thus both the texts that Paul alludes to in Gal. 3:6-9 (Gen. 15 and Gen. 12) appear in the description of the rule of the Davidic king:

Gen. 15:18	Τῷ σπέρματί σου δώσω τὴν γῆν ταύτην ἀπὸ τοῦ ποταμοῦ Αἰγύπτου ἕως τοῦ ποταμοῦ τοῦ μεγάλου, ποταμοῦ Εὐφράτου,
Ps. 71:8	αἱ κατακυριεύσει ἀπὸ θαλάσσης ἕως θαλάσσης καὶ ἀπὸ ποταμοῦ ἕως περάτων τῆς οἰκουμένης.
Gen. 12:3	ἐνευλογηθήσονται ἐν σοὶ πᾶσαι αἱ φυλαὶ τῆς γῆς
Ps. 71:17	καὶ εὐλογηθήσονται ἐν αὐτῷ πᾶσαι αἱ φυλαὶ τῆς γῆς

---

interpretation of the opening of that letter. The focus on Davidic Messiahship and the worldwide kingdom is much less disputable in that passage (Rom. 15:8-12). On Davidic and divine sonship in Rom. 1:2-4, see Wright 2002: 415–19.

47. Alexander 1997: 365.

48. Scott (1995: 129–30) believes that Paul had Ps. 71 LXX in mind, but he does not note this connection.

This link between Gen. 12, 15, and Ps. 71 LXX could allow Paul to claim that Gen. 12:3 is a prophecy. Paul can make such a claim about the Davidic king's role in fulfilling Gen. 12:3 because the author of Ps. 71 LXX makes the same assertion. The author of Ps. 71 LXX says that Gen. 12:3 is a prophecy about a Davidic descendant. In Ps. 71 LXX, he appropriates the Abrahamic promises in four ways. First, he expands the Promised Land to encompass the entire earth. Second, the Son of David, who is likened to the promised seed of Abraham, blesses the nations. Third, the inheritance promised to Abraham's seed is depicted as the worldwide kingdom of the Son. Fourth, the Gentiles' blessing consists of living under the just dominion of the king. Speaking of the connection between Davidic kingship and the Abrahamic blessing in Ps. 71 LXX, Hossfeld and Zenger say:

> A king who realises justice and compassion according to the "program" proposed in Psalm 72 does in fact serve the history of God and Israel begun with Abraham, which is intended to bring Israel and the nations together in such a way that the world may become God's royal dominion, in which the fullness of salvation exists both in the social sphere and in that of nature.[49]

This link in Ps. 71 LXX between the Davidic king, the Gentile blessing, and a worldwide understanding of the Abrahamic inheritance corresponds to Paul's claim that Jesus's death blesses the Gentiles by making them heirs to the Messiah's inheritance alongside believing Jews. By stating that the Gentiles are heirs alongside believing Jews, Paul's claim goes beyond Ps. 71 LXX because in that text the nations had a secondary status (Ps. 71:8-11 LXX). For Paul, all those who trust in Christ share the status of sons and heirs. If this reading is broadly accurate, then claims that Davidic messianism plays a negligible role in Galatians are inaccurate. Instead, the good news of the death, resurrection, and kingdom of the Son undergirds Paul's discussion of justification and the Gentile blessing.

This understanding of justification as the Gentiles' blessing fits well with Paul's words in Gal. 3:9. He says that those who believe are blessed along with believing Abraham (who was also justified by faith).[50] According to Paul, displaying Abrahamic faithfulness assures the Gentiles of their place in the kingdom of the Messiah Jesus alongside their forefather Abraham.

---

49. Hossfeld and Zenger 2005: 218. On the allusion to the Abrahamic promises in Ps. 72 [MT], see McCann 1996: 964.

50. Betz 1979: 143. See also Hunn (2016: 509), who says because Gentiles, "faith is like Abraham's, receive the same benefit as their father Abraham: justification by faith."

4.4. Galatians 3:10-14

4.4.1. Overview

This analysis of Gal. 3:10-14 provides further evidence that Paul presents the cross of Christ as the solution to the covenant curses. By redeeming believing Jews from the covenant curses Jesus's death inaugurates the final realization of the inheritance promise. Thus, the death of Christ in the argument of Gal. 3:10-14 does what Davidic Messiahs were known to do—it brings about the final realization of the inheritance promise, which for Paul encompasses the whole renewed earth.

I present five arguments in favor of a focus on the covenant curses and therefore the inheritance in Gal. 3:10-14. First, Paul's use of Deut. 27:26/28:58/29:19 and Lev. 18:5 in Gal. 3:10-12 reflects a tendency in biblical and Second Temple texts to couple allusions to Deut. 27–29 with Lev. 18:5 when describing the national covenant curses. Second, Paul uses Hab. 2:4 to demonstrate that faith is sufficient to bring believers into Abraham's family on the other side of those same curses. Third, Gal. 3:13 presents Jesus's death as the event that liberates the Jewish Christians from the covenant curses outlined in Deut. 27–29. Fourth, similar to Gal. 3:8, the blessing of the Gentiles in Gal. 3:14 refers to the justification that effects their inclusion in Abraham's seed. I conclude by arguing once more that Paul portrays the promised Spirit as the sign that the Gentiles have indeed been accepted into Abraham's family on the other side of the covenant curses (Gal. 3:2-5). For Paul, the Spirit functions as the initial participation in the inheritance that will be completed when the believers inherit the kingdom alongside their king (Gal. 5:21).

4.4.2. The Covenant Curses and the Use of Deuteronomy 27–29 and Leviticus 18:5 in Galatians 3:10-12

After claiming that faith in the crucified and risen Messiah is sufficient to bring the believer into Abraham's family (Gal. 3:6-9), Paul considers the implications of coming under the works of the Law.[51] In Gal. 3:10 Paul says, Ὅσοι γὰρ ἐξ ἔργων νόμου εἰσίν, ὑπὸ κατάραν εἰσίν γέγραπται

---

51. The meaning of ἔργων νόμου is a contested issue that is not directly relevant to this project. Therefore, it will not be explored in full here. I understand the works of the Law to refer to a variety of practices described in the Torah. It appears that, although Paul highlights circumcision and food laws, those of the works of the Law commit themselves to "live Jewishly" in the sense of obeying what the Torah commands. See Barclay 2015b: 373-4.

γὰρ ὅτι ἐπικατάρατος πᾶς ὃς οὐκ ἐμμένει πᾶσιν τοῖς γεγραμμένοις ἐν τῷ βιβλίῳ τοῦ νόμου τοῦ ποιῆσαι αὐτά. While it is clear that Paul associates coming under the Law with the curse, how Deut. 27:26 supports this claim remains controversial. The confusion arises because Deut. 27:26 seems to pronounce a curse on those who do not keep the Law, while Paul uses the text to pronounce a curse on those who do.[52]

The interpretation of Gal. 3:10 that long dominated Pauline scholarship maintains that Paul deploys Deut. 27:26 to assert that the Law requires absolute perfection.[53] Schnelle says, "Paulus geht hier von der Erfahrung des Scheiterns jedes Menschen am Gesetz...aus, weil kein Mensch Bisher die ganze Tora gehalten hat."[54] Since it is impossible to keep the Law perfectly, those of the works of the Law are cursed.[55] As evidence for this view, advocates posit that the addition of Deut. 25:58/29:19 to Deut. 27:26 extends the potential pitfalls for the Galatians who receive circumcision. Not only must they avoid the twelve prohibitions in Deut. 27:15-26, they must do the entire Torah.[56] Furthermore, Paul's statements in Gal. 5:3 and 6:13 could be read to support the perfect obedience view.[57] Exegetes criticise this interpretation because the Deuteronomic covenant does not require perfection to avoid the curse.[58] Barclay writes:

> Paul's logic does not assume that blessing would require individuals to be perfect in Torah-Observance, but that Israel's history proved her collective and persistent incapacity to be obedient. Understood in this sense, some Jewish texts consider that Israel stood under the covenant curses of Deuteronomy 27–30.[59]

---

52. Betz 1979: 145; Martyn 1997: 309.

53. Schnelle 2014: 292–3. Bruce (1982: 159) says, "he is concerned to stress the unfulfillable character of the Law: by the standard of the Law every one is 'under a curse' because no one is able to keep it in its entirety." See also Das 2014: 313–16; Lightfoot 1902 [1874]: 137; Moo 2013: 202; Schreiner 2010: 203; Fung 1988: 141; Lambrecht 1994: 282 n. 29; Kim 2002: 128–64. Stanley (1990: 481–511) and Witherington (2004: 233) adopt a related reading. They claim that Paul warns the Galatians about the threat of the curse. Paul was telling the Galatians that if they come under the works of the Law and then failed to keep it perfectly, they would be cursed.

54. Schnelle 2014: 305.

55. Moo 2013: 202; Ridderbos 1953: 124.

56. Bruce 1982: 28; Moo 2013: 201–5; Das 2014: 313.

57. On Gal. 5:3, see Matera 1992: 181–2.

58. Dunn 1993: 171; Dunn 2008: 213–26; Lincicum 2010: 143; Fee 2011: 118–19.

59. Barclay 2015b: 405–6 n. 39.

4. *The End of the Curse and the Beginning of the Inheritance*

Barclay's quotation above represents a growing awareness that Paul's use of Deut. 27:26/29:19 arises from his reading of Israel's history.[60] This reading of Israel's history maintains that the nation was under the covenant curses outlined in Deut. 27–30 because of their corporate disobedience.[61] In this reading, Jesus's death redeems the nation from the covenant curses outlined in Deut. 27–29 and enables their justification by faith. Thus, for the Galatians to identify themselves as Abraham's offspring by doing the works of the Law, after Jesus has ended the era of the Law, would move the Galatians back in time to the era marked by national disobedience and the curse.

Those who claim that Paul alludes to the covenant curses call attention to the fact that Gal. 3:10 predicts a curse for failing to do all "γεγραμμένοις ἐν τῷ βιβλίῳ τοῦ νόμου."[62] This phrase is associated repeatedly with predictions of the national curses, including exile and the loss of the land inheritance (Deut. 28:58, 61; 29:19, 20, 26; 30:10). This focus on the loss of the inheritance in this section of Deuteronomy is important for two reasons. First, it shows that the national curses stand in the way of the final realization of the land promises. By removing this curse, Jesus is doing what Messiahs were known to do. Jesus was effecting the final realization of the land promises. Second, establishing the focus on the national curses explains why Paul moves immediately from a discussion of the curse (3:10-14) to the inheritance (3:15-18). To end the curse entails beginning the final realization of the land promises.

---

60. There are various proposals regarding the interpretation of 3:10, and space precludes a full discussion of them all. Instead of an analysis and critique of each position, I have chosen to present fresh evidence that supports a focus on the national curses. For a recent "apocalyptic" reading of Gal. 3:10 that credits Paul's opponents with choosing Deut. 27:26, see de Boer 2011: 200–201. For a claim that Paul saw the Law itself as the curse, see Betz 1979: 149. For a more extensive interaction with these proposals, see Das 2001: 145–70; Morales 2010: 88–95, and more recently Trick 2016: 77–90.

61. See Barclay 2015b: 405–6 n. 39; Wright 2013: 862–7; Lincicum 2010: 145; Watson 2004: 429–34; Hays 2000: 258–9. Hafemann 1997: 327–72; Scott 1993: 657–8; Ciampa 2007: 101–5. Trick (2016: 87) argues that since Deut. 27:26 refers to a curse on an individual, Paul cannot have the national curses in mind. See also Das 2001: 152. For a response, see the discussion of CD 3:1-20 below.

62. Scott 1993: 657–8; Ciampa 2007: 102; Watson 2004: 431; Morales 2010: 92–3.

Support for a national curse reading of Deut. 27:26 in Gal. 3:10 comes from Paul's use of Lev. 18:5 in Gal. 3:12. Using Lev. 18:5 to support a national-curse reading of Deut. 27:26 is controversial because Paul's use of Lev. 18:5 and its relationship to his use of Hab. 2:4 is itself contested. Most assume that in Gal. 3:11-12 Paul contrasts Lev. 18:5 with Hab. 2:4 because the works of the Law require a "doing" that is antithetical to faith.[63]

Others argue that Paul uses Lev. 18:5 to refer to the same national curses alluded to in Gal. 3:10. To support this reading, they point to the use of Lev. 18:5 in biblical and Second Temple texts to summarize the nation's corporate failure to keep the Law in Neh. 9:1-37 and Ezek. 20.[64] Representing this view, Willitts says:

> Ezekiel and Nehemiah place the clause [the one who does these things will live by them] in the context of Israel's failure to maintain its covenant with YHWH. In so doing, the Leviticus 18:5 clause, instead of signifying the positive purpose of the covenant as it did in Leviticus, ironically comes to represent the unrealized covenant potential.[65]

Stated differently, in Ezekiel and Nehemiah, Lev. 18:5 summarizes the nation's history under the covenant: they did not do the Law and live. Therefore, they were cursed. According to Ezekiel and Nehemiah, this curse takes the form of the loss of the land inheritance.

Scholars who adopt this reading, however, do not note that the negative reading of Lev. 18:5 is dependent upon the use of Deut. 27–29 to describe the nation's status in the wider context of the use of Lev. 18:5. Deuteronomy 27–29 functions as a filter that determines the interpretation of Lev. 18:5. Thus, Paul's use of Deut. 27–29 and Lev. 18:5 together reflects a tendency to cluster these texts when describing Israel's covenant failure and subsequent exile in biblical and Second Temple writings. In

---

63. Bruce 1982: 162; Betz 1979: 147; Longenecker 1990: 120; Lightfoot 1902 [1874]: 137. Others who hold to the perfect obedience reading of 3:10 maintain that 3:12 referred to the inevitable failure to do the Law perfectly. See Das 2014: 317.

64. Willitts 2003: 105–22; Sprinkle 2008: 34–44. Grindheim (2007: 557–65) also claims that Paul reads Deut. 27:26 and Lev. 18:5 in light of the prophetic depictions of covenant failure. However, his reconstruction posits that the curse described in Gal. 3:10 occurs because coming under the Law after Christ is a form of apostasy since it represents disobedience to the lord. This apostasy causes the Galatians to be cursed. By contrast, I will argue that the curse of Gal. 3:10 refers to the covenant curses that befell the nation for its disobedience before the coming of Christ.

65. Willitts 2003: 122. See also Morales 2010: 101–4; Grindheim 2007: 561–2; Sprinkle 2008: 44 (italics added).

4. The End of the Curse and the Beginning of the Inheritance

what follows, I demonstrate this clustering tendency in Ezek. 20, CD 3:1-20 and Neh. 9:29-37. I conclude with an interpretation of Gal. 3:10-12 in light of these findings.

Ezekiel 20 combines Lev. 18:5 and Deut. 27–29 in its account of national covenant failure. Ezekiel 20 chronicles Israel's history from the time of the Exodus up through their entry into the Promised Land. According to Ezekiel, Israel's failure to do the Law in Egypt had already earned them the covenant curses (Ezek. 20:8-10).[66] Nonetheless, God mercifully spares the nation and gives them the Torah (Ezek. 20:11). Yet the nation does not observe the commandments by which a person shall live:

> But the house of Israel rebelled against me in the wilderness; they did not observe my statutes but rejected my ordinances, by whose observance everyone shall live [אשר יעשה אתם האדם וחי בהם]. (Ezek. 20:13a)[67]

In Ezek. 20:13, the prophet uses Lev. 18:5 to summarize the nations' covenant failure. He argues that because Israel fails in covenant obedience, they deserve the covenant curses outlined in Deut. 27–29:

> Moreover I swore to them in the wilderness that I would scatter [להפיץ] them among the nations [בגוים] and disperse them through the countries. (Ezek. 20:23)

> The LORD will scatter [והפיצך] you among all peoples [העמים], from one end of the earth to the other; and there you shall serve [עבד] other gods, of wood and stone. (Deut. 28:64)[68]

Ezekiel 20 is important because it contains three elements that are present in Gal. 3:10-14: an allusion to Deut. 27–29 as well as Lev. 18:5, and the likening of the curse to slavery.

CD 3:1-20 is relevant for three reasons. First, the negative portrayal of Israel in CD 3:1-20 relies on Ezek. 20.[69] This is important because it shows that Ezek. 20, a text that uses Lev. 18:5 to summarize corporate disobedience, was in use during the Second Temple period. Second, the author of the Damascus Document alludes to Deut. 27–29 and Lev. 18:5

---

66. Morales 2010: 101.
67. See also Ezek. 20:21.
68. See also Ezek. 20:32, where Ezekiel claims that Israel was determined to worship gods of wood and stone in the context of their impending exile. The scattering of Israel is also predicted in Ezek. 11:17; 12:15; and 22:15.
69. Campbell 1995: 78–80.

when describing the nation's corporate disobedience. Third, CD 3:1-20 uses a text (Deut. 29:18-19) that refers to a curse on an individual or smaller group within the nation to speak about the national curses that befell Israel.[70]

In CD 3:4-5 the author claims that in Egypt the nation walked in the stubbornness of their hearts. It reads, "Jacob's sons strayed because of them and were punished in accordance with their mistakes. And in Egypt their sons walked in the stubbornness of their hearts." Then in CD 3:9-12 he says that the same stubbornness of heart continued after they entered the land. CD 3:9-12 claims, "The very first to enter the covenant made themselves guilty and were delivered up to the sword…having followed the stubbornness of their heart." Because of this stubbornness, God exiles the nation. Based on this structure, we can see that CD 3:1-20 is modeled on Ezek. 20. Both chronicle the nation's disobedience in Egypt and their continued disobedience in the land.[71]

Most agree that the stubbornness of heart in CD 3:4 and 3:9-12 alludes to Deut. 29:18-19, which says:

> All who hear the words of this oath and bless themselves, thinking in their hearts, "I am at peace even though I walk in the stubbornness of my heart [בשררות לבי]"…the LORD will be unwilling to pardon them… *All the curses written in this book* will descend on them, and the LORD will blot out their names from under heaven.[72]

Deuteronomy 29:18-19 is important because Paul refers to a different portion of this text (the things written in the book of the Law) when he describes Israel's national covenant disobedience in the context of an allusion to Lev. 18:5 (Gal. 3:10-12). His use of Deut. 29:18-19 is especially relevant because the author uses a text that describes a curse on an individual (or a smaller group within the nation) to speak about the curse that came upon Israel. This counters the argument that since Deut. 27:26 refers to a curse on an individual, Paul cannot have the national curses in mind in Gal. 3:10.[73] CD 3:1-20 shows that Second Temple authors could use texts that refer to individuals to speak about national curses. I contend, then, that CD 3:1-20 provides important insight into Paul's use of these same texts in Galatians.

---

70. On the importance of the curse on an individual, see the discussion below.
71. See CD 3:5-7 and Ezek. 20:7-8. Campbell 1995: 81.
72. Campbell 1995: 78–80. See his discussion of the extensive influence of Deut. 29:19-28 on this section of the Damascus Document. The quotation from the NRSV was modified (italics added).
73. Trick 2016: 87.

Most interpreters understand CD 3:1-20 to be an example of the positive use of Lev. 18:5 to summarize national obedience.[74] They point out that the author says that his community is doing the Law, and for this reason they are experiencing the restoration:

> But with those who remained steadfast in God's precepts, with those who were left from among them, God established his covenant with Israel for ever, revealing to them hidden matters in which all Israel had gone astray: his holy Sabbath and his glorious feasts, his just stipulations and his truthful paths, and the wishes of his will which *a man must do in order to live by them*...and whoever spurns them shall not live. But they had defiled themselves with human sin and unclean paths. (CD 3:15-17, italics added)

This reading of CD 3:15-16 is accurate, but it ignores the author's statement in CD 3:17 and the narrative frame provided by Ezek. 20.

In CD 3:17 the author contrasts the rest of Israel with the Qumran community. He says that the rest of Israel, "shall not live." This implies that he believes that the rest of Israel is not doing what Lev. 18:5 commands. This is exactly what Ezek. 20 says about the nation. They did not do the Law in order to live. Thus, the author of CD 3:1-20 has retold Ezek. 20 with a crucial difference. While the rest of the nation remains under the curses outlined in Deut. 27–29 because of their failure to do Lev. 18:5, his community is experiencing the restoration.

Ezek. 20	CD 3:1-20
Israel rebelled in Egypt and deserved the covenant curses (20:4-8)	Israel rebelled in the Egypt (3:4-5)
Israel rebelled in the wilderness (20:13)	Israel rebelled in the wilderness (3:6-7)
The generation that entered the land was just like the those who rebelled in Egypt (20:28)	The generation that entered the land rebelled just like the generation in Egypt (3:10-12)
The nation was under the covenant curses for not doing Lev. 18:5 (20:13)	The Qumranites were not under the curse because they were doing Lev. 18:5, while the rest of the nation was under the curse for not doing Lev. 18:5 (3:15-17)

CD 3:1-20 is important for our argument because: (1) it uses Deut. 27–29 and Lev. 18:5 to refer to the national curses that came upon Israel; (2) it shows that Second Temple authors are reading Lev. 18:5 through the

---

74. Sprinkle 2008: 55–68; Grindheim 2007: 562; Willitts 2003: 116.

lens of its use in Ezek. 20; (3) it claims that while one portion of Israel is experiencing the restoration, the rest of the nation remains under the curse. This final point is similar to Paul's claim that those in Christ are experiencing the beginning of the restoration, while those of the works of the Law remain under the covenant curses. In both CD 3:1-20 and Gal. 3:10-12, although the authors claim that the communities in question are no longer under the curse, the final realization of the inheritance still lay in the future.

We encounter the same tendency to couple Lev. 18:5 with Deut. 27–29 in Neh. 9:29-38. First, the author alludes to Lev. 18:5 when summarizing the nation's covenant disobedience. He says:

> And you warned them in order to turn them back to your Law. Yet they acted presumptuously and did not obey your commandments, but sinned against your ordinances, *by the observance of which a person shall live* [אשר יעשה אדם וחיה בהם]. (Neh. 9:29, italics added)

Then the author alludes to Deut. 27–29 in his description of Israel's punishment:

> Even in their own kingdom...and in the large and rich land that you set before them, they did not serve you [לא עבדוך] and did not turn from their wicked works. Here we are...slaves in the land that you gave to our ancestors to enjoy its fruit and its good gifts. (Neh. 9:35-37)

> Because you did not serve [לא עבדת] the LORD your God joyfully and with gladness of heart for the abundance of everything, therefore you shall serve your enemies whom the LORD will send against you... He will put an iron yoke on your neck until he has destroyed you. (Deut. 28:47-48)[75]

Nehemiah's description is relevant for two reasons. First, even though the nation has returned from exile, the author believes that they are still suffering the effects of the Deuteronomic curses. This establishes the fact that for Nehemiah an incomplete restoration is identical to the continuation of the curses. Second, he laments the fact that they are slaves. Again, we observe the same three elements in Neh. 9:28-37 as we find in Gal. 3:10-14: (1) an allusion to Lev. 18:5; (2) an allusion to Deut. 27–29; and (3) the presentation of the curse as slavery.

Nehemiah 9, Ezek. 20, and CD 3:1-20 are important for the interpretation of Gal. 3:10-12 because all three mention the covenant curses outlined in Deut. 27–29 and the national failure to do the Law (Lev. 18:5).

---

75. On the use of Deut. 28:47-48, see Fensham 1982: 233-4.

Nehemiah and Ezekiel refer to slavery in the course of their allusions to Deut. 27–29 and Lev. 18:5. This evidence supports our proposal that Paul alludes to the covenant curses in Gal. 3:10-12. His use of Deut. 27–29, Lev. 18:5, and the slavery motif in Gal. 3:10-14 reflects the tendency to use these texts and motifs when describing the nation's covenant failure. Thus, for Paul, attempting to do the Law would bring the Galatians back into the era defined by the nation's corporate disobedience. Instead of returning to the curse by doing the works of the Law, the Galatians should recognize that those of faith will share in the inheritance given to the Messiah Jesus because of his faithful death, which ends the curse (Gal. 3:11/Hab. 2:4).[76]

In an attempt to understand Paul's argument in Gal. 3:12, Sprinkle also considered the biblical and Second Temple texts discussed above.[77] His work is in basic agreement with my analysis of the use of Lev. 18:5 in Ezek. 20 and Neh. 9.[78] However, we differ in how we understand the implications of this data. Sprinkle believes that Paul finds fault with Lev. 18:5 because "Lev. 18:5 places an unnecessary and inadequate emphasis on human agency in the attainment of eschatological life."[79] According to Sprinkle, the reality of eschatological life as divine gift runs counter to the conditional element of Lev. 18:5.[80] Furthermore, although Sprinkle agrees that the argument of Gal. 3:10-14 reflects a covenantal structure of sin-exile and restoration,[81] he articulates this structure using the language of divine and human agency.[82] Sprinkle's removal of Israel's place in the narrative obscures the question of who the promises are for and what the restoration entails. This removal of Israel is problematic because much of Galatians is about identifying the seed and the heir. This problem is solved when we remember that the human agency in Gal. 3:10 and 12 is the historical failure of Israel and the resulting national curses.[83] The divine agency envisioned is the reversal of those very curses. It is God's agency through his son the king, at this point in Israel's history, that

76. See the discussion of Hab. 2:4 below.
77. Sprinkle 2008: 34–76.
78. See ibid.: 34–44. We differ on CD 3:1–20. See the discussion above.
79. Ibid.: 196. See also Watson 2004: 67–8.
80. Sprinkle 2008: 197.
81. Ibid.: 199–200. Part of this may be explained by his desire to keep traditional nomenclature about faith versus works. See ibid.: 204–5.
82. See a similar critique in Wright 2013: 1467.
83. This interaction need not assume a fundamental disagreement. It is more than fair to extrapolate from Paul's argument in Galatians in order to make broader theological claims about faith and Law obedience, but one must be careful to give Paul's own concerns their due consideration.

marks out Paul's narrative as Davidic and messianic (Gal. 3:13; 4:4-7). It is the removal of Israel's narrative that clouds the messianic shape of Paul's gospel. To put it in other words, if the question in Galatians is only about human and divine agency, then the only role left for Jesus to play is the role of the divine agent who comes to save humans.

In any case, the focus on the national curses in Gal. 3:10-12 supports the argument for a focus on inheritance in Galatians. Paul claims that turning to the Law means returning to the curses that highlight Israel's loss of the land inheritance:

> The Lord will make exceptional your plagues... And he will bring back upon you all the evil pains of Egypt... And every disease and every plague which is not written in the book of this Law [ἐν τῷ βιβλίῳ τοῦ νόμου τούτου] the Lord will bring on you until he utterly destroys you. And you shall be left few in number, instead of the fact that you were as the stars of the sky in multitude, because you did not listen to the voice of the Lord your God... and you shall be removed from the land that you are entering there to inherit [κληρονομῆσαι] it. (Deut. 29:58-63 LXX)

Κληρονομέω and its cognates figure prominently in Deuteronomy.[84] The reception of the inheritance is the reward for Israel's obedience; the loss of the inheritance is the curse that arises from disobedience.[85] Christensen calls these covenant curses, "the complete reversal of Israel's history."[86] In these curses, God nullifies the blessings that he bestowed upon the nation. The relevance of this section of Deuteronomy with its focus on the loss of the inheritance and the return to slavery to Paul's argument in Galatians should be clear. Paul considers a return to the Law a nullification of the cross's redemptive power and a return to slavery after having been granted freedom (Gal. 4:4-7; 5:1). Doing the works of the Law now would be a reversal of the turning point in Israel's history brought about by the crucifixion and resurrection of Jesus.[87] Rather than moving backwards, Paul will encourage the Galatians to maintain their status as heirs (Gal. 3:26-29).

Before concluding this section, it is important to consider Morales' proposal that Paul highlights death as the focus of the covenant curses.[88] Morales alleges that Deuteronomy's climactic statements contrast life and

---

84. Κληρονομέω and its cognates occur some 64 times.
85. See in particular the warnings in Deut. 26:1 and 30:18.
86. Christensen 2002: 695. See also Nelson 2002: 332.
87. This does not make the Law slavery; rather, the curse that the Law pronounces upon the people results in their slavery because of sin (Gal. 3:21-22).
88. Morales 2010: 170–1.

death, the blessing and the curse, not blessing and exile (Deut. 30:11-20).[89] According to Morales, Paul thinks that the restoration is about life and new creation with "no emphasis on a nationalistic return to the land."[90]

Morales' work draws a sharp but unnecessary distinction between death, exile, land, resurrection, and new creation. In many Old Testament texts, resurrection and new creation imagery describes the nation's hope for life with God in the land after exile (Ezek. 36:25; 37:1-14; Isa. 65:17-25).[91] Therefore, there is no reason to place resurrection or new creation in competition with exile and restoration. It is better to say that new creation and resurrection are the shape of Pauline restoration to the inheritance. By connecting the restoration to the new creation, Paul's argument in Galatians bears witness to a worldwide understanding of the inheritance. Stated differently, the resurrection points towards the worldwide kingdom as the locale of the final realization of God's promises.

Morales also cites Dan. 12 as evidence of a shift away from a focus on the land.[92] By citing Daniel, Morales interestingly reflects a tradition that goes back as far as Bousset. Bousset claims that the early Christian use of Daniel demonstrates a shift away from specifically Jewish concerns.[93] But Daniel is a book written from the perspective of exile and serves to encourage Jews to remain faithful while they await restoration (Dan. 9:1-2).

To show the importance of restoration in Daniel, I will provide a brief examination of the context of the reference to the resurrection. Daniel 12:1-3 opens with a discussion of the last day and the vindication of those whose names are written in the book. This discussion of the book recalls Dan. 7:9-14.[94] Daniel 7:9-14 includes a vision of the ancient of days, the Son of Man, and the opening of the book. Daniel 7:9-14 goes on to suggest that those vindicated at the end will participate in the kingdom given to the Son of Man. This kingdom encompasses all creation. Therefore, Dan. 7:9-14 and 12:1-13 do not merely replace the land with life or resurrection. Daniel 7:9-14 and 12:1-3, when considered in light of the whole book, bear witness to the widening of the vision to encompass the exiles enjoying the bounty of all creation. Daniel testifies to a worldwide understanding of the land promises as kingdom after exile. Similarly,

---

89. Morales 2010: 170. Morales does grant that the curses include more than death. See ibid.: 170 n. 4. See also Barclay 2015b: 405–6 n. 39.
90. Morales 2010: 131.
91. Ibid.: 170.
92. Ibid.
93. Bousset 1970 [1913]: 48–9.
94. Goldingay 1989: 306.

Paul believes that the inheritance promised to Abraham's seed would be fulfilled in the worldwide kingdom of the Son after the resurrection.

4.4.3. *Habakkuk 2:4 in Galatians 3:11: Justification by Faith after the Curse*

In our discussion of Paul's use of Deut. 27–29 and Lev. 18:5, we did not consider Paul's claim that the just will live by faith (Hab. 2:4). Narratively, Hab. 2:1-4 is situated at the beginning of the Deuteronomic curses and looks forward to their end. Therefore, Paul's use of Hab. 2:4 fits with our claim that the reality of Deuteronomic curses and participation in the restoration to the inheritance through Christ is crucial to Paul's argument in Galatians. Paul uses Hab. 2:4 to prove that the original terms of the Abrahamic covenant remain in place on the other side of the covenant curses.

Habakkuk opens with a complaint about the unchecked wickedness that pervaded Israel in his day (Hab. 1:4).[95] God responds by telling Habakkuk that he is going to judge national wickedness by sending the Chaldeans to punish Israel and carry them away into exile (Hab. 1:6-9). This appears to be a clear account of the national curses coming upon Israel for their corporate disobedience.[96] But these curses create a dilemma because the Chaldeans are wicked (Hab. 1:12). How will God be just given the impending exile if the people punishing Israel are also evil? By focusing on the theological problems created by the exile, the book of Habakkuk can be seen as a challenge to the role that the Deuteronomic curses play in accomplishing God's purposes.[97] For us it is important to note that Hab. 2:1-4 contains God's response to the problem of exile or the impending loss of the inheritance.[98]

God responds to the problem of the impending curses by commanding Habakkuk to write a vision on the tablet:

> And the Lord answered me and said, Write a vision, and clearly on a tablet, so that the reader might pursue them. For there is still a vision for an appointed time, and it will rise up at the end and not in vain. If it should

---

95. Watts 1999: 5.
96. Robertson (1990: 154) sees an allusion to Deut. 28:49 in the description of the Chaldean army. If this is indeed so, my case is strengthened, though it is not necessary. The logic of this text is surely Deuteronomic.
97. Watts 1999: 7.
98. Smith (1984: 96) says, "The message of Habakkuk was directed to the nation of Judah during the crisis which led to the fall of Jerusalem, the destruction of the Temple, and the deportation of many people."

tarry, wait for it, for when it comes it will come and not delay. If it draws back, my soul is not pleased in it. But the just shall live by my faith. (Hab. 2:1-4 LXX)

Habakkuk 2:1-4 calls upon the people to act faithfully in the context of the impending Deuteronomic curses in the hope of experiencing life. Habakkuk's words are presented as a prophecy that will prove its relevance at a time in the future. This future orientation of Habakkuk's prophecy allows Paul to claim that the followers of Christ are the people who will live by faith after the Deuteronomic curses are over. This prophetic reading of Hab. 2:4 is in keeping with Paul's prophetic reading of Gen. 12:3.

Paul is not alone in believing that Hab. 2:4 is prophecy about Israel's future. 1QpHab 7:1 says, "And God told Habakkuk to write what was going to happen to the last generation."[99] According to the author of the Pesher, God's vision to Habakkuk has a chronological and a theological element. He interprets Habakkuk's vision to mean that faithfulness to the instructions of the Teacher of Righteousness will be vindicated when God acts to deliver his people. In the same way, Paul maintains that Habakkuk's tablets predicted that those of faith will participate in the restoration.

If Paul read Hab. 2:4 as a prophecy, then his use of this text could be more significant than is often appreciated.[100] Paul is not simply taking advantage of a lexical connection with Gen. 15:6. Paul's use of Hab. 2:4 suggests that when the appointed time comes the just would live by faith. Thus, Paul's claim in Gal. 3:11 is not that Hab. 2:4 proves a theological axiom (Gen. 15:6). Habakkuk 2:4 establishes the validity of Abrahamic faith on the other side of the covenant curses. Genesis 15:6 and Hab. 2:4, together, establish the sufficiency of faith at the installation of the Abrahamic covenant and at the beginning of the fulfillment of the promises. For Paul, Hab. 2:4 supports his assertion that the giving of the Law did not fundamentally alter the terms of the Abrahamic covenant (Gal. 3:17). Those who believe are members of Abraham's family. Thus, in Gal. 3:10-12, Paul presents the Galatians with the following options: become a part of Abraham's family through faith or return to the covenant curses.

---

99. See also Heb. 10:37-38.
100. Sanders (1983: 21) claims that the lexical connection with Gen. 15:6 is the only reason Paul uses Hab. 2:4. See also Martyn 1997: 312 and Fung 1988: 143. Betz (1979: 146–7) uses different language to make a similar point.

4.4.4. Galatians 1:4, 3:13: Redemption from the Curse and the Final Realization of the Inheritance

Having shown that Paul's allusions to Deut. 27–29 and Lev. 18:5 are focused on the national curses, I will now consider Paul's interpretation of Jesus's death. Discerning the national focus in Gal. 3:10-12 allows us to appreciate the link between ending the curse and sharing in the Messiah's inheritance after the curse has ended. To establish this link between curse and inheritance, I make the following observations about Paul's interpretation of Jesus's death in Galatians. First, Paul interprets Jesus's death through the lens of the Isaianic servant narrative in Isa. 52:13–53:12 in Gal. 1:4 and 3:13.[101] Second, in the Isaianic servant narrative, the servant's death for sins ends the exile called for in the Deuteronomic curses and enables Israel's post-exilic reception of the inheritance (Isa. 53:12; 54:1-4). The link between the servant's death for sins and the post-exilic reception of an inheritance is under-appreciated in Pauline scholarship. Paul also argues that due to Jesus's death for sins, the believer is now an heir to an inheritance. This link between death and subsequent inheritance in Isa. 53 and Galatians suggests that Paul draws upon the wider Isaianic narrative in his interpretation of Jesus's death. Third, although Gal. 3:13 does not contain lexical links to Isa. 53, the conceptual similarities between Gal. 1:4 and Gal. 3:13 allow us to interpret the latter in light of the former.

Many recognize the allusion to the Isaianic servant's death in Gal. 1:4.[102] They make this observation because the combination of δίδωμι + preposition + sins matches the self-giving of the Isaianic servant. Galatians 1:3b-4 reads:

Ἰησοῦ Χριστοῦ τοῦ δόντος ἑαυτὸν ὑπὲρ τῶν ἁμαρτιῶν ἡμῶν, ὅπως ἐξέληται ἡμᾶς ἐκ τοῦ αἰῶνος τοῦ ἐνεστῶτος πονηροῦ.

Although many highlight the allusion to the servant's death for sins, few note the inheritance given to the Isaianic servant (Isa. 53:12 LXX). Given that Paul also claims that as a result of Jesus's death he too receives an inheritance (Gal. 3:16), the potential relevance of an inheritance following death for sins in Isaiah deserves further exploration.

---

101. Hereafter Isa. 53.
102. Hengel 1981: 35; Wolter 2011: 97, 104–5; Mußner 1974: 51; Schlier 1965: 32–3; Longenecker 1990: 7; Schreiner 2010: 76; Hays 2000: 203; Harmon 2010: 56–66; Moo 2013: 72; Ciampa 1998: 51–62; Dunn 1993: 35; Willitts 2012a: 154.

The importance of the inheritance theme in Isa. 53:12 seems to have been first noted by Hays. He discusses the servant's inheritance during his messianic interpretation of Hab. 2:3-4 in Gal. 3:11.[103] According to Hays, Paul believes that Hab. 2:3-4 is a messianic prophecy.[104] Hays maintains that in Gal. 3:11, ὁ δίκαιος ἐκ πίστεως ζήσεται refers to the Messiah. Isaiah 53:10-12 supports his messianic interpretation of ὁ δίκαιος from Hab. 2:3-4 because Isa. 53:10-12 uses the lexemes σπέρμα and δίκαιος during its account of the servant's death.[105] To bolster the claim that ὁ δίκαιος in Hab. 2:3-4 (and Isa. 53:10-12) refers to the Messiah, Hays points out the fact that God gave the servant an inheritance.[106] According to Hays, the theme of inheritance at the climax of the servant narrative corresponds to the claim that the inheritance belongs to Christ in Galatians.

Hays is correct to note that both Isa. 53:12 and Galatians highlight an individual's reception of an inheritance. He also rightly observes that in Galatians the inheritance belongs to Jesus because he is the messianic seed (Gal. 3:16). However, his reading relies upon a messianic interpretation of Hab. 2:3-4 that is unlikely. Paul's point in Gal. 3:11 is not that the Messiah has come, but that faith in the Messiah's atoning death justifies and brings one into Abraham's family. Furthermore, although I agree that Gal. 3:16 contains a messianic reading of 2 Sam. 7:12, that text did not promise the Son of David an inheritance. The inheritance language appears in Ps. 2:7-8, where God promises the Son an inheritance of the whole earth.

Therefore, I disagree with Hays when he says that Paul thinks that Isa. 53:12 LXX is messianic because it speaks about the righteous one. Instead, I suggest that Paul thinks that Isa. 53:12 LXX is messianic because he believes that it speaks about an inheritance that comes to an individual after his death and resurrection. The death for sins and the subsequent reception of the inheritance in Isa. 53:10-12 is what allows Paul to discern a reference to Christ.

Nonetheless, I agree that Paul's allusion to Isa. 53 extends beyond the death for sins to encompass the wider narrative. This wider narrative includes the fact that Jesus's death ends the covenant curses, including Israel's exile. To support the claim for the wider allusion, I will now

---

103. Hays 2002: 134–6. Morales (2010: 85) makes a similar observation about the inheritance.
104. Hays 2002: 134–6.
105. Ibid.: 137.
106. Ibid.

demonstrate that Isaiah's description of Israel as enslaved and under the Deuteronomic curses matches Paul's description of the state of affairs before the coming of Christ.

Most Old Testament scholars point out that Isa. 52:13–53:12 must be understood within the context of a larger narrative that stretches back at least to 52:1.[107] In Isa. 52:1-12, God speaks to an enslaved Israel announcing her departure from bondage. This narrative climaxes with a call to leave slavery that evokes the Exodus, "For you shall not go out in haste, and you shall not go in flight; for the LORD will go before you, and the God of Israel will be your rear guard" (Isa. 52:12).[108] In the wider context of Isa. 40–55, it is evident that Israel experiences exile as slavery because of covenant disobedience. Stated differently, the slavery of Isa. 52:1-12 is the exile and slavery pronounced by the covenant curses outlined in Deuteronomy.[109] Thus, Isa. 52:13–53:12 presents the servant's ministry as the solution to the problem of Deuteronomic curses, which resulted in slavery. The servant solves the problem of the Deuteronomic curses by suffering the effects of those curses in place of the nation. We can tell that the national Deuteronomic curses are in view because Isaiah draws upon Deut. 28:58-61 in its description of the servant's suffering on behalf of the people.[110]

Deut. 28:59	The Lord will make exceptional your plagues [πληγή] and the plagues [πληγή] upon your offspring, great and marvelous plagues [πληγή] and evil and constant maladies.
Deut. 28:61	And he will bring back upon you all the evil pains [ὀδύνη] of Egypt of which you were in dread before them, and they shall cling to you.
Isa. 53:4	This one bears our sins and suffers pain [ὀδυνάω] for us, and we accounted him to be in trouble and calamity [πληγή] and ill-treatment.

107. Childs 2001: 410. See also Blenkinsopp 2000: 339–40; Baltzer 2001: 393–4.
108. On the New Exodus imagery, see Baltzer 2001: 387.
109. On the influence of Deut. 32 in particular on Isa. 40–55, see Keiser 2005: 486–500; Brueggemann 1968: 191–203. On the influence of Deut. 27–29 on Isa. 52:13–53:12, see Harmon 2016: 8–12.
110. Harmon (2016: 11) says, "The sicknesses…which the servant bears (Isa 53:4) are the sicknesses that Yahweh had promised to bring upon Israel if they broke the covenant (Deut 28:59-61). The servant is 'struck by God'…(Isa 53:4) just as God had vowed to strike rebellious Israel for her covenant unfaithfulness (Deut 28:22, 27-28, 35)." I noticed this link between the servant's suffering and Deut. 27–28 before I encountered Harmon's work.

Deut. 28:61	And every malady [μαλακία] and every plague not recorded in the book of this law the Lord will bring on you until he utterly destroys you.
Isa. 53:5	But he was wounded because of our acts of lawlessness and has been weakened [μαλακίζομαι] because of our sins.[111]

The three lexemes (πληγή, ὀδύνη, μαλακία) that occur in Deut. 28:59-61 and Isa. 53:4-5 provide strong warrant for believing that Isaiah intentionally evokes the Deuteronomic curses in his description of the servant's suffering and death for the nation.

This slavery and Deuteronomic curse background matches Paul's description of the situation in Galatians.[112] He warns the Galatians that turning to the Law means returning to the Deuteronomic curses and slavery (Gal. 3:10-14; 4:22; 5:1).[113] Paul also uses redemption from slavery language when claiming that Jesus's death signals the end of the curse of the Law (Gal. 3:13; 4:4-7). The shared theme of the curse and slavery in the background of the redemptive-restorative death of the servant and Paul's interpretation of the death of Jesus makes it likely that Paul's reading of Israel's history is similar to the one found in Isa. 52–54.

I have argued that both the death of Jesus in Galatians and the death of the servant are presented as solutions to the Deuteronomic curses and slavery. Now I will show that Paul likens the inheritance won by the servant to the inheritance Jesus has as a result of his death and resurrection. Our focus is the climax of the narrative found in Isa. 53:11-12. There, as a result of his death for sins, God gives the servant an inheritance:

Isa. 53:12 MT	לכן אֲחַלֶּק לוֹ בָרַבִּים וְאֶת עֲצוּמִים יְחַלֵּק שָׁלָל
Isa. 53:12 LXX	διὰ τοῦτο αὐτὸς <u>κληρονομήσει</u> πολλοὺς καὶ τῶν ἰσχυρῶν <u>μεριεῖ</u> σκῦλα.

Both the LXX and Hebrew text traditions make it plain that God allots the servant an inheritance because of his death for the sins of many [διὰ τοῦτο αὐτὸς κληρονομήσει πολλοὺς / לבן אחלק לו]. Baltzer, pointing to the resonances with Num. 26:1-4, astutely notices a connection to the

---

111. See also Isa. 53:3, which says, "But his form was without honor, failing beyond all men, a man being in calamity [μαλακία] and knowing how to bear sickness."

112. On the importance of Exodus imagery in Galatians, see Keesmaat 1999; Wilson 2004: 550–71; Wilder 2001.

113. See the discussion below.

distribution of the land.[114] In Num. 26:1-4, God tells Moses to allot [חלק] land to the tribes. Isaiah 53:12, then, imagines that the second Exodus mentioned in Isa. 52:10-12 culminates in a second giving of the inheritance because of the servant's death. Finally, the language of dividing the spoils (יחלק שלל) could refer to the land conquest.[115] Therefore, in Isa. 53, the second Exodus leads to a second reception of the inheritance.

There is a question, however, regarding the inheritance that the servant receives and how it relates to the many [רבים] whose sins he has born. One view suggests that אחלק לו ברבים refers to the servant's inheritance "of" or "from" the many.[116] In this view, God gives the servant an inheritance that he then shares with others. Representing this reading, Lessing says, "Since the Servant is in fact the sole victor...he deserves all the booty."[117]

This reading requires us to take the ב that precedes the רבים to mean "of" or "from" instead of the more natural "among." Advocates present two reasons for this interpretation. First, throughout the narrative, the servant has been the singular actor bringing about Israel's restoration.[118] Given the singularity of his agency, it is strange to conclude the narrative with the servant being equal to the many who receive an inheritance. Second, in the latter half of 53:12 the servant allots the spoils [יחלק שלל] won by his death. This suggests that God gave the inheritance to the servant and then, as a surprising act of grace, he shares that inheritance with others.[119] The second reading takes the more standard interpretation of ב as "among." This would mean that God gave the servant an inheritance along with others and then the servant divides the spoils. This seems to be the more natural reading of the Hebrew text.[120] But the very tension between the shared inheritance and the servant dividing the spoils makes the choice between the two readings difficult.

The LXX tradition reflects the first reading: the servant inherited πολλοὺς and then the servant divides the spoils with the strong [κληρονομήσει πολλοὺς καὶ τῶν ἰσχυρῶν μεριεῖ σκῦλα]. The question remains as to how

114. Baltzer 2001: 425–6.
115. See Josh. 8:2; 11:14; 22:8. It could also refer to the bounty from any battle, see Exod. 15:9 and 1 Sam. 30:16.
116. North 1964: 245, 987; Olley 1987: 342–53; Baltzer 2001: 426–7; Lessing 2011: 603.
117. Lessing 2011: 603 (italics original). See also North 1964: 246.
118. Lessing 2011: 603.
119. For a strong argument that the רבים and עצומים are synonymous, see Olley 1987: 330–41.
120. Oswalt 1998: 406; Hermission 2004: 40–1; Westermann 1969: 255; Childs 2001: 420.

to take the πολλοὺς in Isa. 53:12 LXX. Given that πολλοὺς refers to the nation in Isa. 53:11, it seems that what belonged to the nation passes to the servant because of his death for sins. The servant, however, does not keep it for himself. He divides the spoils with those who sins he has borne. This reading seems to match Paul's argument about the inheritance in Galatians. I suggest that shared themes of (1) slavery and curse; (2) death for sins; (3) reception of an inheritance; (4) sharing that inheritance with others, make it likely that Paul alludes to the servant's death and inheritance in Gal. 1:4 and throughout the rest of Galatians.[121] This means that Paul's claim that Jesus has rescued the believer from the evil age finds its ultimate fulfillment in their sharing in his inheritance.

We have demonstrated that Paul alluded to Isa. 53 in Gal. 1:4. There are also reasons to detect a conceptual link to the servant narrative in Gal. 3:13. First, in Isa. 52:3 the prophet declares that Israel's departure from slavery would occur because of a redemption [λυτρόω] from slavery (Isa. 52:3).[122] Similarly, in Gal. 3:13 Paul presents Jesus's death as the event that redeems [ἐξαγοράζω] believing Jews from slavery and ends the covenant curses.[123] Thus, in Gal. 3:13 and in Isa. 53 the death of an individual brought about the end of slavery. Second, in Isa. 53 and Gal. 3:13 the individual redeems the nation by identifying with their sins. Paul says that Christ redeemed the Jewish Christians from the curse by γενόμενος ὑπὲρ ἡμῶν κατάρα. Jesus becoming a κατάρα is conceptually similar to the servant bearing the sins of the people because the Deuteronomic curses were the result of corporate sinfulness. Speaking of Christ taking upon himself the curse for others, Knöppler says, "Indem Christus die tödliche Wirkung des Fluches übernimmt, tritt er nicht nur (aus Solidarität) neben den Sünder, sondern er tritt (aufgrund von Identifikation) an die Stelle des durch den νομος verfluchten Menschen."[124] Third, in the Isaianic servant narrative, as a result of the servant's death, God ends Israel's exile, restores the nation, and gives the servant an inheritance that he shares with others. Likewise, Paul claims in Gal. 3:14 that the blessing, which enables the inheritance, comes to the Gentiles through Christ because the inheritance belongs to him (Gal. 3:16). This can be displayed visually as follows:

---

121. On the links between the contexts of Isa. 53 and the argument of Galatians, see Morales 2010: 82.

122. See also the mention of a new Exodus in Isa. 52:10-12.

123. I maintain that the redemption from the curse refers to the Jewish Christians because they were the ones under the covenant curses. See the discussion of Gal. 3:10-12 above. See also Trick 2016: 113.

124. Knöppler 2001: 162. What he says about the individual is true for the nation—Christ bears their curse.

Israel experiencing slavery and exile (Isa. 52:10-12)	The death of the servant for sins ends slavery and the exile (Isa. 53:1-11)	The servant receives the inheritance (Isa. 53:12a LXX)	The servant shares the inheritance with others (Isa. 53:12b; 54:1-4)
Returning to the Law means returning to the Deuteronomic curses and slavery (Gal. 3:10, 12; 4:8-11; 5:1)	The death of Jesus for sins frees from slavery and ends the Deuteronomic curses (Gal. 1:4; 3:13; 4:4-7)	The inheritance belongs to the Messiah Jesus (Gal. 3:16, 19)	Those associated with Christ are heirs to the inheritance (Gal. 3:26-29; 4:1-11)

Support for this claim of a shared inheritance comes from Paul's use of Isa. 54:1 in Gal. 4:27-31. Isaiah 54:1-4 describes the immediate aftermath of the servant's work. It chronicles a newly restored Jerusalem giving birth to σπέρμα that expand outward to inherit the nations:

> Enlarge [πλάτυνον] the place of your tents...stretch out to the right and to the left, for your seed [τὸ σπέρμα] will inherit [κληρονομήσει] the nations and they will dwell in the desolate cities. (Isa. 53:3-4)

Many observe that Isa. 54:3 alludes to Gen. 28:14. Both texts used πλατύνω to describe the directional spread of the seed of Abraham in fulfillment of the land promise.[125] In Isa. 53:12–54:4, then, the death of the servant results in his receiving an inheritance that he shares with others after the exile was over. His exile-ending death causes the newly restored people to expand exponentially to inherit the nations. Paul explicitly says that the Galatians are the children predicted in Isa. 54:1-4 (Gal. 4:26-27).[126]

Paul justifies his assertion about the redemptive death of Jesus by citing Deut. 21:23. Paul modifies Deut. 21:23 by inserting the ἐπικατάρατος from 27:26 into 21:23 to make the connection between these curses explicit:

Gal. 3:10 (Deut. 27:26/29:19)	ἐπικατάρατος πᾶς ὃς οὐκ ἐμμένει πᾶσιν τοῖς γεγραμμένοις ἐν τῷ βιβλίῳ τοῦ νόμου τοῦ ποιῆσαι αὐτά.
Gal. 3:13 (Deut. 21:23a)	ἐπικατάρατος πᾶς ὁ κρεμάμενος ἐπὶ ξύλου.[127]

125. Baltzer 2001: 438; Oswalt 1998: 418.
126. See Jobes 1993: 316.
127. On the modification of Deut. 21:23, see Caneday 1989: 204 and Bruce 1982: 165. Brondos (2001: 22) incorrectly argues that Paul has two different curses in mind.

I have demonstrated that the ἐπικατάρατος of Gal. 3:10 referred to the curses that dominated the latter portions of Deut. 27–29. Thus, Paul uses Deut. 23:21 to assert that Jesus's death on the cross involves Jesus taking upon himself the nation's punishment for their disobedience and ending the curse through his death. This is the exact same thing that the servant does when he bears the Deuteronomic curses for the nation so that they might receive a share in his inheritance.

Therefore, to present the cross as the means of redemption from the covenant curses suggests, among other things, that Jesus's death enables the restoration of Abraham's offspring to the inheritance. This claim is not rooted solely in the idea that Deut. 27–29 mentions the loss of the inheritance. There are three reasons to link the inheritance to the end of the curse: (1) the Deuteronomic curses focus on the loss of the inheritance; (2) in the Isaianic servant narrative, which undergirds Paul's interpretation of Jesus's death, the servant's death ends the Deuteronomic curses and the nation shares in his inheritance because of the servant's death for sins (Isa. 53:12–54:4); (3) Paul declares that after the curse the inheritance belongs to Christ because he is the messianic and Abrahamic seed (Gal. 3:16). Paul also says that all those in Christ share in his inheritance (Gal. 3:26-29). Thus, the inheritance that the Galatians will receive because of the death of Christ is a share in the inheritance of the Messiah whose death for sins ends the curse.[128]

Others have asserted that Galatians contains a form of messianism that climaxes in the kingdom.[129] However, they do not organically connect the coming kingdom to the end of the Deuteronomic curses, nor do they explain how ending the curse leads to the inheritance that belongs to Christ.[130] Connecting the redemption from the curse to the restoration to the inheritance as kingdom creates a natural link between Jesus's

---

128. Trick (2016: 118–19) argues that Christ did not bear the nation's curse. According to Trick, Christ bore the curse he rightly deserved because he hung on a tree (Deut. 21:23). Trick does not understand how Christ as Messiah can bear the curse for the nation because he neglects the Isaianic interpretation of Jesus's death offered above. This Isaianic interpretation of Jesus's death explains how an individual can bear the Deuteronomic curses for the nation.

129. See the discussion in Chapter 1.

130. On the connection between the inheritance and the kingdom, see Hester (1968: 36–7), who says, "possession of the inheritance depends on a relationship to the Heir. The inheritance to which he gives access is the Kingdom of God." I agree that the inheritance is the kingdom of God, but Hester's work did not explain how, by removing the Deuteronomic curses, Jesus's death made the Galatians heirs. Hester also fails to examine the role the Davidic Messiahs play in restoring Israel to the

curse-ending death and the inheritance that believers have in Christ. Furthermore, this reading of curse and inheritance unites the two halves of Gal. 3:1–4:11. Paul can say that the death of Jesus makes the Galatians heirs to the inheritance because to redeem from the curse entails beginning the restoration to the inheritance. Finally, understanding the redemption from the curse in this manner also allows us to discern how the death of Jesus could be seen as royal or messianic. Jesus's death is a manifestation of Davidic messianism because it allows believing Jews and Gentiles to share in the king's inheritance (Ps. 2:7-8). Thus, Jesus's death in the argument of Galatians accomplishes what was achieved by other means in Second Temple depictions of royal figures. It leads to the final realization of the land promises.

4.4.5. *Galatians 3:14: The Blessing of Abraham and the Promised Spirit*

Paul concludes this section by returning to the Abrahamic blessing and the promised Spirit (Gal. 3:14). The majority view argues that Paul believes that the blessing promised to the Gentiles in Gen. 12:3 is the promised Spirit of Gal. 3:14b.[131] Furthermore, since believing Gentiles are the promised seed of Abraham, the Spirit is also the blessing promised to Abraham's seed in Gen. 12:7, 15:8, and 22:17.[132] Since the Spirit is the blessing promised to Abraham's seed, there is no longer a place for the land inheritance.[133] This interpretation leads many to conclude that the Spirit is the inheritance that belongs to Christ the seed in Gal. 3:16, 18, 26-29.[134] Thus, in Galatians the inheritance is fully realized. De Boer sums up the majority position well when he says:

> The reception of the Spirit through faith, meaning the faith of Christ, has made Gentile believers, no less than Jewish believers, the…"sons of Abraham," thus the rightful heirs of the promise that God made to the faithful patriarch. That promise concerned the gift of the Spirit, which is the "blessing of Abraham."[135]

inheritance in Second Temple texts. See also Beale 2011: 249; Davies 1980 [1948]: 37–41; Forman 2011: 189–91; Martin 2015: 137; Schweitzer 1998 [1931]: 21–5. See the much fuller discussion in Chapter 1.

131. Burton 1980 [1921]: 177; de Boer 2011: 215; Bruce 1982: 168; Betz 1979: 152–3; Martyn 1997: 323.

132. De Boer 2011: 215.

133. Burton 1980 [1921]: 185; Witherington 2004: 245–6, 292; Das 2014: 390; Martyn 1997: 342–3; Williams 1997: 96–7; de Boer 2011: 185; Garlington 2007: 206–7.

134. Das 2014: 356; Burton 1980 [1921]: 185; Bruce 1982: 191.

135. De Boer 2011: 215.

This interpretation requires the Spirit to function in three ways: (1) the Spirit makes the Galatians heirs; (2) the Spirit is the inheritance promised to them as heirs; (3) the Spirit fulfills the promise that God would bless the Gentiles.

What evidence has been presented to substantiate these claims? Moo notes that the parallelism of the two clauses in Gal. 3:14 leads many to believe that the promised Spirit is the blessing promised to Abraham's seed.[136] But this parallelism does not require us to make this interpretative leap.[137] Grammatically, the promised Spirit and blessing of Abraham could be coordinate results of the redemption of the Jewish Christians from the curse of the Law.[138] Thus, the interpretation of the relationship between these two clauses depends upon an analysis of the wider argument of the letter. Paul's wider argument speaks against equating the blessing of Abraham with the promised Spirit.

The primary reason for maintaining that there is a distinction between the blessing of Abraham and the promised Spirit is that Paul just said that Gen. 12:3 foresaw the justification of the Gentiles by faith (Gal. 3:8).[139] This leaves us with three options: (1) we can assume that when Paul speaks of justification in Gal. 3:8 he really means the Spirit;[140] (2) Paul defines the blessing of Abraham differently in Gal. 3:8 and 3:14;[141] (3) justification is the blessing of Abraham that comes to the Gentiles, and therefore the Spirit is not the blessing.[142]

---

136. Moo 2013: 216.

137. De Boer (2011: 215 n. 311) claims that the parallelism indicates an identification.

138. Moo 2013: 216.

139. Fung 1988: 141; Moo 2013: 216; Witherington 2004: 228.

140. De Boer (2011: 194–6) acknowledges that in Gal. 3:8 Paul defines the blessing as justification, but according to de Boer his opponents' arguments forces him to speak in this way. They believe that the Spirit enables Law obedience and facilitates their eschatological justification. According to de Boer, Paul believes that justification occurs in the past because of the faithfulness of Christ. For de Boer, the gift of the Spirit in the present brings the Galatians into Abraham's family and fully sets the Galatians right with God. Stated differently, for de Boer, when Paul refers to justification in Gal. 3:8, he really means the Spirit. De Boer is correct that the Spirit testifies to justification by faith, but he is wrong to conclude that Paul only speaks of justification by faith to rebut his opponents.

141. See Watson (2004: 186–7), who acknowledges that in Gal. 3:8 Paul defines the blessing as justification, but then suggests that Paul later defined the blessing of Abraham as justification and the Spirit. His interpretation will be considered below.

142. Witherington 2004: 228; Moo 2013: 216.

Regarding the first option, I have shown that the Spirit functions as evidence of justification because God promised to pour out his Spirit upon his people when the covenant curses were over. Thus, to be justified on the other side of the curses entails the reception of the Spirit. Therefore, the promised Spirit and justification are linked because those justified by faith receive the Spirit. Nonetheless, justification and Spirit reception are not the same thing. The second option fails because we need not assume that Paul contradicts himself in the span of a few sentences unless all other options fail.

Having eliminated the first two options, I will now provide fresh evidence that the blessing of the Gentiles is the justification that makes them a part of Abraham's family by pointing to a neglected allusion to Gen. 28:4 in Gal. 3:14a.[143] This allusion supports the claim that the blessing of Abraham is indeed their justification.

The phrase ἡ εὐλογία τοῦ Ἀβραάμ is uncommon in the LXX. It only occurs in Gen. 28:4.[144] In Gen. 28:1-4 Isaac blesses Jacob by asking God to make Jacob into a gathering of nations [συναγωγὰς ἐθνῶν]. Then Isaac asks God to give the blessing of Abraham to Jacob and to the seed that he says will become a συναγωγὰς ἐθνῶν. This Abrahamic blessing is this seed's participation in the inheritance. It reads, "may he give the blessing of Abraham [τὴν εὐλογίαν Αβρααμ] my father to you and to your seed [σπέρματί] in order to inherit [κληρονομῆσαι] the land" (Gen. 28:5).[145] Genesis 28:1-4 is pertinent because it looks to the ἔθνη being gathered into a singular seed and thereby becoming heirs to the inheritance. This corresponds to Paul's claim that Jesus's death has given the blessing of Abraham (justification) to the Gentiles so that they might be gathered into the seed that will inherit. That Gal. 3:15-19 immediately turns to the question of the seed and the inheritance strengthens the likelihood that Paul has this text in mind. Therefore, the best reading of the "blessing of Abraham" is one that focuses on the justification that brings the Galatians

---

143. Morales (2010: 110) maintains that Paul alludes to Isa. 44:3 because in that text God promises to pour out his blessing on Jacob's descendants in the form of the Spirit. Genesis 28:4 has a stronger warrant for being the source of Paul's allusion because Gen. 28:1-4 refers to the blessing of Abraham, the Gentiles, the inheritance, and the seed.

144. De Boer (2011: 214) and Watson (2004: 188) note, but do not develop, the allusion. Moo (2013: 215) claims that an allusion to Gen. 28:4 would be unnecessary because Paul is simply thinking of the Abrahamic blessing as a general concept. The appearance of seed, inheritance, and the notion of Gentiles being gathered into a seed suggests that Paul's allusion to Gen. 28:4 is intentional.

145. My translation.

into Abraham's family. Seeing the blessing of the Gentiles as their incorporation into Abraham's family through justifications allows for a better reading of Galatians. If the blessing brings the Gentiles into the family that stands to inherit, then Paul's discussion of heirship and inheritance in the latter portions of the letter becomes readily explainable.

If the Spirit should not be identified with the blessing of Abraham, can we nonetheless say that Spirit replaces the land as the inheritance promised to Abraham and his seed? There are six reasons to doubt that the Spirit replaces the land. First, the idea that the Spirit replaces the land promise is "unattested in any other contemporary literature."[146] Second, in Gal. 4:27-31 Paul compares those born of the Spirit to Isaac, who is the heir. Isaac's heirship is important because in the Genesis passage that Paul alludes to, Isaac does not yet have the inheritance (Gen. 21:6-14). Third, in Rom. 4:13 Paul says that God promised Abraham and his seed the world, not the Spirit.[147] Fourth, in Gal. 5:5 Paul says that the Spirit empowers the believer to wait for the hope of δικαιοσύνης. This suggests that the gift of the Spirit and justification have their completion in something greater, namely participation in the Son's inheritance.[148] A major problem with the "Spirit replaces the land" view is that advocates assume that attaining the status of Abraham's seed entails the immediate reception of the full inheritance.[149] Fifth, the "Spirit replaces the land" view separates resurrection, life, new creation, and inheriting the kingdom from the fulfillment of the Abrahamic land promise. The problem with this division is that the Pauline nomenclature in Galatians (the end of the curse, life, inheriting the kingdom, new creation) implies a belief in the post-exilic fulfillment of the Abrahamic land promise (Deut. 30:11-19; Ezek. 37:1-28). Finally, presenting the Spirit as the inheritance promised to the Abrahamic seed encounters insurmountable difficulties when we arrive at Gal. 3:15-18 and 26-29.[150] In Gal. 3:15-18, Paul claims

---

146. Kwon 2004: 109. De Boer (2011: 185) says that the fact that the Spirit replaces the land was common ground between Paul and his opponents. But this seems only to beg the question.

147. Kwon 2004: 114.

148. While Paul's words in Gal. 5:5 are terse, his later discussion of eschatological hope in a similar context is relevant. In Rom. 8:20-24, the believer's hope is tied to the hope that creation itself will be set free from bondage and decay when God finally acts to redeem his people. In the meantime, the Spirit aids the believers while they await being fully conformed to the image of the Son who reigns over all. See also the concept of abounding in hope in Rom. 15:8-13.

149. Forman 2011: 174; Kwon 2004: 113.

150. See the fuller discussion in the next chapter.

that the promises (plural) were made to Christ. Replacing the land with the Spirit would mean that Paul believes that the Spirit is the content of the promises made to Christ.[151] But Paul does not argue that Jesus himself receives the Spirit as his inheritance because of his death and resurrection. Instead, Paul consistently proclaims Jesus's rise to sovereignty over creation as a result of his death and resurrection (Phil. 2:9-11; 1 Cor. 15:25). It is this sovereignty that he shares with his people (Rom. 8:17; 1 Cor. 4:18). This emphasis on Jesus's universal sovereignty suggests that Jesus shares his worldwide inheritance in the age to come with those who have been justified by faith.

If the Spirit does not replace the land, why does Paul associate the Spirit with the Abrahamic blessing? We need not repeat the arguments of Gal. 3:2-5 in full. Instead, I will reaffirm the influence of the prophetic texts that associate the Spirit with the post-exilic transformation of the people and the land on the other side of the curses:

> A new heart I will give you, and a new spirit I will put within you; and I will remove from your body the heart of stone and give you a heart of flesh. I will put my spirit within you, and make you follow my statutes and be careful to observe my ordinances... And they will say, "This land that was desolate has become like the garden of Eden." (Ezek. 36:26-27, 35a)

According to Ezekiel, a mere return to the land is insufficient without the transformation of the heart that would prevent Israel from disobeying the covenant again and returning to exile.[152] By focusing on the transformation of the heart, Ezekiel mirrors the circumcision of the heart mentioned in Deut. 30:6.[153] According to Ezekiel, then, the Spirit prepares those being restored for their new life in the land that itself will become like the garden of Eden. Therefore, Paul could relate the promised Spirit to the blessing of Abraham because, as Abraham's seed, the Galatians have received the transformed hearts through the Spirit on the other side of the curses. But this transformed heart is for life in the kingdom. This is why, for Paul, life outside of the Spirit defines those

---

151. De Boer (2011: 223) says, "Between the promise and Christ, therefore, there were no offspring of Abraham, no heirs of the promise that God made to Abraham. The inheritance, the Spirit, became available only with the coming of Christ." But here he seems not to follow his argument fully. The question is not when the "inheritance" became available. The question is to whom the promises had been made.

152. On the influence of Ezek. 36:26-27 on Gal. 4:5, see Martyn 1997: 391–2 and Morales 2010: 127.

153. See also Rom. 2:28-29.

who will not inherit (Gal. 5:21).[154] Thus, the Spirit is the sign that the Gentiles are Abraham's seed and the beginning of their participation in the inheritance.

Watson disagrees with our understanding of the inheritance as the worldwide kingdom of the Messiah. Instead, he says that Paul interprets the blessing as justification in 3:8 and the Spirit in 3:14.[155] For Watson, "blessing" is multivalent. Therefore, justification and the gift of the Spirit can both be seen as blessings that come to the Gentiles in Christ.[156]

Watson's multivalent understanding of blessing does not lead him to maintain that the Spirit replaces the land inheritance. Instead, Watson suggests that salvation replaces the land.[157] Watson believes that salvation replaces the land even though he acknowledges that Paul believes that Abraham is "heir of the world."[158]

Watson rightly recognizes that many often conflate the content of the blessing with the content of the inheritance. His work also separates the blessing that brings the Gentiles into Abraham's family (Spirit reception and justification) from the inheritance (salvation) that the Gentiles receive because they are members of Abraham's family. Furthermore, his work reveals that the interpretation of the inheritance will in large part depend upon the type of argument that exegetes believe Paul is making. Watson believes that inheritance is salvation because he believes that Paul's argument focuses on the fact that God takes "total responsibility for human salvation."[159] By contrast, those who believe that Paul is really talking about the Spirit make the Spirit the inheritance.

Nonetheless, Watson's proposal that we define the inheritance as salvation leaves open the question of how Paul relates the location in which the saved reside to the inheritance promised to the Messiah Jesus (Gal. 3:16).[160] For example, in Rom. 8:17-32 the believer's life in the transformed creation is the ultimate outcome of salvation from sin and judgment. Therefore, in Galatians we cannot define the inheritance as salvation without highlighting the fact that the outcome of that salvation, at the climax of one of his most important letters, includes the reign of

---

154. See the discussion of 5:21 in the next chapter.
155. Watson 2004: 186–7. Here Watson advocates for position two outline above, namely that Paul has two definitions of "blessing." I argued above that assuming Paul contradicts himself should be the last resort.
156. Ibid.: 192.
157. Ibid.: 200.
158. Ibid.: 201. Here he relies upon Rom. 4:13.
159. Ibid.: 196.
160. See Chapter 1.

the Messiah Jesus over a transformed creation. It is important to point out again that Galatians does not use the language of salvation; it refers to the inheritance. If we can bring in the language of salvation from Romans and elsewhere, then it is fair to highlight how Paul describes that salvation in that letter. Put differently, I concur that Paul believes that the Christians are saved from sin, judgment, and the present evil age. However, in Galatians Paul focuses on participating in the Son's inheritance of the whole earth that is his by right as the designated heir of Abraham and David.

4.5. Conclusion of Chapter 4

This chapter has shown that Paul presents the cross of the Messiah Jesus as the solution to the problem of the Deuteronomic curses. These curses focus to a large extent on the loss of the inheritance. While not denying the emphasis placed on death as an element of the Deuteronomic curses, I highlighted the final realization of the inheritance as a central feature of the end of the curse in Galatians and Deuteronomy. I called attention to the inheritance because of: (1) the presence of the inheritance theme in the Abrahamic narrative; (2) the link between inheritance and Spirit reception in Israel's prophetic texts; (3) and the inheritance given at the climax of the Isaianic servant narrative. I showed that these three sources (the servant narrative, the Abraham cycle in Genesis, and restoration texts that emphasize the Spirit) all influence Paul's understanding of the inheritance in Galatians. Nonetheless, I do not see an essential conflict between resurrection, life, inheritance, and new creation.[161] For Paul, they are all outcomes of God's rescue of his people from the curse.

This rescue through the cross is good news for believing Jews and Gentiles because the sole requirement for membership in the family that will inherit on the other side of the curse is faith in the Messiah Jesus. To counter the claim that doing works of the Law is necessary to make one an heir, Paul goes to great lengths to show that faith has always been the sole criterion for participation in the Abrahamic covenant. He pursues this goal by showing that God's justification of Abraham before the giving of the Law, and Habakkuk's prediction that those of faith will live on the other side of the curse, reveal that faith is sufficient to make the Galatians sons and heirs.

---

161. This stands in contrast to Morales 2010: 170–1. See the discussion above.

4. The End of the Curse and the Beginning of the Inheritance 143

A consistent theme in the prophetic accounts of restoration is the idea that God will transform the hearts of those being restored. This theme appears in Gal. 3:1-14 when Paul turns to the evidence of the Spirit to prove that the Galatians are heirs apart from the Law. In his depiction of the Spirit, Paul relies upon accounts of the gift of the Spirit in Israel's prophetic literature. In those texts, God pours his Spirit upon those who are being restored. Thus, the reception of the Spirit by faith supports Paul's claim that the Galatians are heirs. Rather than replacing the Spirit with the land, Paul portrays the Spirit as the beginning of the inheritance to be completed at the resurrection.

Although we have repeatedly mentioned the inheritance in this chapter, Paul addresses the question of the inheritance and identity of the rightful heir most directly in Gal. 3:15–4:7. We now turn to a discussion of 3:15–4:7 to further establish the relationship between Davidic messianism and the inheritance. There I will argue that when Paul speaks about believers being heirs to the inheritance through Christ in fulfillment of the promises made to Abraham, we should take his language seriously. According to Paul, through the death and resurrection of Christ, believing Jews and Gentiles have become heirs to the inheritance that belongs to Jesus as Messiah: the whole earth.

Chapter 5

SHARING IN THE SON'S INHERITANCE: DAVIDIC MESSIANISM AND THE ABRAHAMIC LAND PROMISE IN GALATIANS 3:15–4:7; 5:21

5.1. Introduction

In the previous chapter, I argued that Paul presents the cross of the Messiah as the solution to the problem of the covenant curses. These covenant curses stood in the way of Israel obtaining its promised inheritance. I argued that ending the covenant curses should be described as a royal or messianic act because it began the final realization of the land inheritance, expanded to encompass the whole earth under the rule of Israel's Messiah, Jesus.[1]

Through an analysis of Gal. 3:15-19, 26-29, 4:1-7, and 5:21, this chapter continues my argument that Paul believes that the Messiah Jesus has enabled the eschatological participation in his inheritance of the renewed earth. We will see that Paul believes that the Abrahamic covenant designates the Messiah Jesus as the ultimate heir to promises made to Abraham. As king and heir, Jesus is entitled to the whole earth as his inheritance and kingdom (Gal. 3:15-19). Furthermore, Paul depicts the believer as an heir who will share in the Son's inheritance in Gal. 3:26-29 and again in 4:1-7. This inheritance begins with the Spirit and will be completed in the kingdom. This reading of inheritance as kingdom will be confirmed through an analysis of Gal. 5:21. Despite claims to the contrary, Paul's inheritance language in Gal. 5:21 is in accord with his inheritance language in Gal. 3:15–4:7. Throughout the epistle, Paul argues that the believer will share in the king's inheritance of the whole earth.

---

1. On the link between royal figures and the restoration to the land, see Chapters 2 and 3.

Few if any considerations of Gal. 3:15–4:7 and 5:21 focus on kingship and inheritance. Therefore, the presence of kingship and inheritance is not so much disputed as it is ignored. That is understandable because different readers come to Galatians with varying agendas. It is not my intention to claim that readings of Galatians that highlight other elements of Paul's argument (such as the primacy of faith over Law obedience) are incorrect. Instead, I attempt to show that, in the course of making his argument about the primacy of faith over Torah, Paul reveals his belief in the worldwide inheritance of the Messiah. This claim about the singular inheritance of the Messiah given and shared is not the sole pillar of Paul's argument in Gal. 3:15–4:7, but it is a pillar that Pauline scholarship neglects. In the course of making the case for Jesus's messiahship and his inheritance in Gal. 3:15–4:7, I will interact, often in at least partial agreement, with those who bring different questions to the text.

5.2. *Galatians 3:15-19*

5.2.1. *Overview*

What follows is not an analysis of all the contested issues in Gal. 3:15-19. Instead, I make two points in support of the claim that Paul's argument focuses on the Messiah's inheritance. First, Paul reads the covenant of Gen. 17:1-21 in light of the promises made to the seed of David in 2 Sam. 7:12-14.[2] Paul links these two texts because the emphasis in Gen. 17:1-21 on kingship arising from Abraham's seed corresponds to God's promise to David that he would raise up a seed to succeed him. For Paul, both the Abrahamic and Davidic texts foretell the coming of the Messiah Jesus, the rightful heir to the inheritance. Paul's adoption of a messianic reading of seed also entails adopting a messianic reading of inheritance as kingdom. In the Davidic seed texts, the rise of the seed leads to the establishment of his kingdom, which in the Royal Psalms spans the entire earth. Second, we can be confident that Paul has the Messiah's inheritance in mind because he alludes to Gen. 49:10 in Gal. 3:19.[3] Paul's allusion to Gen. 49:10 is important because that text was being read as a prediction about the Messiah and his kingdom in the Second Temple period.

---

2. Hays (2002: 137) makes a similar claim, but he does not highlight the inheritance promised to the Messiah nor did he emphasize the prediction of kingship in Gen. 17. See the discussion below. In addition to Hays, see Juel 1992: 85–6; Duling 1973: 55–77; Wilcox 1979: 2–20; de Boer 2011: 222–3; Collins 2003: 75–86; Novenson 2012: 140–2.

3. Dahl 1977: 130–1; Juel 1992: 85–6; Jervis 1999: 73.

5.2.2. Galatians 3:15-18: The Inheritance Belongs to the Messiah

In Gal. 3:15 Paul opens by making an analogy about human covenants or wills (διαθήκη) to make a point about God's covenant with Abraham and his seed.[4] Paul maintains that God's covenant with Abraham is just as unchangeable as a human διαθήκη. Many question Paul's meaning here because, based upon what we know of human wills of the period, they could be amended.[5] Despite our lack of clarity on Paul's reference, his basic point is clear: once God put the covenant in place, the terms of that covenant could not be changed or amended 430 years later by the addition of the Law.

Paul's comment on the terms of the covenant leads to one of his most controversial exegetical claims. According to Paul, the promises were not made to many seed [σπέρμασιν], but to a singular seed [σπέρμα] who is Christ (Gal. 3:16). Scholars criticize Paul because in many of the Genesis passages that deal with the Abrahamic promises, σπέρμα is a collective singular. Authors usually choose one the following solutions to this problem: (1) they argue that Paul uses an exegetical technique that would be accepted by his contemporaries, even if we find it odd;[6] (2) they claim that Paul refers to a Genesis text that does focus on a singular seed;[7] (3) they assert that Paul has the singular family of the Messiah's people in mind when he speaks about the singular seed;[8] (4) they declare that Paul's interpretation of seed is messianic and looks to the Messiah Jesus as the designated heir of the Abrahamic promises.[9]

The first option is not really an explanation of Gal. 3:16; it is an apologetic for Pauline exegesis. As valuable as such an apologetic might be, it does not aid in our interpretation. The second option fails because Gal. 3:16 included καὶ in the quotation. I mention the καὶ because, according to many advocates, Gen. 22:18 is the text that contains the singular σπέρμα that Paul has in mind in Gal. 3:16.[10] But Gen. 22:18 says, καὶ ἐνευλογηθήσονται <u>ἐν τῷ σπέρματί σου</u> πάντα τὰ ἔθνη τῆς γῆς, ἀνθ' ὧν ὑπήκουσας τῆς ἐμῆς φωνῆς. The phrase ἐν τῷ σπέρματί σου does not

---

4. Schröter 2013: 170.
5. Moo 2013: 227–8; Dunn 1993: 182; Burton 1980 [1921]: 180; Hahn 2009: 258–60; Schröter 2013: 171.
6. Moo 2013: 229. On Paul's rabbinic exegesis, see Daube 1944: 227–30.
7. See the discussion below.
8. Most recently Wright 2013: 868–9.
9. Hays 2000: 264; Novenson 2012: 141; Wright 2013: 868; Pyne 1995: 215–16. See also the discussion of the new interpretation offered by Trick 2016 below.
10. Collins 2003: 75–86; Hahn 2009: 262–4.

correspond to Paul's allusion in Gal. 3:16, which says καὶ τῷ σπέρματί σου. Hahn tries to overcome this problem by arguing that Paul alludes to Gen. 22:18-20 because of a typological correspondence between Jesus and Isaac.[11] Thus, for Hahn, Jesus is the ultimate singular seed who brings blessing to the world. Collins, on the other hand, maintains that Gen. 22:18 must be the source because it is an Abrahamic text that contains a promise that God will bless the Gentiles.[12] For Collins, since Galatians focuses on Gentile inclusion, Paul's source text in Gal. 3:16 must also mention Gentiles. Therefore, according to Collins, the main alternative to Gen. 22:18, namely Gen. 17:8, fails because it does not look to the inclusion of the Gentiles even though it conforms more closely to Paul's language in Gal. 3:16. Genesis 17:8a reads, καὶ δώσω σοι καὶ τῷ σπέρματί σου μετὰ σὲ τὴν γῆν, ἣν παροικεῖς. In addition, Collins notes that the similarity between Gen. 22:17-18 and Ps. 72:17 allows Paul to read Gen. 22:17-18 as a messianic prophecy.[13] Collins' argument fails for two reasons. First, the lexical overlap between Gen. 17:8 and Gal. 3:16 is too compelling to ignore. Second, Gal. 3:16 is not about the mediation of blessing to the Gentiles; it is about identifying the rightful heir to the inheritance. Paul's argument is that the inheritance belongs to Christ and those united to him by baptism and faith (Gal. 3:26-29).

The third reading has been championed by N.T. Wright. He says, "the points of verses 15-18 can be expressed quite simply: (a) God promised Abraham a single family, not two families; (b) the Law threatens to create two families…; (c) the Law cannot be allowed to overthrow the original promise and intention."[14] I agree with the first and third point. Paul believes that God promised Abraham a single family, and he maintains that the Law cannot overrule that promise. This family consists of those united to Christ the seed. The problem arises with the middle proposition. Paul could not be arguing that by installing the Law his opponents would create two families because his opponents deny family membership to those outside the Law. Their claim is that the Law does create a single family, that of Torah-obedient Jews and (former) Gentiles. The disagreement, then, is about two different ways of defining the one family of Abraham, not the potential creation of two families. According to Paul, Abraham's family consists of those united to Christ, the heir (3:16, 26-29).

---

11. Hahn 2009: 262–4.
12. See Collins (2003: 75–86), who relies upon the grammatical observations of Alexander (1997: 363–7) to argue that in Gen. 22:18-20 the seed is singular.
13. Collins 2003: 75–86.
14. Wright 2013: 868.

Recently Trick has offered a new interpretation.[15] He argues that Christ is the singular seed because the διαθήκη that Paul refers to in Gal. 3:15 actually describes God's testamentary adoption of Abraham.[16] According Trick, if God adopted Abraham into his family, then the promised seed of Abraham must be a son of Abraham and a son of God. For Trick, Jesus, the divine Son who is also of Abrahamic descent, meets this criterion. Therefore Christ is the promised heir, not Isaac.[17] Trick posits this interpretation as an alternative to the messianic reading of seed.[18] The major problem with this interpretation is that the Davidic king is described as the Son of God in Ps. 2:7-8.[19] In Ps. 2:7-8, God also promises the Son an inheritance. Furthermore, we know that Paul uses Son language to describe Jesus's divinity and status as Messiah (Rom. 1:3-4). Thus, there is no need to highlight Jesus's divinity in such a way that it rules out an allusion to his status as the promised seed of Abraham and David. Stated differently, I agree that Paul believes that the divine Son is heir to the promises. Yet, I maintain that he also believes that the divine Son is Israel's Messiah who was promised the world as his inheritance.[20]

The final view, and the one supported in this book, focuses on a messianic reading of seed.[21] To understand Paul's messianic interpretation, it is important to identify his source text. The most likely candidate is Gen. 17:8 because the wider context of Gen. 17:8 emphasizes the covenant, and it matches Paul's language in 3:16.[22]

Gen. 17:8   καὶ στήσω τὴν διαθήκην...διαθήκην αἰώνιον εἶναί σου θεὸς καὶ τοῦ σπέρματός σου μετὰ σέ. καὶ δώσω σοι <u>καὶ τῷ σπέρματί σου</u> μετὰ σὲ τὴν γῆν

Gal. 3:16   τῷ δὲ Ἀβραὰμ ἐρρέθησαν αἱ ἐπαγγελίαι καὶ τῷ σπέρματι αὐτοῦ. οὐ λέγει· καὶ τοῖς σπέρμασιν, ὡς ἐπὶ πολλῶν ἀλλ' ὡς ἐφ' ἑνός· <u>καὶ τῷ σπέρματί σου</u>

---

15. Trick 2016.
16. Ibid.: 137–82.
17. Ibid.: 177–80.
18. Ibid.: 140.
19. It is interesting to note that he never cites or discusses Ps. 2:7-8 even through Jesus's sonship and inheritance are central pillars of his thesis. See ibid.: 374.
20. See also the discussion of sonship and messianism below.
21. Views two and three also rely on a messianic interpretation of seed, but follow the exegetical paths outlined above.
22. See also Gen. 13:15, but that text does not mention the covenant.

5. Sharing in the Son's Inheritance

If Paul has Gen. 17:8 in mind, then his claim about the singular and messianic σπέρμα may have been facilitated by the ambiguity of σπέρμα throughout Gen. 17:1-21. Harmon rightly notes that God refers to his διαθήκη with Abraham five times in Gen. 17:7-10. In Gen. 17:7-10, the covenant seems to be between God, Abraham, and his corporate σπέρμα.[23]

But things are not that simple. Genesis 17:15-19, which looks back to the covenant of Gen. 17:7-10, focuses on Isaac, Abraham's singular σπέρμα (Gen. 17:19).[24] God's words to Abraham about Isaac in Gen. 17:19 come on the heels of Abraham's request that God would establish his διαθήκη with Ishmael. God rejects that request and promises Abraham that he will have a son through Sarah and that God will establish his covenant with him. Given that the covenant language of Gen. 17:19 corresponds exactly to the language of Gen. 17:7-8, it is possible to read Gen. 17:7-8 in light of Gen. 17:19 such that in Gen. 17:8 God establishes his covenant with Isaac, the singular seed:

Gen. 17:7   καὶ στήσω τὴν διαθήκην μου ἀνὰ μέσον ἐμοῦ καὶ ἀνὰ μέσον σοῦ καὶ ἀνὰ μέσον τοῦ σπέρματός σου μετὰ σὲ εἰς γενεὰς αὐτῶν εἰς διαθήκην αἰώνιον

Gen. 17:19   καὶ στήσω τὴν διαθήκην μου πρὸς <u>αὐτὸν</u> εἰς διαθήκην αἰώνιον[25]

It is surely relevant that Genesis and the rest of the Pentateuch repeatedly emphasize the fact that the covenant promises were made to the individual patriarchs and secondarily their corporate offspring. Put differently, as it is recalled in the Pentateuch, Gen. 17:1-19 does not move from Abraham to the corporate σπέρμα, but from Abraham to Isaac, then to Jacob, and finally the nation:

> God heard their groaning, and God remembered his covenant with Abraham, Isaac, and Jacob. (Exod. 2:24)[26]

> Then will I remember my covenant with Jacob; I will remember also my covenant with Isaac and also my covenant with Abraham, and I will remember the land. (Lev. 26:42)[27]

---

23. Harmon 2010: 150.
24. Ibid.
25. Ibid.: 151.
26. See also Gen. 35:9-11, which uses the language of Gen. 17:7-8 to speak about the promises made to Abraham, Isaac, and Jacob.
27. See also Exod. 6:8; 32:13.

> Is not because of your righteousness or the uprightness of your heart that you are going in to occupy their land; but…in order to fulfill the promise that the LORD made on oath to your ancestors, to Abraham, to Isaac, and to Jacob. (Deut. 9:5)

Paul's reading of a singular σπέρμα in Gal. 3:16, then, could have been influenced by the interpretation of Gen. 17:7-10 in Gen. 17:15-19, which focuses on the covenant with Isaac.[28] Furthermore, this focus on the covenant with Isaac and the individual patriarchs is repeated throughout the Pentateuch. But this still leaves open the question of how Paul could claim that the Messiah is the ultimate heir to these promises.

Hays and others claim that Paul's reference to Christ as the singular σπέρμα is based upon the catchword σπέρμα found in Gen. 17:8 and 2 Sam. 7:12-14. It reads:

> I will raise up your offspring after you [καὶ ἀναστήσω τὸ σπέρμα σου], who shall come forth from your body, and I will establish his kingdom…and I will establish the throne of his kingdom forever. (2 Sam. 7:12-14)

According to Hays, "Paul implicitly links the promise to Abraham with the promises to a 'seed' that will come forth from David, the Messiah… This sort of catchword linkage, known as *gezerah shawah*, was commonly employed by Jewish interpreters in Paul's day."[29] Hays is right to note that Gen. 17:8 and 2 Sam. 7:14 are linked by "τὸ σπέρμα σου." Outside of Gen. 17:8, this phrase usually occurs in connection with a promised descendant of David (2 Sam. 7:12-14, Ps. 89:3-4; 1 Chr. 17:10-14).[30] As further justification for Paul's messianic reading of σπέρμα in Gal. 3:16, some cite 4Q174. 4Q174 also contained a messianic reading of the seed from 2 Sam. 7:12-14.[31] If the messianic reading is correct, then Paul's argument would be that as Israel's Messiah, Jesus is the ultimate heir to the promises made to Abraham and his σπέρμα in Gen. 17:8.

This argument is a good start. However, there are other links between Gen. 17:1-21, Israelite kingship, and kingdom that Hays and others neglect. These links suggest that Paul's messianic reading of seed is based

---

28. We can be sure that Paul has the particular covenant with Isaac in mind because he too contrasts Isaac, the singular heir with Ishmael in Gal. 4:21–5:1.

29. Hays 2000: 264; Novenson 2012: 141.

30. Novenson 2012: 141. Trick (2016: 140–1) says that a messianic reading based up *gezerah shawah* would be easily refuted by Paul's opponents. My argument for a messianic reading of seed goes beyond the lexical connection between Gen. 17:8 and 2 Sam. 7:12-14. See the discussion below.

31. See Juel 1992: 81–8; de Boer 2011: 223.

upon more than mere lexical connections. Paul's reading is rooted in the idea that the Messiah would bring about the final realization of the land promises as kingdom.[32]

First, Gen. 17:1-21, the source of Paul's seed language in Gal. 3:16, emphasizes the fact that Abraham and his σπέρμα will give birth to βασιλεῖς. Genesis 17:6-7 reads:

καὶ αὐξανῶ σε σφόδρα καὶ θήσω σε εἰς ἔθνη, καὶ βασιλεῖς ἐκ σοῦ ἐξελεύσονται. καὶ στήσω τὴν διαθήκην μου ἀνὰ μέσον ἐμοῦ καὶ ἀνὰ μέσον σοῦ καὶ ἀνὰ μέσον τοῦ σπέρματός σου μετὰ σὲ εἰς γενεὰς αὐτῶν εἰς διαθήκην αἰώνιον εἶναί σου θεὸς καὶ τοῦ σπέρματός σου μετὰ σέ.[33]

Then, in Gen. 17:16, God repeats this kingship language in his promise to Sarah or possibly Isaac. In the manuscript tradition, there is a lack of clarity as to whether the kings would come forth from Sarah or Isaac.[34] While the majority of extant Hebrew manuscripts contain a reading that says kings would come forth from Sarah, some Septuagint manuscripts predict that kings will come forth from Isaac:

Gen. 17:16   εὐλογήσω δὲ αὐτὴν καὶ δώσω σοι ἐξ αὐτῆς τέκνον· καὶ εὐλογήσω αὐτόν, καὶ ἔσται εἰς ἔθνη, καὶ βασιλεῖς ἐθνῶν ἐξ αὐτοῦ ἔσονται.[35]

Gen. 17:16   וברכתי אתה וגם נתתי ממנה לך בן וברכתיה והיתה לגוים מלכי עמים ממנה יהיו

If the covenant promise with Isaac contains a promise about kings coming from him, then God's covenant promise to Abraham and Isaac both mention land, people, and kingship. It is also important to note that the covenant promises to Jacob mention kingship as well. When God

---

32. See also the very brief reflections on the passages discussed below in Diffey 2011: 313–16.

33. Thiessen (2016: 126) notes that Isa. 11:1 looks to a descendant of David "coming out of" the stump of Jesse.

34. See Wevers 1974: 180. The best evidence suggests that kings will come forth from Sarah, but it is possible that Paul had access to a text that said that kings will come forth from Isaac. In any case, to claim that kings will come from Sarah is in effect a claim that kings will come from Isaac because he is the only child of Sarah and Abraham. This discussion of kingship arising from Isaac is important because, as I will argue below, Paul is drawn to this passage because of its emphasis on kingship.

35. This is the reading suggested by Rahlfs 2006. The *BHS* cites one Hebrew manuscript that contains this reading. According to Brayford (2007: 309), "the Hellenistic ideology of the Alexandrian translator" causes him to say that kings will come from Isaac not Sarah.

reaffirms his promises to Jacob in Gen. 35:10-11, he uses the same language about kings that we encounter in Gen. 17:6 and 17:19. Genesis 35:10-11 says:

καὶ εἶπεν αὐτῷ ὁ θεός Τὸ ὄνομά σου Ιακωβ· οὐ κληθήσεται ἔτι Ιακωβ, ἀλλ' Ισραηλ ἔσται τὸ ὄνομά σου. εἶπεν δὲ αὐτῷ ὁ θεός Ἐγὼ ὁ θεός σου· αὐξάνου καὶ πληθύνου...καὶ βασιλεῖς ἐκ τῆς ὀσφύος σου ἐξελεύσονται.

All three of these texts (Gen. 17:6; 17:16-19; 35:10-11) are important because these reaffirmations of the promises to the Patriarchs (Abraham, Isaac, and Jacob) emphasize kingship. Thus, Paul's claim that Jesus, as σπέρμα of David and Abraham, is the ultimate heir of the promises could be based upon the shared emphasis on the succession of kings that Paul observes in Gen. 17:1-21 and 2 Sam. 7:12-14.

We have shown, then, that Gen. 17:1-21 and 2 Sam. 7:12-14 are linked by their shared focus on kingship and offspring. Now we will consider the neglected issue of the inheritance. In Gen. 17:1-21 the covenant promises include the land and the people. Genesis 17:5 focuses on the multiplication of Abraham. Genesis 17:8 focuses on the land. Some scholars acknowledge the fact that the land is a central feature of Gen. 17:1-21. They also grant that Gen. 17:1-21 is Paul's source text in Gal. 3:16, but they dismiss the emphasis on land in Gen. 17:1-21 because they claim that the land, even when expanded to encompass the whole earth, plays no role in Paul's theology.[36] The claim that Paul cares little for the land neglects the fact that Paul reads Gal. 3:16 as a reference to the Davidic as well as the Abrahamic seed. In the same way that "seed" is read in light of the Abrahamic and Davidic promises, the same must be said of "the inheritance."

In the Davidic texts that emphasize the seed, the "rise" of the Davidic king means the establishment of his kingdom as the physical space over which he reigns. This is what makes his coming important. Thus, to look for the coming of a messianic seed is to look for the coming of the kingdom that belongs to that seed, otherwise his coming loses its purpose. Therefore, if Paul reads Gen. 17:8 in light of 2 Sam. 7:14, then he links the covenant promises of a land, people, and kingship in Gen. 17:1-21 to the king and kingdom of 2 Sam. 7:12-14. This link allows the definition of the Davidic kingdom in the Psalter to influence Paul's interpretation of the inheritance in Galatians.

While Gen. 17:8 claims that the land of Canaan is the κατάσχεσιν of the seed of Abraham, Ps. 2:7-8 says that the seed of David, as the Son of God, has the whole earth as his κατάσχεσιν:

---

36. De Boer 2011: 224; Watson 2004: 200; Martyn 1997: 339.

> I will tell of the decree of the LORD: He said to me, "You are my son; today I have begotten you. Ask of me, and I will make the nations your inheritance [κληρονομία], and the ends of the earth your possession [τὴν κατάσχεσίν]."

Psalm 2:7-8 is relevant because it makes a unique claim about the Davidic monarch. The Son of Ps. 2:7-8 is the only individual outside of the Patriarchs whose singular inheritance is a point of emphasis.[37] Thus, when looking for texts that help explain how Paul can say that the promises and inheritance belong to Christ, Ps. 2:7-8 is a logical place to begin. In Ps. 2:7-8 the singular κληρονομία consists of the peoples and territories of the earth.[38] This corresponds to the claims in Gen. 17:1-21 that the seed will receive both people and territory. Thus, it is because Paul reads Gen. 17:8 messianically that he can look to the Messiah's inheritance of and rule over the renewed earth. Furthermore, it is because Paul believes Jesus to be the Messiah that he can claim that the "inheritance" is his alone (Gal. 3:15-18).

Although other psalms do not mention the Davidic king's singular inheritance, the worldwide kingdom of the Davidic offspring is a feature of some royal psalms. Psalm 89 predicts a worldwide kingdom for the seed of David, whom God claims as his own Son:

> You said, "I have made a covenant with my chosen one, I have sworn to my servant David: 'I will establish your descendants [τὸ σπέρμα σου] forever, and build your throne for all generations...' I will set his hand on the sea and his right hand on the rivers. He shall cry to me, 'You are my Father, my God...I will make him the firstborn, the highest of the kings of the earth.'" (Ps. 89:2-4, 25-27)

Psalm 89:4 is important because its use of τὸ σπέρμα σου corresponds to the language of Gen. 17:8 and 2 Sam. 7:12-14.

This reading of the inheritance as the whole earth enables a better reading of Gal. 3:15-18 than the claim that the Spirit replaces the land because the whole earth (as kingdom) is something that can be plausibly promised to the multiple heirs under consideration in Galatians: Abraham, Christ, and the believer as the co-heir in Christ.[39] Put differently, it makes

---

37. On the importance of Ps. 2 in Jewish and early Christian texts, see Janse 2009: 51–133.

38. Our previous analysis of Ps. 72:8-16, which stated that the worldwide rule of the Son of David would fufil God's promises to Abraham and mediate blessings the Gentiles, is also relevant. See the discussion in Chapter 4.

39. Trick (2016: 189) claims that the inheritance is "blessed Gentiles." However, according to Trick, the blessing promised to the Gentiles is the promised Spirit. Therefore, his interpretation of the inheritance is subject to the criticism of the "Spirit

conceptual sense to believe that God promises Abraham, the Messiah, and his followers the kingdom.

Moo offers a different interpretation of inheritance in Gal. 3:18. He says: "For Paul (and other NT authors) the inheritance is Christ himself and all the blessings Christ provides his people."[40] This interpretation is difficult to understand because that would entail Christ as the singular σπέρμα being promised himself. Dunn, on the other hand, claims that the inheritance is salvation, which is begun by the Spirit.[41] While Dunn rightly observes that the Spirit begins the inheritance, we are still left wondering how Christ as the σπέρμα of 3:16 is promised salvation. In Gal. 3:15-18 Paul is speaking about who has a rightful claim to the κληρονομία. Paul concludes that the Messiah is this heir. Thus, it would be more accurate to say that in Galatians salvation takes the form of experiencing eternal life with the Messiah in the renewed earth. Translating inheritance as salvation in Galatians is problematic because it de-centers the concept of place present in both the Abrahamic and Davidic seed texts.

The question, then, is whether Paul is actually speaking about the Abrahamic covenant and the rightful heir to the inheritance promised to Abraham and his seed or whether the Abrahamic covenant functions as a rhetorical device to speak about something else entirely (salvation, the gift of the spirit, etc.). I contend that the Abrahamic covenant and its provision of a place for God's people never falls from view, even if that place has been transformed into the eschatological kingdom of the Messiah.

5.2.3. Galatians 3:19: The Inheritance Belongs to the Messiah Continued

This messianic reading of seed and inheritance in Gal. 3:15-18 is supported by a neglected allusion to Gen. 49:10 in Gal. 3:19.[42] In Gal. 3:19 Paul's claim that the Law cannot nullify the promises gives rise to the question of why the Law was put in place at all. The answer to that question is not

---

replaces the land" view offered in Chapter 4. Further, if the inheritance is blessed Gentiles, then how can the Gentiles receive themselves as their inheritance in Christ? Trick's view here is similar to the reading offered by Hammer (1960: 272), who says, "We may say that for Paul the *synklēronomoi Christou* become historically with Christ not only heirs but also the inheritance. That is, with Christ they become the means to and the content of the inheritance." See the criticism of Hammer and this reading of inheritance in Chapter 1.

40. Moo 2013: 231.
41. Dunn 1993: 186. See also Watson 2004: 200.
42. Dahl 1977: 131; Juel 1992: 85–6. See also Jervis (1999: 73), who briefly mentions Juel (1992: 85–6) but offers no fresh analysis or support.

directly relevant to the question of the inheritance, but Paul's description of the seed in Gal. 3:19 is pertinent. Paul says that the Law was put in place because of transgressions ἄχρις οὗ ἔλθῃ τὸ σπέρμα ᾧ ἐπήγγελται. This phrase is usually incorrectly translated as "until the offspring would come to whom the promise had been made."[43] But the passive ἐπήγγελται looks back to the subject of Gal. 3:18, which is ἡ κληρονομία. Galatians 3:18-19 reads, εἰ γὰρ ἐκ νόμου ἡ κληρονομία, οὐκέτι ἐξ ἐπαγγελίας· τῷ δὲ Ἀβραὰμ δι' ἐπαγγελίας κεχάρισται ὁ θεός...ἄχρις οὗ ἔλθῃ τὸ σπέρμα ᾧ [ἡ κληρονομία] ἐπήγγελται.

Paul's point in Gal. 3:19 is that God put the Law into place until the coming of the seed to whom was promised the κληρονομία.[44] This is an awkward way of making a similar point that Paul makes in Gal. 3:16. Paul's awkwardness can be explained. He is alluding to Gen. 49:10, which he believes predicts the coming of the Davidic Messiah. Juel notes the allusion to Gen. 49:10 in Galatians and elsewhere.[45] This allusion to Gen. 49:10 in Gal. 3:19 is important because Gen. 49:10 figures prominently in many Second Temple messianic texts. Furthermore, this claim about an allusion to Gen. 49:10 in Galatians has not been refuted. It has largely been ignored in the secondary literature on Galatians.[46] Juel cites three uses of Gen. 49:10 that are similar to Paul's allusion, but he neglects the fact that all three follow the formula found in Gal. 3:19. In all four uses of Gen. 49:10, one can discern: (1) the prediction of the Messiah's coming; (2) the insertion of a messianic title; (3) and a statement of what belongs to that individual as Messiah.

> The sceptre shall not depart from the tribe of Judah. While Israel has the dominion... Until the Messiah of righteousness [*prediction*] comes, the branch of David [*messianic title*]. For to him and to his descendants has been given the covenant of royalty [*what belongs to them as kings*]. (4Q252 5:1-4)

> Until the King Messiah comes [*prediction and title*], to whom belongs the kingdom, and him shall nations obey [*what belongs to him as Messiah*]. (Tg. Onq. Gen. 49:10)[47]

---

43. ESV, NRSV, NAB, NJB.
44. Soards and Pursiful (2015: 149) translates this correctly.
45. Juel 1992: 85–6. On the importance of Gen. 49:10 in Second Temple messianic texts, see Oegema 1998a: 294–9 and Novenson 2012: 57.
46. Jervis (1999: 73) is a notable exception. See also the discussion of Trick 2016: 198 below.
47. Grossfeld 1990: 158.

Until the King Messiah shall come [*prediction and title*], to whom the kingship belongs; to him all the kingdoms be subject [*what belongs to him as Messiah*]. (Tg. Neof. Gen. 49:10)[48]

ἄχρις οὗ ἔλθῃ [*prediction*] τὸ σπέρμα [*messianic title*] ᾧ ἐπήγγελται [*what belongs to him as Messiah*]." (Gal. 3:19)

All four of these interpretations are based upon reading the שלה in Gen. 49:10 differently than the extant Hebrew manuscripts:

| Gen. 49:10 MT | עד כי יבא שילה |
| Proposed revision | עד כי יבא ש לה |

In the proposed revision, Gen. 49:10 says that the sceptre will not depart from Judah until he comes to whom it [the sceptre] belongs.[49]

This revised reading of the Hebrew gives rise to the forms we outlined above. These authors believe that Gen. 49:10 predicts the coming of a king to whom something is due. These authors then insert a messianic title to indicate that Gen. 49:10 predicted the coming of the Davidic Messiah. They conclude with an explanation of what belongs to him. In Gal. 3:19, Paul claims that as the "Seed" of David and Abraham the inheritance rightly belongs to Christ.

An allusion to Gen. 49:10 in Ezek. 21:27 [21:32 MT] supports this reading of Gal. 3:19.[50] Ezekiel 21:32 does not contain a messianic interpretation of Gen. 49:10. Instead, Ezekiel believes that Gen. 49:10 refers to the blessing promised to the tribe of Judah. Ezekiel ironically turns the prophecy about Judah's future prosperity into a prophecy of Judah's doom. What is crucial for our argument is Ezekiel's use of the language of Gen. 49:10 to make his point. It reads:

| Ezek. 21:27 | A ruin, a ruin, a ruin—I will make it! (Such has never occurred.) Until he comes to whom judgment belongs and I will give it to him. |
| Ezek. 21:32 [MT] | עוה עוה עוה אשימנה גם זאת לא היה עד בא אשר לו המשפט ונתתיו |

In Ezekiel's corporate interpretation of Gen. 49:10, he makes the same exegetical decisions as the authors of 4Q252, the Targums, and Paul.

48. McNamara 1992: 220.
49. On this emendation, see Hamilton 1995: 659–61.
50. The allusion to Gen. 49:10 in Ezek. 21:32 LXX [21:27 MT] is widely recognized in Old Testament scholarship. See Allen 1990: 28 and Block 1997: 693.

Ezekiel also thinks that Gen. 49:10 foretells the "coming" of someone [Judah] to whom something is owed. In Ezekiel's reading, what belongs to Judah is judgment and exile.

Most important for Galatians is the LXX translation of Ezekiel's use of Gen. 49:10. It is similar to Paul's allusion to Gen. 49:10 in Gal. 3:19:

Ezek. 21:32	ἕως οὗ ἔλθῃ ᾧ καθήκει
Gen. 49:10	ἕως ἂν ἔλθῃ τὰ ἀποκείμενα αὐτῷ
Gal. 3:19	ἄχρις οὗ ἔλθῃ τὸ σπέρμα ᾧ ἐπήγγελται

This lexical correspondence is important because it demonstrates what form a Greek allusion to Gen. 49:10 might take.[51] The lexical evidence of Ezek. 21:32 shows that Paul is referring to Gen. 49:10 in Gal. 3:19 even if his interpretation of Gen. 49:10 is far from what we find in Ezekiel.

Paul's allusion to Gen. 49:10 in Gal. 3:19 is important for a variety of reasons. First, it shows that Paul believes that the seed referred to in Gen. 17:8 is also described in Gen. 49:10. This supports the claim that Paul attends to the trajectory of Genesis and its focus on a singular descendant. According to Paul, this trajectory climaxes in the coming of the king predicted in Gen. 49:10. Second, many Second Temple authors use Gen. 49:10 in their descriptions of kings of Israel. Furthermore, as we showed above, when these authors adopt messianic readings of Gen. 49:10, they focus on what belongs to the king. Third, in Gal. 3:18-19 Paul claims that the seed was promised the κληρονομία.

Psalm 2:7-8 describes that king's κληρονομία as the whole earth. This supports our argument that Paul has the singular inheritance of the Messiah's worldwide kingdom in mind in Gal. 3:16. Finally, if Paul believes that the inheritance, which belongs to the seed, is his kingdom, he would not be alone. The Targums assert that Gen. 49:10 speaks of the king and his kingdom as well.

Trick dismisses this reading of Gal. 3:19.[52] He calls the echo of Gen. 49:10 weak and claims that the lexical connection is not strong. Furthermore, he says that Gen. 49:10 is irrelevant to the argument that Paul makes in Galatians.[53] However, I have shown that Gal. 3:19 is similar to a known Greek allusion to Gen. 49:10 (Ezek. 21:32). In addition, Gal. 3:19 fits the Second Temple pattern of messianic readings of Gen. 49:10 outlined above. In those Second Temple texts, Gen. 49:10 is used to

---

51. The only difference between Ezek. 21:32 LXX and Gal. 3:19 is the use of ἄχρις instead of ἕως.
52. Trick 2016: 198.
53. Ibid.

explain what belongs to the Messiah. Similarly, Paul's argues that since Christ is the promised seed, the inheritance belongs to him. Therefore the claim that a messianic reading of Gen. 49:10 would be irrelevant to Paul's argument in Galatians is incorrect.

I have put forward three strong pieces of evidence in favor of a messianic reading of seed and inheritance in Gal. 3:15-19. First, I showed that Paul's claims about the singular seed in Gal. 3:16 are rooted in his belief that Jesus is Israel's king and Messiah. As seed of David and Abraham, Jesus is the rightful heir to the inheritance promised to that seed. Then I demonstrated that the Royal Psalms contain language that suggests that the Davidic king will inherit the peoples and territory of the earth. Since Paul's reading of the seed is messianic, we are justified in assuming that his reading of the inheritance is messianic because the purpose of the seed's arrival is to establish his kingdom. Finally, I pointed to Paul's use of Gen. 49:10 to claim that the inheritance belongs to the messianic seed. Together, this evidence suggests that Paul's interpretation of the Abrahamic promises and the inheritance is inexplicable apart from his belief that Jesus is Israel's Messiah who shares his inheritance with those united to him by faith.

De Boer maintains that Paul's argument in Gal. 3:16 is messianic, but he means something very different. According to de Boer, Paul relies upon a messianic reading of seed to assert that between Abraham and Christ there were no descendants of Abraham.[54] He writes:

> between the promise and Christ, therefore, there were no offspring of Abraham, no heirs of the promise that God made to Abraham. The inheritance, the Spirit, became available only with the coming of Christ.[55]

This reading is difficult to maintain for a variety of reasons. First, such reasoning entails denying Abrahamic descent to the succession of heirs in the Genesis narrative. For example, in Gen. 17:1-21 God promises Abraham that Isaac will receive Canaan. Then, later in Genesis, God predicts that Jacob will receive the land (Gen. 28:13). According to de Boer's reasoning, the promise that Jacob will inherit the land necessitates claiming that Isaac was not really Abraham's offspring. No one would maintain this. Stated differently, Genesis itself makes a claim about the succession of heirs without denying Abrahamic descendant to previous generations. Second, de Boer's reading ignores that fact that Paul is able to make his claim about Jesus as the heir precisely because of the role

---

54. De Boer 2011: 223; see also Longenecker 2002: 67–8.
55. De Boer 2011: 223.

that Jesus plays in Israel's story. Stated differently, there is within the Jewish scriptures the idea that the king will bring about the fulfillment of God's promises to Abraham and the Gentiles (Ps. 72:8-17). This idea is present in early Christian and Pauline texts (Matt. 1:1; Luke 1:68, 73-74; Rom. 15:7-15). As Hooker rightly notes, "God has not 'bypassed' Israel's story, for God has used her promised Messiah to fulfil God's purposes."[56] Finally, de Boer does not take Paul's discussion of the Deuteronomic curses seriously enough. According to Paul, Israel did not have the inheritance before Christ came because they were under the curse. Therefore, Christ does not take the inheritance from Israel; he makes it available.

Paul's claim that the Messiah is the singular seed supports his central theological claim: obedience to Torah is not the means by which one becomes an heir to the inheritance. For Paul, identifying Christ as the seed confirms the gracious nature of the promise because Christ's death for sins (and subsequent resurrection) secures his right to his inheritance, an inheritance that he shares with all who believe (3:26-29). According to Paul, to assert that the Abrahamic covenant was amended at Sinai such that the inheritance comes through Israel's corporate obedience to Torah would change the very nature of the promise, which was given as an act of grace (χαρίζομαι). Paul finds this idea problematic because: (1) the original requirement of the covenant with Abraham is faith (Gal. 3:6-9); (2) Israel's history has proven that the Torah did not lead to the inheritance; it led to slavery (3:10-14); (3) the covenant itself looks to the coming of the messianic seed (3:15-19).

This reading of the Abrahamic covenant, which divides the Abrahamic covenant from the covenant at Sinai, leads Paul to consider the purpose of the Law (Gal. 3:19-25). Since our focus is on the inheritance, Paul's interpretation of the role of the Law in Israel's history before the coming of Christ is not directly relevant. Instead, we will consider what Paul has to say about the heirs in Gal. 3:26-29, 4:1-7, and 5:21.

5.3. *Galatians 3:26-29*

5.3.1. *Overview*

Paul concludes the argument that he began in 3:1 by stating that those who belong to the Messiah are κληρονόμοι (Gal. 3:29).[57] Discerning the

---

56. Hooker (2002: 91) responding to Longenecker (2002: 58–84).
57. Paulsen (1980: 74–5) says, "Sicher wird zunächst zu sagen sein, daß Gal. 3 26-29 eine konkrete Aufgabe nicht allein für die Gedankenführung von Gal. 3, sondern auch im Blick auf die Argumentation des gesamten Briefes hat."

meaning of κληρονόμος is crucial to deciphering Paul's concept of the inheritance because κληρονόμος could refer to an heir who is still awaiting his inheritance or could refer to an heir who has come into his inheritance.[58] If Paul refers to the Galatians as heirs in possession of the inheritance, then the most likely definition of "inheritance" is the Spirit.[59] However, if Paul describes the Galatians as heirs still awaiting their inheritance, then Paul is looking to life in the kingdom as the time when the Galatians will come into their full inheritance.

I offer two pieces of evidence in support of the heir-in-waiting reading. First, by relying on baptism to support his argument about sonship, Paul reveals the future orientation of κληρονόμος. Paul customarily uses baptism to speak about a status that gives birth to a future hope (Rom. 6:1-11; 1 Cor. 6:9-11; 15:25-30). Second, what the Law says about the land inheritance provides the key to interpreting Gal. 3:28. Rather than making a general statement about Christ overcoming divisions in society, in Gal. 3:28 Paul speaks about overcoming the distinctions the Law makes regarding who can be a κληρονόμος to the land inheritance. Overcoming these distinctions is necessary because the Torah prevents Gentiles, slaves, and in most cases women from being named heirs. Paul's point in Gal. 3:28-29 is that the Torah plays no role in determining who can share in the Messiah's inheritance of the whole earth.

5.3.2. *Galatians 3:26-27: Baptism Makes the Believer an Heir in Waiting*

First, we will consider the link between sonship, baptism, and an heir-apparent reading of κληρονόμος in Gal. 3:29. In Gal. 3:26 Paul claims that all who believe are sons of God through faith in Christ. Paul bases his claim about believers' sonship on their baptism. Paul's use of baptism to ground their status as sons supports an heir-in-waiting reading of κληρονόμος.[60] Paul refers to the baptism of believers in Rom. 6:1-11; 1 Cor. 6:9-11; 12:13-14, and 15:25-30. With the exception of 1 Cor. 12:13-14, in each case Paul uses baptism to speak about a present status in Christ that gives birth to a future hope.[61]

---

58. LSJ, "κληρονόμος," 1940.

59. Matera 1992: 143; Das 2014: 356; de Boer 2011: 224; Burton 1980 [1921]: 185; Bruce 1982: 191.

60. On baptism as the basis for their Galatians' heirship, see Fee 2011: 139–44 and Becker 1998: 59.

61. In 1 Cor. 12:13-14 Paul uses baptism to affirm Christian unity in a way that does not speak to the future status of the baptized.

Furthermore, in the four direct references to baptism in Paul's undisputed letters, three of them have direct links with either the kingdom (1 Cor. 15:20-29; 6:9-11) or the journey to the inheritance (1 Cor. 10:1-5). Therefore, in Galatians, when Paul uses the baptism to speak about the Galatians' status as sons and heirs, unless we have strong reasons to suggest otherwise, we should assume that Paul uses baptism to describe the Galatians' status as "heirs in waiting" for the promised inheritance.

We begin with 1 Cor. 6:9-11. In 1 Cor. 6:9-11 Paul speaks about those who will not inherit the kingdom of God. Then Paul says that before the Corinthians' conversion they were like those who had no hope of inheriting (1 Cor. 6:10).[62] He then contrasts their previously hopeless situation with the Corinthians' present status as baptized believers.[63] Paul says, "And this is what some of you used to be. But you were washed, you were sanctified, you were justified in the name of the Lord Jesus Christ and in the Spirit of our God" (1 Cor. 6:11). According to Paul, then, baptism moves the Corinthians from a place in which they had no hope of inheriting into a situation in which they now stand to inherit the kingdom. 1 Corinthians 6:9-11 is important because Paul uses their reception of the Spirit and baptism to prove that they will inherit the kingdom.[64] Similarly, Paul uses the Spirit as evidence that the Galatians are members of Abraham's family in Gal. 3:1-5 and 3:14. As baptized sons, who have received the Spirit, the Galatians (like the Corinthians) are heirs to the kingdom.

Similar to 1 Cor. 6:9-11, 1 Cor. 15:25-30 uses baptism to speak about the future inheritance of the kingdom. Many acknowledge that what Paul means when he refers to baptism on behalf of the dead in 1 Cor. 15:25-30 is difficult to understand.[65] Nonetheless, this baptism's relationship to the kingdom discussed in 1 Cor. 15:20-28 is relatively straightforward. In 1 Cor. 15:20-28 Paul claims that Christ is the first fruits of the resurrection, which will eventually include all of God's people. According to

---

62. See Ciampa and Rosner 2010: 243.

63. Dunn (1970: 121–3) argues that Paul does not have baptism in mind, but the whole conversion experience. It is true that Paul would not assume that baptism effects conversion apart from faith. Nonetheless, the reference to "washed" in the context of conversion does support an allusion to the baptismal rite as a part of the Christian conversion experience. See Thiselton 2000: 454; Conzelmann 1975: 107; Perkins 2012: 97.

64. Ciampa and Rosner 2010: 244.

65. See Conzelman 1975: 275. For a review of recent options, see Hull 2005: 7–21, and, more recently, Sharp 2014: 36–66.

Paul, when the resurrection occurs, and death is defeated, Jesus will hand over the kingdom to the father. This kingdom encompasses all creation.[66] Then Paul says that if this kingdom is not coming, then baptism for the sake of the dead is futile. Regardless of who benefits from this "baptism for the sake of the dead," it is clear that those benefits will be experienced in the kingdom described in 1 Cor. 15:20-28.[67]

Paul refers to baptism a third time in 1 Cor. 10:1-5. There Paul likens baptism to passing through the Red Sea.[68] If this analogy is to be taken seriously, then baptism is the beginning of a journey whose endpoint is life in the promised inheritance. Paul warns the Corinthians to avoid the fate of the Israelites who were "baptized" but nonetheless died in the wilderness before they received the inheritance. In 1 Cor. 10:1-5, baptism does not make the believer an "heir in possession" of the inheritance. Baptism begins a journey that should end with an inheritance.

Finally, there is Rom. 6:1-11. In Rom. 6:1-11 Paul uses the reality of baptism to speak about the Christian dying and rising with Christ. According to Paul, since the Christian has died and been raised with Christ, they are no longer in the realm of death or under the power of sin.[69] Therefore, they should live into the freedom Christ has granted them. However, this freedom has not been fully realized. The discussion that begins in Rom. 6:1-11 climaxes in Rom. 8:1-32, where the baptized Christian is declared an heir with the Messiah to the new creation.

5.3.3. *Galatians 3:28-29: The Law Plays No Role in Determining the Heir*

Having shown that Paul uses baptism to speak about the Galatians' hope for an inheritance in the future, we now turn to Gal. 3:28. Scholars have long acknowledged that Paul encourages a reevaluation of ethnicity, class,

---

66. Paul's allusions to Pss. 8:6 and 110:1 in 1 Cor. 15:25-27 suggest Jesus's sovereignty over all creation.

67. Hull (2005: 40–3) notes that there is no evidence that baptism was done on behalf of those already dead. Based upon this lack of evidence, Hull argues Paul refers to believers being baptized for the sake of the dead so that they might experience the resurrection alongside the faithful departed. See also Ciampa and Rosner 2010: 783–4. Wright (2003: 338) notes that Hull's interpretation, "seems possible, but equally possible, I think, is the more traditional reading, that some people who had come to Christian faith in Corinth had died before being baptized, and that other Christians had undergone baptism on their behalf, completing vicariously in their own persons the unfinished sacramental initiation of the dead."

68. Thiselton 2000: 724–5.

69. Wright 2002: 538.

and gender among believers in Gal. 3:26-29.[70] Furthermore, the statement that there is neither Jew nor Greek bears an uncontested relationship to his larger argument about the Torah. However, his need to negate the distinction between slave and free, as it pertains to the argument of Galatians, is less clear. His negation of "male and female" may be the most perplexing. Why these three pairs here?

Attending to the importance of the inheritance as life in a physical space helps explain all three negations under a single principle, and it links the negations to the role that the Torah plays in the life of the believer. In Gal. 3:26-29 Paul wants the Galatians to know that because they were baptised into Christ, the seed of Abraham, the Galatians are all equally κληρονόμοι to the inheritance. Paul contrasts this equal status as heirs to the distinctions that the Torah makes regarding who can be a κληρονόμος to the land inheritance. Jewish inheritance laws, which were still the subject of debate in the Second Temple period, excluded slaves and Gentiles from inheriting. In addition, women could usually only become heirs if their father failed to produce a male κληρονόμος. Therefore, in most cases, women only received an inheritance as a part of a male and female pair. Paul's argument for women would be that in Christ, apart from any other considerations, women are heirs to the inheritance.

There are four common explanations for the pairs in Gal. 3:28: (1) the pairs form a part of a pre-Pauline baptismal liturgy;[71] (2) the pairs represent the fundamental divisions in society;[72] (3) the negations counter a rabbinic prayer of gratitude in which one thanks God you were not born a Gentile, a female, or a slave;[73] (4) Paul refers to the return to the original state of man and woman before sex difference was introduced.[74] I will consider each in turn before explaining how inheritance laws help us understand the negations of Gal. 3:28.

Those who support the baptismal argument outline four elements: (1) negating pairs of opposites; (2) baptism into Christ; (3) clothing in Christ or garments; (4) a proclamation of unity.[75] However, Martin rightly

---

70. See Hays 2000: 272–3; Longenecker 1990: 156–7; Betz 1979: 189–90. A notable dissenter is Miller 2002: 9–11. He does not believe that Gal. 3:26-29 is "the great egalitarian text."
71. Martyn 1997: 378; de Boer 2011: 243; Schlier 1965: 174–5.
72. Garlington 2007: 230; Schreiner 2010: 255; Matera 1992: 142; Williams 1997: 105; Oakes 2015: 128.
73. Longenecker 1990: 158; Bruce 1982: 187.
74. Meeks 1974: 165–208.
75. Ibid.: 179–80; Betz 1979: 186–201; Martyn 1997: 378; Williams 1997: 104.

observes that Col. 3:11 and 1 Cor. 12:13, the supposed parallels to Gal. 3:28, lack the negation of male and female.[76] If Paul simply quotes a liturgy, why does he quote the extended liturgy in Gal. 3:28 while omitting it elsewhere?[77] This baptismal argument becomes even more difficult to explain when we observe that many who claim that Paul alludes to a baptismal liturgy assert that the final two negations in Gal. 3:28 have nothing to do with Paul's argument.[78] If Paul could expand or omit irrelevant material in other allusions to the liturgy, why include the entire liturgy in Galatians and omit irrelevant elements elsewhere?[79]

Furthermore, many who believe that Paul alludes to a baptismal ceremony maintain that Paul makes a radical statement of equality that few passages of the New Testament can rival, but does so by means of a baptismal liturgy that was widespread in early Christianity.[80] It was either radical or commonplace. It cannot be both. If all Christians, including Paul's rivals, heard that there was neither Jew nor Gentile in Christ, it is hard to imagine that anyone could mount such a strong advocacy for Law obedience.[81] In any case, identifying a pre-Pauline fragment does not alleviate the need to explain Gal. 3:28 in its context. Instead, pride of place must go to the interpretation that explains how Paul's negations relate to the argument of Galatians.

The most common explanation of the three-fold denial is that they represent the three most readily identifiable divisions in society: slave/free, Gentile/Jew, male and female.[82] Advocates argue that Paul believes that, as it relates to salvation, all are equal. While this may be true, it is not directly related to what Paul is arguing.[83] In Gal. 3:15-29 Paul is not

---

76. Martin 2003: 113.
77. Ibid.
78. Betz 1979: 195; Williams 1997: 104.
79. Williams (1997: 104) calls the formula "loose." Martin (2003: 113) rightly states that if the formula is loose, then the formula cannot be used to explain the shape it takes in Galatians. See also Trick 2016: 222.
80. This criticism is noted in Lategan 2012: 277–8. For the idea that Paul reaches this egalitarian highpoint only to retreat, see Schüssler Fiorenza 1983: 206–7.
81. Martyn (1997: 378–82) claims that in the original liturgy it referred to an internal state of mind that Paul actualized. This seems unlikely.
82. Garlington 2007: 230; Schreiner 2010: 255; Matera 1992: 142; Williams 1997: 105; Oakes 2015: 128.
83. Moo (2013: 252) admits as much when he says, "This well known saying about the way traditional religious, social, and gender barriers are transcended in Christ is not explicitly tied to its context." See also Soards and Pursiful 2015: 182.

talking about the divisions in society; he is speaking about the divisions put in place by Torah as it relates to making one an heir. This lack of connection to the argument of Galatians does not bother some because Gal. 3:28 provides the opportunity to affirm the egalitarian spirit of early Christianity in the face of modern claims about the church's historic role as an oppressor.[84] Paul, however, is not warding off modern critics; he is attempting to persuade the Galatians not to come under the Law. In addition, the claim that these three distinctions represent the most fundamental divisions in society is not completely accurate. The household codes, for example, also highlight the distinction between the parent and child (Eph. 6:1; Col. 3:20).

Others contrast the pairs with the Jewish morning prayer in which a Jewish man thanks God that he was not born Gentile, a slave, or a woman.[85] But, as Uzukwu has shown, the earliest forms of this prayer do not contain the three elements negated by Paul.[86] Secondly, this prayer is connected to the synagogue liturgy that arose in the wake of the destruction of the Temple and the Jewish attempt to reorder its religious and institutional life. We simply cannot say with certainty that Paul is in direct dialogue with this prayer or that he would feel the need to counter such a prayer at this point in Galatians.

Meeks attempts to explain the male/female negation by referring to the idea of the androgyne. Originally Adam was neither male or female; the image of God was asexual. In Christ, this division is overcome and the image of God is restored.[87] The problem with this view is three-fold. First, the material adduced as a parallel is later and likely more an interpretation of Paul than an influence on his thought.[88] Second, Christ as the image of God is never tied to his asexuality, but rather his moral and

---

84. Longenecker (1990: 157) says, "The second and third couplets have no relevance for Paul's immediate argument... But these three couplets also cover in embryonic fashion all the essential relationships of humanity, and so need to be seen as having racial, cultural, and sexual implications as well. And that is, as I have argued elsewhere, how the earliest Christians saw them—admittedly, not always as clearly as we might like, but still pointing the way toward a more Christian personal and social ethic" See also Kartzow 2010: 366.

85. Bruce 1982: 187.

86. Uzukwu 2010: 370–92. Uzukwu (2015: 8–11) suggests that the earliest forms of the prayers are found in the Babylonian Talmud and the Tosefta. These forms do not correspond to Paul's pairs of opposites.

87. Meeks 1974: 165–208.

88. Williams 1997: 105.

ontological likeness to his father.[89] Finally, it does not seem likely that Paul is speaking about the post-resurrection loss of gender at this point in the argument of Galatians.[90]

Witherington notes this lack of concern for context and attempts to explain the gender negation of Gal. 3:28c by drawing attention to the circumcision rite and the calendar discussion in Galatians.[91] Men are circumcised and women are not.[92] According to Witherington, purity laws limit a woman's full participation in the festivals and thereby renders her full obedience to the Law's commands impossible. In his reconstruction, concerns over women's status led Paul's opponents to stress the need for them to be married and produce children in order to secure their place in the covenant community.[93] Witherington helpfully places Paul negations in explicit conversation with elements of the Torah. Nonetheless, we lack evidence that Jewish Christian missionaries were forcing marriage on the Galatian women or that absence from festivals because of purity made women deficient.

Hays points to new creation. While gender, race, and class divide in the old creation, they should not in the new creation.[94] For Hays the question is not why the gender negation occurs here, but why Paul omits it in 1 Cor. 12:13. Hays conjectures that in 1 Cor. 12:13 the controversy about sexual ethics and marriage led Paul to omit the male/female pair.[95] When Hays discusses new creation, he surpasses previous proposals because his thesis ties Paul's use of the pairs to the themes of the letter. Nonetheless, his explanation of 1 Cor. 12:13 is unconvincing. First, if the liturgy is as common as Hays claims, then omitting elements would have drawn as much attention as including them. Second, the language of new creation suggests that Paul is working within a redemptive framework in which old divisions under Torah no longer apply. This raises the question of what the Torah has to say about the three pairs that Paul negates.

---

89. 1 Cor. 15:49; Rom. 8:3, 29; Col. 1:15-20; Phil. 2:5-11.

90. Uzukwu (2015: 17) says, "I do not perceive how Paul within the framework of his approach to the Galatians about their inappropriate understanding of the Law could be talking about the image or form humanity will assume in the resurrection."

91. Witherington 1981: 593–604.

92. Lieu (1994: 364–9) disputes the claim that a woman's inability to be circumcised is the central issue in Gal. 3:28. Nonetheless, she demonstrates that the means of signifying Gentile female conversion was a live issue in the Second Temple period.

93. Witherington 1981: 596; 2004: 279–81.

94. Hays 2000: 272.

95. Ibid.: 273.

Having reviewed previous proposals, I will now show that a focus on inheritance law explains these pairs.[96] Jewish inheritance laws limit the inheritance rights of slaves, Gentiles, and single women.[97] Thus, when Paul claims that there is no male and female, Jew nor Gentile, slave nor free, he means that the coming of the Messiah ends the distinctions that the Torah made regarding who could be an heir to the inheritance.

First, we will look at what the Torah says about Gentiles and slaves before turning to a discussion of the inheritance rights of women. Various texts show that foreigners had no inheritance rights in Israel. One example should suffice. In Exod. 22:21, God commands the Israelites to have mercy upon גרים because the Israelites were גרים when they were in Egypt. While in Egypt, as גרים, the Israelites could not own property. The point is clear; the foreigners have no inheritance rights. In addition, we know that some Second Temple texts explicitly exclude Gentiles from the land during the author's depiction of Israel's post-exilic restoration. Speaking of the actions of the Davidic king, *Pss. Sol.* 17:28 says, "And he shall distribute them according to their tribes upon the land, and no resident alien and foreigner shall sojourn among them any longer."

In *Pss. Sol.* 17:28 the author directly opposes Ezek. 47:21-23. In one of the more radical expansions of inheritance rights to foreigners in the Old Testament, Ezekiel says:

> You shall allot it as an inheritance for yourselves and for the aliens who reside among you and have begotten children among you. They shall be to you as citizens of Israel; with you they shall be allotted an inheritance among the tribes of Israel. (Ezek. 47:22)[98]

Ezekiel extends inheritance rights to foreigners who live among the people and keep the Law. Stated differently, in order to inherit, foreigners have to meet the same standards as native-born Israelites. This seems to be the

---

96. Lategan (2012: 282) comes close to this when says that the Galatians have the "legal status" as heirs, but he does not follow that up with a consideration of Old Testament inheritance law.

97. Oakes (2015: 129) says there is no evidence that Jews of the Second Temple period thought that slaves and women were excluded from God's people. There is evidence that some Second Temple Jews believed that women (in most cases) and slaves could not be heirs.

98. Allen (1990: 281) says, "Elsewhere in the Old Testament the latter [foreigners] are represented as incapable of owning land." See also Warren 2014: 421–4; Darr 2001: 1602. See also Isa. 56:1-3.

line of argument that Paul's opponents pursued. If the Galatians wanted to become heirs, they must submit to Torah or be cursed. Paul counters by asserting that it is the Torah which says that Gentiles cannot inherit. Therefore, Gentiles turning to the Torah to become heirs is a mistake. According to Paul, faith is sufficient to make them sons and heirs.

Paul then contends that there is neither slave nor free in Christ. Again, in Galatians Paul is not highlighting the distinctions that society makes between different groups. The question is the distinctions made by the Law. According to the Torah, slaves can be circumcised and participate fully in the festivals of Israel, but they cannot own property (Exod. 12:44). The Torah describes three classes of slaves: (1) Jewish slaves who must be released after seven years (Exod. 21:1-3);[99] (2) Jewish slaves who make the decision to remain in their master's household and become lifelong slaves (Exod. 21:6); (3) lifelong foreign slaves (Lev. 25:44-46).

There is no evidence that Second Temple Jews adhered to the practice of freeing Jewish slaves after seven years.[100] As practiced in the Second Temple period, slaves did not have an equal status when it came to inheriting. We see the importance of slaves inheriting in Colossians, where Paul specifically highlights the rights of a slave to the inheritance (Col. 3:22-24). Paul's point in Gal. 3:28b is that the Law says that a slave could not inherit, but in Christ all are heirs to the inheritance.

The final and most contested division consists of the denial of male and female. Some recognize an allusion to Gen. 1:27 in the language of Gal. 3:28c, but explaining how Gen. 1:27 advances the argument about the Torah in Galatians is far from clear.[101] I suggest that Paul's allusion to Gen. 1:27 refers to the man and woman in marriage. We have Second Temple examples of this practice. First, Jesus uses Gen. 1:27 to speak about marriage in Mark 10:6. Second, the author of the Damascus Document also uses Gen. 1:27 as a shorthand for marriage (CD 4:21). When Paul says that there is no male and female in Christ, he asserts that one's marriage status or gender has no bearing on the ability to become an heir. This claim stands in contrast to the Torah, which usually names the firstborn son the heir. Speaking of Jewish inheritance law, Lightfoot

---

99. The freed slave could expect to regain his legal status in Israel. He could inherit property after he gained his freedom.

100. Hezser (2005: 31–2) says, "In the Greek Jewish writings of the Hellenistic and early Roman period the distinction between Jewish and non-Jewish slaves is almost completely absent and the biblical rules concerning Hebrew slaves' manumission in the seventh year of their service is ignored."

101. Bruce 1982: 189; Hays 2000: 273.

says, "by Jewish [law], the sons inherited unequally, and except in default of male heirs the daughters were excluded."[102]

Numbers 27:1-11, which recounts the story of the daughters of Zelophehad, addresses the inheritance rights of women. Their father died without producing sons. Because he lacked a male heir, his daughters inherited his share of the land. However, under normal circumstances women lacked inheritance rights. They could only share in the inheritance of their fathers and later their husbands.

Tobit 3:7-14 also considers the inheritance issue. In the narrative, Sarah marries seven husbands and fails to produce an heir. Lacking sons, Sarah does not consider herself to be a suitable heir. She says:

> You know, O Master, that I am innocent of any defilement with a man, and that I have not disgraced my name or the name of my father in the land of my exile. I am my father's only child; he has no other child to be his heir; and he has no close relative or other kindred for whom I should keep myself as wife. (Tob. 3:14-15)

I am not suggesting that Paul's opponents believe that women have to be married in order to participate in the resurrection. Instead, I am positing that Paul believes that making the Torah the basis for making one an heir introduces inequalities in the community that is one in Christ. Witherington comes close to this position when he says that women were second-class citizens because they could not participate in all the festivals and ceremonies outlined in the Torah.[103] There is no evidence of this idea in the Second Temple period. However, there is evidence about status insecurity when it comes to women's status as heirs in the Old Testament and the Second Temple period. We have already mentioned the story of Sarah in Tobit. We also note the case of Naomi. She could not simply pass her family's inheritance on to Ruth. Instead, they needed a redeemer that would allow Ruth to inherit as a part of a male and female pair. For those in Christ, no such qualifications are needed. All, including slaves, Gentiles, and females (married or not) are heirs.

I have argued that Paul maintains that ethnicity, legal status, and marriage status (and therefore gender) have no bearing on the right to be named a co-heir to the Messiah's inheritance. This stands in contrast to the Torah, which would introduce inequalities. Since our focus is the inheritance in Galatians, space precludes a full discussion of the implications

---

102. Lightfoot 1902 [1874]: 170. He is commenting on Gal. 4:7, but his point still stands.

103. Witherington 1982.

of this reading for Paul's larger theology. This much can be said here: Paul's understanding of the inheritance is more concrete than we realize. For Paul, the new creation is a place where the Messiah reigns as lord over all. Thus, to proclaim to a mixed congregation that includes Gentiles, females, and slaves that all are equally heirs to that inheritance is not a mere spiritualization.[104] It speaks to the question of who is valued as a citizen in the Messiah's kingdom. Paul's message to women, slaves, and Gentiles that they are "heirs" in Christ would be theologically and socially significant to them. It may be that it is only in a modernized Western culture like ours where everyone can own land that such statements could be deemed a spiritualization.

In conclusion, Gal. 3:26-29 does not directly address the question of the scope of the inheritance. But it does suggest that the inheritance is not fully realized. In support of an heir-apparent reading of κληρονόμος, I demonstrated that Paul customarily uses baptism to refer to an heir who would inherit in the future rather than to emphasize a fully realized inheritance. Secondly, I showed that the three-fold negation of Gal. 3:28 is best explained as a polemical insight about the inheritance regulations in the Torah. This focus on inheritance laws implies that Paul is making an argument about who has the right to inherit in the future.

5.4. *Galatians 4:1-7, 5:21*

5.4.1. *Overview*

I have shown that in Gal. 3:1-29 Paul demonstrates that faith in Christ suffices to make the Galatians heirs alongside Christ of his messianic inheritance of the whole earth. In Gal. 4:1-7 he continues his argument by using the analogy of an heir who, while he is a minor, remains under the supervision of ἐπίτροποι and οἰκονόμοι until the time set by his father. Paul then compares the situation of this heir to the Jewish Christians before the coming of Christ.[105] Paul ends this section with a different analogy, that of a slave's move from slavery to sonship through adoption.

As with Gal. 3:26-29, we must seek to discern what type of κληρονόμος Paul refers to in Gal. 4:1-7. Does Paul intend to portray the Galatians as heirs in full possession of the inheritance or as heirs in waiting?[106] The

---

104. For a spiritual-equality reading, see Soards and Pursiful 2015: 182.

105. Whether Paul has in mind the Jewish Christians exclusively or all believers is a matter of debate. See the discussion below.

106. Again, most of those who believe that the heir is in full possession of the inheritance claim that the inheritance is the Spirit.

answer to this question is pertinent because if Paul refers to the Galatians as heirs in waiting, then he looks to their sharing in Christ's own inheritance of the kingdom.

I present five arguments that support the contention that in this passage Paul believes that the Galatians are κληρονόμοι of the Messiah's worldwide kingdom. First, the Jewish belief that Abraham's offspring will inherit the earth causes Paul to depict the κληρονόμος of Gal. 4:1-2 as κύριος πάντων. Second, when Paul applies the heir analogy in Gal. 4:3-7 he does not focus on the reception of the inheritance in the present, but the removal of the enslaving power of τὰ στοιχεῖα τοῦ κόσμου. This focus on the removal of oversight supports the claim that Paul does not focus on believers receiving the inheritance in the fullness of time, but rather the heir's new-found freedom. Third, the one sent to liberate them is God's Son. This description of Jesus as Son speaks to his status as the divine and kingly Son whom the Father sent to liberate the Galatians so that they might share in the Son's inheritance. Fourth, Paul's final metaphor is adoption. Greco-Roman adoption makes one an heir to a future inheritance alongside other members of the family. This future orientation of adoption speaks against the idea that Paul believes that the Spirit is the content of the inheritance. I conclude with a brief analysis of Gal. 5:21. Attempts to separate Paul's inheritance language in Gal. 5:21 from Gal. 3:15–4:7 are unnecessary. Paul assumes throughout the letter that believers will inherit the kingdom (i.e. the world) alongside their king.

5.4.2. Galatians 4:1-2: Believers as Future Heirs of All Things

Paul begins this section with a brief illustration whose origins are debated. The majority interpretation assumes that Paul describes a situation in which a paterfamilias dies before his heir comes of age.[107] In such a situation, until the heir reaches adulthood, the child remains under the care of administrators and overseers who the paterfamilias placed in charge of the child in his will.[108] This situation continues until the child comes into the inheritance at the time set by the father. Since, in many cases, these overseers and managers would be slaves, the heir's experience of his supervision could be compared to slavery. According to the standard reading, Paul believes that the Law functioned as the overseer until the time set by God. Then God sent his Son to free believers from the Law

---

107. Matera 1992: 148–9; Lightfoot 1902 [1874]: 164; Longenecker 1990: 163; Burton 1980 [1921]: 211; de Boer 2011: 259; Moo 2013: 258; Schreiner 2010: 265; Hays 2000: 281.

108. Becker 1998: 61; Oepke 1973: 127.

whose time of oversight has past. This reading has gained wide acceptance because it allows for a straightforward application of an illustration drawn from a common Greco-Roman practice to Paul's argument about the temporary role of the Law.

The first question we must answer is why Paul refers to the heir in the illustration as κύριος πάντων and what light that sheds on his understanding of the inheritance.[109] Scott argues that the heir to an estate is not usually described as a κύριος πάντων.[110] Furthermore, he says that this phrase is often used to describe the universal sovereignty of a ruler over a certain area.[111] For example:

> Now consider those of our antagonist Philip. In the first place, he was the despotic commander of his adherents... He was responsible to nobody: he was the absolute autocrat, commander, and master of everybody and everything [κύριος πάντων].[112]

Scott's insight is part of a larger proposal. Scott contends that Paul did not refer to a Greco-Roman analogy at all. Instead, Paul retells the story of Israel in Gal. 4:1-7.[113] According to Scott, κύριος πάντων reflects the Jewish belief, found in Paul's own letters, that Israel is the heir to the entire earth (Rom. 4:13).[114] Goodrich, however, disagrees. He says, "κύριος πάντων is such a compact and ambiguous phrase, and κύριος was so often used for property ownership (e.g., Mt. 20.8; Lk. 12.43), that there is no reason why this expression must be interpreted either way a priori."[115] Goodrich rightly observes that κύριος πάντων is capable of multiple meanings. However, it is the use of κύριος πάντων in a discussion about heirs, which will soon be applied to Israel's status before the coming of Christ, that provides the rationale for interpreting κύριος πάντων as a reference to universal sovereignty.

Since Scott put forward a new reading of the illustration of 4:1-2, whether Paul refers to Israel as the heir to the entire earth has been linked to a larger debate regarding the origin of the illustration. But settling the

---

109. This phrase is usually ignored even though it is universally acknowledged that Paul shapes the illustration to fit the application. See the discussion below.
110. Scott 1992: 130.
111. Ibid.: 131–5. See also Rom. 10:12 and Acts 10:36.
112. Demosthenes, *On the Crown* 18.235.
113. Scott 1992: 121–86.
114. See Dunn (1993: 211), who does not follow Scott, but nonetheless sees a reference to the Jewish belief that Israel would inherit the earth.
115. Goodrich 2010: 262.

question of the illustration's origin need not decide the meaning of κύριος πάντων. I make this assertion because those who argue for a Greco-Roman origin of the illustration grant that Paul shapes his presentation with an eye to its application, especially when he compares the heir's oversight by the guardians and taskmasters to slavery.[116]

This claim about shaping allows them to skip over the fact that Paul's description of testamentary oversight does not correspond to the best reconstructions of the practice. If Pauline shaping explains the slavery claim, then the same can be said of his description of the heir as κύριος πάντων. Paul refers to the heir in the illustration as the lord of all because he believes that Christ, the seed of Abraham and David, shares his status as the heir of all things with those who believe. That Paul casually alludes to a belief in the believer's possession of all things in Galatians should not be surprising given Paul does so on another occasion: πάντα γὰρ ὑμῶν ἐστιν…εἴτε κόσμος εἴτε ζωὴ εἴτε θάνατος, εἴτε ἐνεστῶτα εἴτε μέλλοντα πάντα ὑμῶν (1 Cor. 3:21b-22). The question, then, is not whether κύριος πάντων could refer to an heir's reception of the entire estate. The question is: Given Paul's statements elsewhere, and the connotations of the phrase in the Roman world, how would the Galatians understand the phrase κύριος πάντων when it is applied to their status as sons and heirs? Stated differently, Paul makes his point about God the Father's plan for the fullness of time through an illustration in which an extremely wealthy landowner gives his heir the entirety of his estate. It is not unreasonable to suggest that the "estate" which God gives to his Son (the heir) and his adopted sons (believers) is the whole earth.

I conclude this discussion of κύριος πάντων with an analysis of texts that are cited as parallels to Gal. 4:1-2 in the New Testament, namely Matt. 20:8 and Luke 12:43.[117] Scholars use these texts to show that κύριος could mean lord or owner of property. But Matt. 20:8 and Luke 12:43 prove more than proponents realize. The κύριος of the vineyard in Matt. 20:8 illustrates God's sovereign ownership of Israel, his vineyard. The return of the κύριος to the house in Luke 12:43 is likened to Jesus's return to earth as the Son of Man. Thus, Jesus' return in power is a return to that which is his, the earth. In the same way, the application of the estate illustration in Galatians would naturally be that the estate owned by God

---

116. Mußner 1974: 267; Betz 1979: 203; Schreiner 2010: 266; Moo 2013: 259. Martyn (1997: 386) says that "Paul is altering the picture somewhat, in order to make it altogether serviceable to his application."

117. Matera 1992: 148; Moo 2013: 259.

the Father (the whole earth) has been given to Christ and those adopted into God's family.

The importance of κύριος πάντων does not rest on the origin of the analogy. Nonetheless, discerning the origin of the illustration in Gal. 4:1-2 will assist in understanding the application in Gal. 4:3-7, especially the timing of the inheritance. As stated above, the majority interpretation assumes that Paul has in mind a situation in which a paterfamilias dies before his heir comes of age.[118]

James Scott argues that certain difficulties make this reading untenable.[119] His best arguments against the standard interpretation are as follows: (1) in the analogy of Gal. 4:1-2 the father is dead, and in Gal. 4:3-7 the father is alive; (2) the child comes of age in Gal. 4:1-2, while in 4:3-7 the child is outside of the family, enslaved, and then adopted; (3) the language of νήπιός and προθεσμίας are not technical terms for a minor or the time set in a will; (4) Roman law does not allow the father to set the time for the reception of the inheritance; (5) οἰκονόμος was never used to refer to the guardianship of a heir whose father had died.[120]

According to Scott, these problems suggest that Paul does not have in mind a Greco-Roman analogy. Instead, Paul makes a typological argument about the Exodus. According to Scott, Paul sees Israel's experience of slavery as the "type" and the situation of the believer before Christ's redemptive death as the "antitype."[121] In Scott's proposal, Israel as the type is heir to the entire world, but remains enslaved until the time set by the father. This time is the 400 years of slavery in Egypt. During the time of slavery, Israel suffered at the hands of the Egyptian taskmasters (ἐπίτροποι and οἰκονόμοι). Then, because God is committed to being faithful to his promises to Abraham, he acts to redeem Israel by removing them from slavery and making them sons. According to Scott, in the same way, all humanity was enslaved to τὰ στοιχεῖα τοῦ κόσμου until God sent his Son to redeem humanity from slavery. This redemption from slavery brings about the believer's adoption. For Scott, Christian adoption is based upon the promise of a coming Davidic son (2 Sam. 7:14). According to Scott, instead of the Abrahamic promise, Paul relies upon a Jewish eschatological expectation found in 4QFlor 1:11, *Jub.* 1:24, and *T. Jud.* 24:3. This eschatological expectation assumes that the divine

---

118. Matera 1992: 148–9; Lightfoot 1902 [1874]: 164; Longenecker 1990: 163; Burton 1980 [1921]: 211.

119. Scott 1992: 126–31. What follows is a summary of his argument.

120. Becker (1998: 61) says, "Nicht mit den üblichen Rechtsgepflogenheiten vereinbar ist der Umstand daß Paulus von Vormündern und Hausverwaltern spricht."

121. Scott 1992: 150.

adoption promised in 2 Sam. 7:14 would be given to the Messiah and his people at the time of the second Exodus.[122]

Despite the recent popularity of Scott's view, it has problems.[123] First, as Goodrich points out, Scott builds much of his criticism on the lack of attested evidence for οἰκονόμους, νήπιός, and προθεσμίας in Greco-Roman guardianship documents. But apart from νήπιός in Hos. 11:1, Scott does not have strong lexical evidence that links the analogy of Gal. 4:1-2 with the Exodus.[124] This is especially true of ἐπίτροπος and οἰκονόμος, which Scott does not convincingly tie to the Exodus tradition.[125]

Recognizing this lack of explicit connection with the Exodus narrative, Hafemann suggests a modification of Scott's proposal. Rather than a reference to the Exodus, Hafemann thinks that Paul describes the entire history of Israel before the coming of Christ as childhood and slavery.[126] He comes to this conclusion in part based on the use of νήπιος in Hos. 11:1 and its discussion of Israel's idolatry. According to Hafemann, although "Israel by covenant status…is the eventual 'lord' (κύριος), i.e. rightful owner, of the 'earth' as her estate," she remained in slavery because of her covenant disobedience until the time set by the father.[127] Hafemann's proposal has more warrant than Scott because he does not limit Paul's focus to the first period of enslavement.[128] But as Hafemann himself acknowledges, his proposal is not really dependent upon a denial of a Greco-Roman analogy.[129]

---

122. Scott 1992: 178. According to Scott, Galatians points to the nationalization of the Davidic covenant through the believer's shared participation in Christ. He also points to 1 Cor. 6:14–7:1 as support for this view.

123. Supporters include: Hafemann 1997: 329–72; Wright 2013: 656; Keesmaat 1999: 302–3; Wilder 2001: 83–5.

124. Goodrich 2010: 255–6. According to Scott, νήπιός could be linked to the Exodus via Hos. 11:1.

125. Goodrich (2010: 264) says, "even the most sympathetic reader is left without the impression that ἐπίτροπος and οἰκονόμος were established titles for the Egyptian slave drivers during the first century." See also Moo 2013: 259.

126. Hafemann 1997: 338.

127. Ibid.: 339. It is interesting to note that Hafemann acknowledges that Paul refers to Israel's eventual inheritance of the world in Gal. 4:1-2. Hafemann then argues that this Spirit is the inheritance in Gal. 4:3-7. It would seem more reasonable to suggest that Paul still believes that the newly reconstituted people of God remain heirs to the whole earth. See Hafemann 1997: 350.

128. See also Schreiner (2010: 266–7), who takes a mediating position. He believes that Paul's illustration contains aspects of Greco-Roman practices and Exodus imagery. This is close to the argument I pursue below.

129. Hafemann 1997: 339.

One could make the same exegetical points about Israel's long enslavement before the coming of Christ on the basis of the application of the illustration in Gal. 4:3-7. Put differently, Paul's point could be that just as the heir in the illustration experiences a long period of slavery, so did the Jewish people before the coming of the Messiah. The new Exodus theme is present in Gal. 4:3-7 because Paul speaks about the heir's slavery and subsequent freedom. A new Exodus motif, then, does not depend on an Exodus origin of the illustration.

If the guardianship analogy has flaws, and Scott has failed to demonstrate that Paul is concerned with the first Exodus, where does that leave us? It leaves us with a third and often-neglected view. This is the view that Paul describes the situation of a youth who had yet to come of age in a Greco-Roman household with a living father.[130] In this reading, Paul's thinking is much the same as that of Gal. 3:24-25. In Gal. 3:24-25 Paul speaks of the temporary function of the Law and uses the imagery of the παιδαγωγός. This παιδαγωγός exercises a certain authority over the son until he comes of age. However, the child's coming of age does not entail the reception of the inheritance. Coming of age results in the removal of the oversight and the granting of new freedoms. In the same way, in Gal. 4:1-2 Paul refers to the administrators and overseers who have power over the father's estate, and therefore the son, while the heir is a youth.

In the case of an heir with a living father, the minor does not have direct access to the father's funds. Instead, the management of the father's estate is usually overseen by the ἐπιτρόποι and οἰκονόμοι.[131] Although ἐπιτρόπος could refer to one tasked with the oversight of a minor whose father had died, it could also be used to refer to any manager or steward.[132] Οἰκονόμος was never used in guardianship situations and often refers to someone who oversees property on behalf of the owner of an estate.[133] I contend that Paul has these basic roles as estate managers in view. Paul is saying that, as it relates to the estate and its management, these ἐπιτρόποι and οἰκονόμοι have authority over the heir and his future estate during the heir's youth.[134]

---

130. Hester 1967: 118–25; Duncan 1934: 127; and George 1994: 293–4, all adopt this reading, but do not develop it as I do below.

131. Goodrich 2010: 265.

132. See *Ant.* 18.194; Matt. 20:8; Luke 8:3.

133. Goetzmann, "οἰκονόμος," *NIDNT* 2:254.

134. Hester (1967: 122) says, "Perhaps what Paul is referring to is not a full-blown guardianship in the sense of tutor or curatorship, but a situation in which the son was dependent on managers and stewards of his father's estate for his livelihood. They controlled the purse-strings so to speak, and he was dependent on their good will for his support."

When the heir came of legal age his situation would change. The adult heir now has the right to marry, begin military training, and enter into contracts on his father's behalf.[135] In most cases, once the son came of age he received a peculium to start his own household. The father also had the option of giving him an annual allowance.[136] Saller rightly points out that aristocrats were under "social pressure" to make sure that their adult sons had the resources to be successful.[137]

Therefore, the reception of a peculium or an allowance dramatically affects the lives of sons who come of age while the father is still alive. Paul, then, refers to the following situation in Gal. 4:1-2: an heir had no direct access to the father's resources during his childhood, but once he became an adult, and at the father's leisure, the father gives the heir access to portions of his future estate.

This reconstruction allows for a more coherent reading of Gal. 4:1-7. First, it does not require Paul to be unaware of the fact that deceased fathers do not decide when the son inherits. This is set by Roman law.[138] Second, unlike the whole estate, the gift of the peculium or an allowance is fully at the father's discretion. Third, this reconstruction uses ἐπίτροπος and οἰκονόμος according to their normal meanings at the time.[139] Fourth, this view does not require Paul to assume that the father is dead, something that all agree is irrelevant to the argument Paul was making.[140] Fifth, many highlight the parallels between Gal. 3:24-25 and 4:1-7.[141] This proposal brings those sections into closer alignment. Both envision oversight for a limited period of time. Sixth, this reconstruction highlights the removal of oversight at the time set by the father. This is Paul's focus in the application (Gal. 4:3-7).

---

135. Saller 1994: 118–19.
136. Ibid.: 124.
137. Ibid.
138. Hays 2000: 281. Goodrich (2010: 261 n. 14) argues that the father in his will could delay the heir's reception of the inheritance. It is true that the father could prevent the heir from inheriting at the age of fourteen. We lack evidence that it could be delayed beyond the age of 25 when the heir would be declared fully independent. See Saller 1994: 188. Thus, the heir could look to a date set by the state when he would inherit.
139. Martyn (1997: 387) says that the use of ἐπίτροπος and οἰκονόμος together to refer to those who oversee the heir of a deceased father is "without linguistic precedent."
140. Longenecker 1990: 163.
141. Moo 2013: 258.

Even if we assume that Paul has testamentary guardianship in mind, this need not imply that the Spirit is the full inheritance. Goodrich, a strong proponent of the testamentary reading, makes the following qualification, "Although in Paul's thought believers have yet to take full possession of the inheritance, they have already received an initial endowment in their adoption through the Spirit."[142] But this "initial endowment" corresponds much more closely to a peculium or an annual allowance given to adult sons. Put differently, claiming that Paul refers to the expanded rights of the adult heir accounts for the initial endowment of the Spirit, which confirms that the Galatians are indeed sons and heirs (Gal. 4:6-7).

I have argued that in Gal. 4:1-2 Paul describes the situation of a son who is destined to inherit the entire estate, but during his childhood has no direct control over the resources of the estate. He is, by some accounts, in a lower position than the ἐπίτροποι and οἰκονόμοι who oversee the expenditure of funds. This lower status, which Paul exaggerates by likening it to slavery, lasts until the son comes of age and the father grants him access to some of the funds of the estate. Now he is no longer under the authority of the ἐπίτροποι and οἰκονόμοι. Instead, the son has begun to access an inheritance whose fullness lay in the future. This corresponds to Paul's words about believers receiving an initial endowment of the Spirit while their full inheritance is still to come.

5.4.3. *Galatians 4:3: The* στοιχεῖα τοῦ κόσμου *and the Covenant Curses*

In Gal. 4:3-7 Paul applies the analogy of the heir in 4:1-2 to the situation of the Jewish believers before and after the coming of Christ. Paul says that just as the heir, who is destined to be κύριος πάντων, remains under the oversight of ἐπίτροποι καὶ οἰκονόμοι, the Jews were enslaved by the στοιχεῖα τοῦ κόσμου. Explaining the meaning of στοιχεῖα τοῦ κόσμου is difficult for two reasons. First, it is not clear how we should understand the phrase στοιχεῖα τοῦ κόσμου. Second, it is hard to explain how Paul could claim that life under the Law led to slavery to the στοιχεῖα τοῦ κόσμου.

In this section I argue that the στοιχεῖα τοῦ κόσμου describes the fundamental elements of the world: earth, wind, air, and fire that were being worshipped as gods in Gentile circles. Paul claims that these Gentile gods enslaved the Jews under the Law because the covenant curses predicted that Israelite disobedience to the Law would lead to slavery to foreign gods (Deut. 28:64).[143] Thus, for Paul, because Jesus's death redeems the

---

142. Goodrich 2013: 74 n. 30.
143. See also Hardin (2008: 133–8), who also argues for an allusion to the Deuteronomic curses in Gal. 4:3. I came to this conclusion before consulting his work.

nation from the covenant curses, it also liberates Jewish believers from slavery to foreign gods.[144]

This interpretation of the liberation from the στοιχεῖα τοῦ κόσμου is pertinent to our proposal about the Messiah and the inheritance because it supports my claim that Paul maintains that the cross ended the covenant curses and began the final realization of the inheritance. I link the end of the curse to the beginning of the inheritance because Paul transitioned from discussing redemption from the Law (4:4-7) to proclaiming that those who have been redeemed now stand to share in the son's inheritance through their adoption into God's family (Gal. 4:5b). This move from slavery to heirship in Gal. 4:4-7 is similar to the transition from redemption from the curse (3:10-14) to sharing in the Messiah's inheritance (3:15-29).

The term στοιχεῖα usually describes basic principles or elements.[145] When added to κόσμος it can refer to the fundamental elements of the universe. The problem comes when we try to apply slavery to the fundamental elements of the universe to the argument of Galatians. Recognizing the difficulties of a reference to the elements of the universe, some argue that Paul alludes to the "fundamental principles" of religion that enslaved the Jews before the coming of Christ. For them this slavery to an early form of religious belief has been overcome now that Jewish believers (or humanity as a whole) have reached their maturity in Christ.[146] The problem with this view is that Paul does not portray the problem in Galatians as being mere immaturity. He presents the στοιχεῖα τοῦ κόσμου as a power from which the Jewish Christians are in need of rescue. The primary contrast in Galatians is not maturity and immaturity; it is slavery and freedom (Gal. 4:8; 5:1). Secondly, στοιχεῖα usually describes the elements of the universe, not principles of religion.[147]

The most plausible reading is that the στοιχεῖα τοῦ κόσμου denote the fundamental elements of the world: earth, wind, air, and water, which were venerated as gods in Gentile circles.[148] As evidence for this view,

---

144. Paul would also affirm that the Gentiles have been liberated as well. He discusses their liberation in Gal. 4:8-11.

145. For a much fuller discussion, see Mußner 1974: 293–304, and more recently de Boer 2011: 252–61.

146. Matera 1992: 150; Lightfoot 1902 [1874]: 164; Witherington 2004: 284–7.

147. Moo 2013: 262. For a review of the evidence, see Rusam 1992: 119–25.

148. Schreiner 2010: 268–9. A third view claims that στοιχεῖα refers to spiritual beings, but we have no extant sources that use the term in this way during the New Testament era. See Moo 2013: 261. Finally, Trick (2016: 238) argues that στοιχεῖα

de Boer cites Paul's own words in Gal. 4:8-11, where he describes the στοιχεῖα τοῦ κόσμου as beings that are by nature not gods.[149]

If Paul does have these elements in mind, then how could he equate life under the Law with slavery to these elements? For de Boer, the link between the Law and the elements is the calendar.[150] According to de Boer, when the Gentiles worship these deities, seasonal worship and the observance of certain days is a central feature of the practice.[151] De Boer argues that the Jewish calendar, with its connection to the seasons of the year, is also tied to the old world that is dominated by the στοιχεῖα τοῦ κόσμου.[152]

The problem with de Boer's reconstruction is that he contends that Paul does not focus on the slavery of the *Jewish* people to the στοιχεῖα τοῦ κόσμου. This is part of a larger proposal in which he maintains that Paul's "we" statements do not refer to Jewish Christians, but all of humanity, which is enslaved to the Law on one hand and the στοιχεῖα on the other.[153] This view is hard to square with the repeated claim that those rescued from the curse were those under the Law (Gal. 3:10-14; 4:4-7) that had been given to Israel (Gal. 3:19).[154] Thus, I agree that the στοιχεῖα τοῦ κόσμου refers to the elements worshipped by the Gentiles, but Paul's point is that those same στοιχεῖα τοῦ κόσμου enslaved the Jews before the coming of Christ. But how could Paul link the στοιχεῖα τοῦ κόσμου to the Torah?

Paul could link the slavery to the elements to the slavery pronounced by the Law because the Law itself predicts that covenant disobedience will lead to Israelite slavery to foreign gods:

τοῦ κόσμου refers to the elements that divide humanity. According to Trick, the Law enslaves because the Law "makes its adherents Jews, i.e. divides them from the rest of humanity." This reading has two problems. First, this meaning of στοιχεῖα τοῦ κόσμου is not well attested in the contemporary literature. The three parallels that he cites (Rom. 3:6; 5:12; 11:12) do not establish this interpretation. Second, he assumes that becoming Jewish does not return adherents of the Law to the covenant curses. See the discussion of Gal. 3:10-14 above and our discussion of 4:3 below.

149. De Boer 2011: 253-4.
150. Ibid.: 257; Longenecker 1998: 49–50.
151. De Boer 2011: 257.
152. Hays 2000: 283.
153. Hays (ibid.: 282) and Becker (1998: 60) also argue that this "we" statement refers to all humanity.
154. See the argument that the curse of the Law refers to the covenant curses that befell Israel in Chapter 4.

> The LORD will scatter you among all peoples, from one end of the earth to the other; and there you shall serve other gods, of wood and stone, which neither you nor your ancestors have known. (Deut. 28:64)[155]

> The LORD will scatter you among the peoples; only a few of you will be left among the nations where the LORD will lead you. There you will serve other gods made by human hands, objects of wood and stone that neither see, nor hear, nor eat, nor smell. (Deut. 4:26-28)

This prediction about slavery to foreign gods is picked up in Israel's prophetic texts that use Deuteronomic language to foretell the impending covenant curses:

> Because you have behaved worse than your ancestors... Therefore I will hurl you out of this land into a land that neither you nor your ancestors have known, and there you shall serve other gods day and night, for I will show you no favor. (Jer. 16:11-13)

It is important to recognize the irony in this covenant punishment. Israel served foreign gods in Israel, therefore Israel will serve foreign gods in other lands. The punishment for idolatry is the continuation of their idolatry.

Wisdom of Solomon 13:1-10 provides important support for our thesis that for Paul the στοιχεῖα τοῦ κόσμου are the foreign gods described in Deuteronomy. In Wis. 13, the author says that the elements of the cosmos are false gods made by human hands, which cannot answer. This is the same language that Deut. 4:26-28 uses to describe the foreign deities that would enslave Israel if they disobeyed:

> For all people who were ignorant of God were foolish by nature...nor did they recognize the artisan while paying heed to his works; but they supposed that either fire or wind or swift air, or the circle of the stars, or turbulent water, or the luminaries of heaven were the gods that rule the world... But miserable, with their hopes set on dead things, are those who give the name *"gods" to the works of human hands*, gold and silver fashioned with skill, and likenesses of animals, or a useless stone, *the work of an ancient hand*. (Wis. 13:1-2, 10)[156]

---

155. On the importance of Deut. 27–29, see the discussion of Gal. 3:10–14 in Chapter 4.

156. Many note the importance of Wis. 13:1-10 for understanding Paul's argument, but they do not highlight the connection to the Deuteronomic idolatry warnings. See Schreiner 2010: 268–9 (italics added).

> There you will *serve other gods made by human hands*, objects of wood and stone that neither see, nor hear, nor eat, nor smell. (Deut. 4:28, italics added)

Therefore, the author of Wisdom claims that the elements that the Gentiles worship are the non-gods described in Deuteronomy. This evidence is important because it shows that Second Temple authors did equate the elements of the cosmos to the non-gods described in Deuteronomy and elsewhere. If the στοιχεῖα τοῦ κόσμου could be equated to the non-gods of Deuteronomy in the Second Temple period then we can see how Paul can say that the elements enslaved Israel. This is exactly what the Deuteronomic covenant predicted.

Paul's point, then, goes beyond the belief that a return to the calendar equalled a return to slavery. Paul contends that turning to the Law would bring the Galatians into a situation in which they would be at the mercy of foreign powers that enslaved Israel because of their disobedience to the Law. Paul could make this claim because he believed that Israel, as defined by Torah, remained under the covenant curses.

Therefore, those who claim that Paul focuses on all of humanity and not the Jewish situation under the Law in Gal. 4:3 miss the polemical edge of his argument. It was Israel's covenant disobedience that caused it to be enslaved to the foreign gods, and in that sense they ended up in the same situation as the Gentiles. The difference was that for the Jews, life under the Law ended in slavery to the στοιχεῖα, while the Gentiles had always been in slavery. Paul's point, then, is that the Gentiles are not escaping the elements by coming under the Law. They would be returning to slavery to the deities that once held sway over their lives (Gal. 4:8-11).

Thus, when Paul describes God's actions through his Son to redeem Israel in Gal. 4:4-5, this act of redemption at the same time addresses the Gentile enslavement to the beings that were by nature not gods (Gal. 4:8-11). This is why Paul could easily shift from describing the situation of the Jews in Gal. 4:1-7 to discussing the Gentiles in 4:8-11. God had set both groups free from the στοιχεῖα τοῦ κόσμου.

5.4.4. *Galatians 4:4-7: Adoption Makes the Believer an Heir in Waiting*

In Gal. 4:4-7 Paul describes God's response to Jewish (and therefore also Gentile) slavery. In the fullness of time, God sent his Son, born of a woman, born under the Law to redeem those under the Law so that all might receive adoption as sons and become heirs. There are three elements of Gal. 4:4-7 that are relevant to the question of the Messiah and the inheritance. First, Jewish messianism informs Paul's description of Jesus as Son. Second, Paul's assertion that the Son brings about believers' adoption into God's family and thereby makes them heirs is conceptually similar to the claim that the believer stands to inherit the kingdom (Gal. 5:21). I make this claim because, for Paul, the believer's sonship is clearly derivative of Jesus's sonship. Thus, whatever it is that believers will inherit alongside God's Son must be a share of that which belongs to Jesus as Son. As Son, Jesus is heir to the world as his inheritance and kingdom. Third, the adoption metaphor itself suggests that the inheritance will occur in the future. In Greco-Roman society, one did not inherit at the moment of adoption. This future orientation of adoption means that, for Paul, the Spirit is not the full inheritance.

First, we must consider Paul's son language. In Galatians Paul has already referred to Jesus as "Son" in 1:16 and 2:20. The question is what to make of this description. The standard definition of sonship denies or significantly limits the influence of Davidic messianism. Longenecker says:

> It may be claimed that "Son of God" is a title carried over from both Paul's Jewish and his Christian past, and that he uses it here as a central Christological ascription because (1) it was ingrained in his thinking as a Jewish Christian, and (2) it was part of the language of his opponents, who were also Jewish Christians.[157]

Hengel's classic work on sonship summed up the two strands of interpretation of the Son that persist to this day. He says that Paul emphasizes, "(1) the sending of the pre-existence Son into the world; (2) his being given up to death on a cross."[158] According to Hengel, sonship is about Christology and soteriology.

While I affirm Paul's belief in Jesus's ontologically unique relationship with God, it is unclear how this rules out messianism. The assumption seems to be that the higher Paul's Christology, the lower his concern for Jewish messianism must be.[159] This is difficult given that it is likely that

---

157. Longenecker 1990: 31. I do not think it is likely, given the way that Paul describes his opponents elsewhere in Galatians, that he would adopt their language of sonship to curry their favor or to affirm their point of view. See also Fung 1998: 64–5.

158. Hengel 1976: 12. On the importance of divine sonship to the apparent exclusion of messianism, see more recently Trick 2016: 240–6.

159. This assumption goes back at least to Baur (1876: 3), who set out to explain "how Christianity, which was at one time so closely interwoven with Judaism, broke loose from it and entered on its sphere of world-wide historical importance." See the discussion in Chapter 1.

the earliest Christology was both Jewish and high.[160] Put differently, if the earliest Christology combines Jewish messianism with the belief that Jesus shares in the divine identity of YHWH himself, then Jesus's divinity need not be emphasized to the exclusion of Jewish-Christian messianism. Therefore, it seems more likely that "Son" encompasses Jesus's status as Messiah and his ontologically unique relationship with the Father. "Son" is such a fitting designation for Jesus precisely because it speaks to his kingly (and therefore human) and divine nature simultaneously. If "Son" evokes Jesus's kingly and divine characteristics, then the relevant elements of Jewish messianism can still be included within our analysis of Paul's Christology in Galatians. It is his status as the messianic Son that sheds light on Paul's understanding of the inheritance as kingdom in the letter.

The claim that Paul's focus is soteriological and therefore not concerned with Jewish messianism is equally unconvincing.[161] For example, Kramer asserts that:

> the only fact which clearly prompted Paul to chose this particular title is that for him the title suggests the Son's solidarity with God. So 'his Son'… indicates the very close relationship between the one who brought salvation and God himself.[162]

Kramer's soteriological (and therefore not messianic) interpretation of sonship assumes that Jewish messianism was unconcerned with saving activity. That is incorrect. 4Q174, among others, speaks about the Davidic Branch's saving work:

> He is "the Shoot of David" who will arise with the Interpreter of the Law, who…in Zion in the last days; as it is written, "And I shall raise up the tabernacle of David that is fallen." That is the tabernacle of David that is fallen is he who will arise to save Israel. (4Q174 I 10-13)

The difference between Jewish messianism and Pauline sonship is not that Paul displayed soteriological concerns while others do not. The difference lies in the means by which that salvation is accomplished and the nature of the salvation that the royal figure achieves. 4Q174 focuses on the defeat

---

160. This debate about early high Christology is extensive and cannot be discussed here. See Wright 2013: 644–708; Bauckham 1998; Hurtado 2003; Capes 1992; and, most recently, Fletcher-Louis 2015: 1–30.
161. Schreiner 2010: 100–101.
162. Kramer 1966: 185.

of Israel's enemies in eschatological war, while Galatians highlights the death of the Messiah for sins so that Jew and Gentile might enter his kingdom.

Not only has a messianic interpretation been neglected, it has been explicitly denied. Martyn says:

> Paul does not say that God sent his son into the salvific history of Israel (or even into the unsalvific history of Israel), but rather the malignant orb in which all human beings have fallen prey to powers inimical to God and to themselves.[163]

By referring to the "unsalvific history" of Israel, Martyn is responding to those who want to affirm Jesus's relationship to Israel's story. These advocates argue that Jesus does not come at the climax of a series of positive steps toward an inevitable kingdom. Instead, Israel's story includes failure, exile, and curse.[164] Martyn denies that this history forms the background of Paul's theologizing. According to Martyn, because the gospel is about God's invasion of the world, and the worldwide enslavement to powers, it is not about Jesus's relationship to Israel's story as the messianic Son of God.[165] This is difficult to maintain when we note that Paul's own description of his call harkens back to elements of Israel's prophetic literature in which Israel's restoration would have worldwide implications (Gal. 1:15-16). Secondly, we have shown that Second Temple authors could and did claim that the coming of the king would have worldwide implications.[166] Third, we have seen that slavery to foreign powers was an element of the covenant curses, which were undone by the coming of the Messiah Jesus.[167] I fail to see how the liberation of people under slavery, even to foreign deities, could be portrayed as unrelated to Israel's story when the idea that a royal figure would liberate the people of God and restore them to their inheritance has been shown to be a thoroughly Jewish concept.

Paul claims that Jesus's redemptive death allows believers to move from being slaves to sons through adoption. The implications of this adoption metaphor, and its relationship to the timing of the inheritance,

---

163. Martyn 1997: 390.
164. See the discussion of Gal. 3:10-14 in the previous chapter.
165. For a criticism of this reading of Paul, see Novenson 2016, who says, "In my opinion, interpretation of Paul continues to suffer under a clunky and quite unnecessary dichotomy between Heilsgeschichte and apocalyptic."
166. See Chapters 2–3.
167. See the discussion of Gal. 4:3 above.

have not always been appreciated. To understand the image of adoption, it is important to understand the situation in which adoption was likely to occur. In contrast to modern adoption, most ancient adoptions were of adults.[168] These adoptions assured the stable transfer of the inheritance from one generation to another.[169] According to Peppard, adoption was most common among the rich. He says, "those with little property or status had little cause for adoption; but for patricians and emperors, the stakes were high indeed."[170] Most prominent among these adoptions were the imperial adoptions, which made the adopted son an "heir in waiting" to rule over the entire empire. Thus, the most public and well-known adoptions did not result in the immediate reception of the inheritance. It made the adoptee an heir in waiting.[171]

Therefore, when Paul says that the Galatians are heirs through adoption, he means that they are now a part of the family that will inherit in the future. Speaking of adoption, Moo says the following, "Paul therefore uses the word to highlight the status enjoyed by believers, heirs of all that God has promised to his people."[172] If Paul maintains that the believer is heir to all that God promised to his people, then Moo's previous statement that κληρονόμος referred to heirs in possession of the inheritance is untenable.[173]

The adoption of believers as sons arises from the action of the Son. Scott has argued that Paul draws upon a tradition that nationalizes the adoption formula of 2 Sam. 7:14.[174] According to Scott, a variety of Second Temple Jews believed that God would adopt both the king and the people at the time of the second Exodus. Scott has indeed shown that

---

168. Peppard 2011: 52.

169. Trick 2016: 144.

170. Peppard (2011: 52), quoting *OCD*, 13, says, "Therefore, adoption was performed neither for the sake of a child's welfare nor to satisfy a 'nuclear' couple's desire to nurture, but for the sake of a father, who needed to pass on his wealth, name, honor and family cult. Since all property and status were concentrated in the *paterfamilias*, even bachelors could adopt in Roman culture. On the whole, 'adoption of adult men was a convenient resource for childless aristocrats and for emperors in need of successors'."

171. Matera (1992: 151) says, "adoption leads to the right of inheritance."

172. Moo 2013: 268. Despite making this point, Moo claims that Paul's use of "heir language" emphasizes heirs in possession of the inheritance. See Moo 2013: 256. It seems improbable that Paul thinks that believers are already in possession of all that God promised.

173. Ibid.: 256.

174. Scott 1992: 174–80.

2 Sam. 7:14 could be applied to the nation. He has also demonstrated that Paul applies that tradition to believers who participate in Christ's sonship and thereby become sons and heirs.[175] Whether there was a "tradition" of nationalizing the Davidic covenant is not necessary for this proposal.[176] What is clear is that Paul thinks that believers participate in Christ's sonship and for this reason they can be described as heirs. Thus, the inheritance given to Jesus as Son now belongs to all those united to him by faith. This leads to a question that is central to this book: What belongs to Christ as the Son of God? The most likely interpretation is the renewed earth as his kingdom. Paul has already alluded to Christ's possession of this kingdom as his messianic inheritance in Gal. 3:16 and 3:19.

The sequence of events in Gal. 4:5 has again been the cause of much debate. Does Paul imply that the believer's prior sonship gave rise to the Spirit, such that conversion precedes the gift of the Spirit? Paul does not appear to be interested in providing an ordo salutus. His point is that the gift of the Spirit confirms believers' status as sons by allowing them to cry out to the father in the same way that Jesus did.[177] Calling the Spirit the "Spirit of the Son" testifies to the fact that believers' sonship comes from the work of the Son. As sons who share in the Son's Spirit, they can be sure that they are indeed heirs to the coming inheritance.[178]

Galatians 4:1-7 shows that Paul believes that the inheritance is the whole earth.[179] The description of the heir as "lord of all" in Gal. 4:1-2 is rooted in the belief that Israel as the collective heir is destined to receive the world. The liberation and adoption that leads Paul to call the believer an heir in Gal. 4:3-5 suggests that they will inherit alongside Jesus, the Son of God. Paul uses this adoption metaphor because he wants to remind the Galatians of what is theirs as God's own children. They are heirs in Christ to the whole of creation. This inheritance is possible because of the redemptive death of Jesus. Jesus has, through his death, done what Messiahs were known to do. He has enabled Abraham's offspring (believing Jews and Gentiles) to share in the inheritance promised to them.

---

175. Ibid.
176. Rightly Schreiner 2010: 271.
177. Scott 1992: 182–3.
178. Schreiner 2010: 271. Hays (2000: 285) calls the Spirit a "pledge."
179. Johnson Hodge 2007: 70; Wright 2013: 658.

5.4.5. Galatians 5:21: Inheriting the Kingdom

Paul refers to the Galatians' future inheritance on one other occasion. In Gal. 5:21, he warns the Galatians that those whose life is characterized by works of the flesh will not inherit the kingdom of God. This statement is a major problem for those who want to define the inheritance in Galatians as the Spirit. Paul's words in Gal. 5:21 leave them with two options: (1) Paul provides two definitions of the inheritance in Galatians; (2) the inheritance is not the Spirit.

The following arguments are usually put forward to avoid defining the inheritance in Galatians as a place in the Messiah's kingdom: (1) Paul does not refer to the kingdom very much, therefore it must not be important to him;[180] (2) the kingdom of God is a fragment of Jewish Christian tradition;[181] (3) Paul uses a negative phrase about "not inheriting the kingdom";[182] (4) the inheritance cannot be the kingdom because it is the Spirit.[183]

Those that highlight the lack of kingdom language in Paul's letters do not provide any criteria by which to judge this claim.[184] Stated differently, they do not establish how often Paul must refer to a concept in order for it to be considered important to his theology. In the undisputed letters, Paul speaks about the kingdom in Rom. 14:17; 1 Cor. 4:20; 6:9; 15:24, 50; 1 Thess. 2:12, and Gal. 5:21.[185] For the sake of comparison, we note that Paul mentions the kingdom more times and across more letters than he mentions spiritual gifts, baptism, or the Eucharist.[186] Few would claim

---

180. Longenecker 1990: 258; de Boer 2011: 360–1.

181. See Martyn 1997: 498. Betz (1979: 285) says, "The language contains a number of non-Pauline terms and, therefore, is in some tension with Paul's theology." This assumes that because the terms did not originate with Paul, they must reflect a different theology. However, Paul's description of the Eucharist contains non-Pauline terms. Few would argue that those words are in conflict with this theology. See 1 Cor. 11:23-26.

182. De Boer 2011: 360–1.

183. Ibid.

184. On the rarity of the kingdom language, see Witherington 2004: 406; Moo 2013: 362.

185. See also Col. 1:13: 4:11; Eph. 5:5; 2 Thess. 1:5. This list does not include Rom. 15:12, in which Paul applies Isa. 11:10, a text about the return of the Davidic monarchy and the king's worldwide rule, to the resurrection of Jesus to rule the Gentiles.

186. In the undisputed letters, Paul mentions baptism in 1 Cor. 6:9-11; 10:1-5; 12:13-14; 15:20-28; Gal. 3:27; Rom. 6:1-11. Paul mentions the Eucharist in 1 Cor. 10:17-22; 11:23-32. The spiritual gifts are listed in 1 Cor. 12:4–11; Rom. 12:3-8, and Eph. 4:7-16.

that the spiritual gifts, baptism, and the Eucharist are minor elements of his theology because of the paucity of Paul's references. The number of times a term is used cannot be the sole criterion for determining importance.[187]

Nor can it be said that Paul never goes into detail about the kingdom in his letters. In 1 Cor. 15:24-28 Paul speaks about Jesus's reign over all creation and uses a Davidic Psalm that lauds God's decision to give humans sovereignty over all creation (Ps. 8:6) to do so. Thus, for Paul, the universal sovereignty of the man Jesus fulfills God's purpose in creation. Therefore, we do have some insight into how Paul understands the kingdom. Absent other data, it would seem reasonable to suggest that his shorter remarks on inheriting the kingdom should be read in light of his more detailed discussion in 1 Corinthians.

Others claim that Paul's kingdom language is a fragment of Jewish Christian tradition.[188] But identifying something as traditional does not mean that it is unimportant or in conflict with Paul's theology. It simply means that it is traditional. Using its traditional nature to dismiss Paul's kingdom language is based upon the faulty assumption that the only things important to Paul are his innovations. We have no evidence that this is the case. Furthermore, Paul's statement that he told the Galatians before about the kingdom (Gal. 5:21) suggests that during his previous visit to them he instructed them about the kingdom.[189] If Paul can casually remind the Galatians about his teaching on the kingdom, then it was probably a stable and coherent feature of his instruction to his churches. Furthermore, if Paul did instruct the Galatians about how to inherit the kingdom, it is unlikely that he also defines the inheritance as the Spirit.

Third, some assert that Paul uses the phrase negatively. He warns them about "not inheriting the kingdom."[190] But a negative warning implies a positive alternative. If Paul issued a warning about losing the kingdom, then avoiding the prohibited behavior would enable the Galatians to obtain it.

Paul's warning about not inheriting the kingdom occurs in the course of his description of the works of the flesh. Paul then describes the fruit that comes from a Spirit-led lifestyle (Gal. 5:22-24). Thus, in Gal. 5:22-24 life in the Spirit marks out those who will inherit in the future. This

---

187. If we follow the "mention frequency rule" then kingdom (mentioned one time) is more important in Galatians than salvation (not mentioned at all).
188. Martyn 1997: 498; Betz 1979: 285.
189. Bruce 1982: 251; Moo 2013: 362.
190. De Boer 2011: 360-1.

corresponds to Paul's claim in Gal. 3:1-5, 3:14, and 4:4-7 that the Spirit functions as evidence that the believer is indeed a son and heir.[191]

The final argument against a kingdom reading of the inheritance is that the kingdom cannot be the inheritance in Galatians because Paul has already defined the inheritance as the Spirit.[192] But we have already shown that this interpretation of Gal. 3:1-5, 3:14, and 3:18 is flawed.[193]

5.5. Conclusion of Chapter 5

This chapter has shown that Paul's belief that Jesus is the promised seed of Abraham and David shapes his reading of the Abrahamic covenant in Gal. 3:15-19.

According to Paul, as the seed of David and Abraham, Jesus is the rightful heir to the renewed earth as his kingdom. Therefore, all those united to Christ are also sons and co-heirs to the Messiah's inheritance. In our analysis of Gal. 3:26-29 and Gal. 4:1-7, we demonstrated that Paul portrays the Galatians as "heirs in waiting" whose initial experience of the Spirit functions as a foretaste of their sharing in the Son's inheritance of the kingdom. We concluded by demonstrating that Paul's language about inheriting the kingdom in Gal. 5:21 cannot be explained away. Paul believes that through Jesus's death and resurrection he made believing Jews and Gentiles heirs of the kingdom. Therefore, Paul does not abandon the land inheritance in Galatians. He expands it because he looks to the worldwide rule of the Messiah Jesus, the Son of God.

---

191. See the fuller discussion on the Spirit as evidence of family membership in Chapter 4.
192. De Boer 2011: 360–1.
193. See Chapter 4.

Chapter 6

CONCLUSION

So when they had come together, they asked him, "Lord, is this the time when you will restore the kingdom to Israel?" (Acts 1:6)

Then comes the end, when he hands over the kingdom to God the Father, after he has destroyed every ruler and every authority and power. (1 Cor. 15:24)

And if you belong to Christ, then you are Abraham's offspring, according to the promise: heirs. (Gal. 3:29)[1]

6.1. *The Land and Messiah in Pauline Scholarship on Galatians Revisited*

In the book of Acts, before his ascension, the disciples ask Jesus if he is now going to restore the kingdom to Israel. The debate surrounding the answer to that question need not detain us. What matters for our purposes is the link the disciples articulate between Jesus's status as Lord and Messiah and the coming kingdom. I have demonstrated that the link between the Messiah and his kingdom as the locale of the final realization of the Abrahamic land promise explains Paul's interpretation of the inheritance in Galatians.

We began by looking at the history of interpretation of the land promise in Galatians. We discovered that despite the prominence of the Abrahamic promises in Galatians, especially Paul's focus on who has the right to be named an heir, his interpretation of the land promise has received little attention. Furthermore, our sketch of the history of interpretation showed that few scholars make the distinction between an a-territorial and worldwide definition of the inheritance.[2] Many scholars

1. My translation.
2. Davies 1979: 179.

assume, incorrectly, that a worldwide interpretation of the inheritance is synonymous with spiritualization. But worldwide interpretations of the land promises are present in biblical and Second Temple texts. These interpretations are not called spiritualizations. Another consistent problem in interpretations of the Abrahamic land promise is the faulty deduction that defining Christ as the inheritance renders the spacial aspects of the Abrahamic land promise irrelevant.[3] But we argued that for Paul one's status "in Christ" secures something further, namely life under the reign of the Messiah in the new creation. Finally, many claim that because Paul rejects the ongoing role of Torah in the life of the believer, he must also abandon any concern for the land.[4] But Paul never connects the end of the Torah to a lack of concern for the land as worldwide kingdom.

Besides the claim that Paul abandons the Abrahamic land promise, two other interpretations of the inheritance in Galatians figure prominently. First, many say that the Spirit is the inheritance promised to Abraham and his offspring. Others assert that salvation is the inheritance. We delayed a full discussion of these two proposals for our exegesis, but we did note two things. First, the claim that the Spirit replaces the land runs into difficulty when we move from the interpretation of Gal. 3:14 on to 3:15-18. Second, defining the inheritance as salvation in Galatians makes it hard to explain Paul's claim that the promises were made to the Messiah (3:16). This would entail asserting that God did not promise salvation to Abraham, but to the Messiah Jesus. In addition, focusing on salvation leads to a neglect of the adoption imagery in Gal. 4:1-7 because Paul's point in Gal. 4:1-7 is that the believer shares in the inheritance that the Father gives to the Son.

Turning to the question of the importance of messiahship in Galatians, we noticed two trends. First, many scholars argue that Second Temple portrayals of messianic figures are so diverse that there is no script for Jesus to act out. Second, others say that neither Jewish or Christian messianism plays a specific role in Paul's argument. In response, we noted that those who have argued for the messiahship of Jesus in Galatians have, in various ways, focussed on the importance of the inheritance as kingdom. Stated differently, for proponents of messianism, what makes Galatians messianic is the fact that it climaxes in the kingdom. This review left us with a testable hypothesis: Did other Second Temple authors link Davidic Messiahs to the establishment of kingdoms such that Paul's affirmation of the same provides a warrant for deeming Galatians a messianic text?

3. Hammer 1960: 272; Davies 1979: 220.
4. Davies 1979: 220; Baur 1876: 3.

Despite this periodic emphasis on the kingdom by other scholars, previous affirmations of the link between messianism and inheritance in Galatians have either been cursory or rooted in a reading of Gal. 3:1–4:7 that left many questions unanswered. One of these unanswered questions was how to relate the removal of the curse to the final realization of the inheritance in the kingdom of the Messiah.

Our review of history left us with two agenda items. First, we wanted to show that Second Temple authors did link royal and messianic figures to the final realization of the land promises. Second, we sought to show that Paul makes similar claims about Jesus in Gal. 3:1–4:7 and 5:21.

6.2. *The Evidence of Qumran and the Pseudepigrapha*

Chapters 2 and 3 addressed the question of the link between royal and messianic figures and the final realization of the land promises. In Chapter 2 we considered four texts: *4 Ezra, 2 Baruch, Psalm of Solomon* 17, and 1 Maccabees. In *Pss. Sol.* 17 the author said that the Davidic king would personally parcel out the land to the twelve tribes. He also referred to the land as the inheritance in a way that evoked the Abrahamic promises. In addition, in *Pss. Sol.* 17 the kingdom of the Davidic Messiah was not limited to Israel. He assumed a rule over the world. Finally, obedient Gentiles were blessed through their participation in his worldwide kingdom.

2 Baruch also looked to the worldwide kingdom of the Davidic Messiah as the locale of the fulfillment of God's promises to Abraham. In the course of our analysis of that text, we noted that the letter written to the exiles and the location in which Baruch received the visions (the oaks of Mamre) suggested a connection between the kingdom described in Baruch's vision and the fulfillment of God's covenant promises.

Turning to *4 Ezra*, we acknowledged that the presentation of the Messiah in that text varied. Nonetheless, in the course of the document, the author made it plain that he believed that the Messiah would liberate the oppressed remnant and rule over the world. That this messianic age served as a point of transition to the age to come did not render it meaningless. Once the remnant received the land in the context of the Messiah's worldwide rule, they never lost it again. His reign was a turning point in history.

We concluded Chapter 2 with a discussion of 1 Maccabees. This text differed from the others we studied because Simon did not claim Davidic descent. Nonetheless, the author of 1 Macc. 13–14 used Davidic texts in his description of Simon and his accomplishments. We highlighted the fact that the author credited Simon with breaking the yoke of Gentiles, an idea associated with the post-exilic restoration of Israel. The use of these Davidic texts demonstrated that the author wanted to show that what God promised to do through David's descendants was happening through Simon. Together these four texts showed that Second Temple authors could and did associate royal and messianic figures with the final realization of the land promises. We also noted that explicit affirmations of Davidic Messianism often led to claims of a worldwide kingdom and not merely a restoration to the Promised Land.

Turning to the material from Qumran, we examined four texts: 4Q174, 4Q252, 4Q161, and 1QSb. Again, we observed an explicit link between messianic figures and the final realization of the land promises. In 4Q174 the author asserted that the rise of the Davidic Branch would mean that his community, as the faithful remnant, was planted in the land. 4Q174 was particularly important because it contained a messianic reading of 2 Sam. 7:12-14, a text that Paul also read messianically in Gal. 3:16.

4Q252, by contrast, looked at Gen. 49:10. It claimed that the Davidic Branch would realize the land promises through his leadership in the second Exodus. This second Exodus would climax in a second conquest of the land. Again, in 4Q252, the Davidic king's rule was not limited to Israel. Instead, the author looked to the worldwide dominion of the Branch. Similar to 4Q174, the use of Gen. 49:10 in 4Q252 was directly pertinent to the question of messianism in Galatians because in Gal. 3:19 Paul alluded to Gen. 49:10 when he claimed that the inheritance was promised to Christ, the messianic seed.

4Q161 interpreted a variety of texts from Isaiah. During the course of the author's interpretation, he maintained that while the rest of Israel had forfeited their right to the Abrahamic promises, the Qumranites would be restored to the land. This restoration would come about through the work of the Davidic Branch who would defeat Israel's enemies and establish the worldwide rule predicted in Isa. 11:1-5.

Our final Qumran text was 1QSb. Our focus in 1QSb was the prayer for the Prince of the Congregation. In that prayer the author asked God to renew the Davidic covenant with the Prince of the Congregation so that he might establish the kingdom. This kingdom would be worldwide. The expansive nature of that kingdom could be seen in the fact that the nations would serve him.

What are we to make of these eight texts from the Second Temple period? It would go beyond the evidence to suggest that they all articulated the same hope. These authors had, in many ways, divergent visions for the present and future of Israel. Nonetheless, they were united in their belief that the arrival of a messianic or royal figure meant that

God's promises of a place for his people would be realized through their community's participation in the kingdom brought into being by his rule. Thus, it is fair to say that the link between Davidic Messiahs and the final realization of the land promises was a stable feature of Second Temple discourse about royal and messianic figures.

6.3. *The Curse, the Inheritance, and the Spirit in Galatians 3:1-14*

Having established the link between messianic figures and the final realization of the land promises in some Second Temple Texts, we turned to a close reading of the central section of Galatians. Even if we grant that such a focus existed in Second Temple texts, could one discern a concern for the final realization of the land promises as kingdom in Galatians? To show that Paul did display a concern for the land inheritance we began with Gal. 3:1-14. Our argument in Gal. 3:1-14 had a negative and positive agenda. Negatively, we demonstrated that the reception of the Spirit described in Gal. 3:1-5 and 3:14 did not replace the eschatological reception of the inheritance. Positively, we showed that ending the Deuteronomic curses could be directly linked to the final realization of the inheritance as kingdom.

My analysis of Gal. 3:1-5 supported the claim that Paul has Jesus's curse-ending and inheritance-enabling death in mind throughout in two ways. First, I showed that by accusing his opponents of casting the evil eye on the Galatians, Paul equated his opponents to those who were under the covenant curses outlined in Deut. 28:53-61. If the Galatians came under their spell, they too would join the community that was alienated from the inheritance. Second, we looked to the evidentiary power of the Spirit in 3:2-5. There I showed that rather than replacing the land, the Spirit proved that the Galatians were a part of the community that would inherit in the future. I made this claim based upon the prophetic texts that said that God would pour out his Spirit on his people once the Deuteronomic curses were over. Given that many of these texts predicted a transformation of the people and the land on the other side of the covenant curses, the claim that the gift of the Spirit replaced the land was unwarranted. Instead, the transformation of the people was the sign that they would experience life in a transformed creation.

Turning to Gal. 3:6-9, we demonstrated that (1) Paul explicitly stated that faith was sufficient to justify Abraham; (2) the blessing of Abraham promised to the Gentiles was their justification by faith; (3) Paul claimed that Gen. 12:3 was a prophecy about the gospel because it looked to the coming of the Messiah who would end the curse and enable the justification of Jews and Gentiles by faith. Paul could consider Gen.

12:3 a prophecy because he read Gen. 12:3 in light of Ps. 71:17 LXX. This latter text said that the promised blessing of the Gentiles would be realized through their participation in the worldwide kingdom of the seed of David.

Galatians 3:10-14 may be the most controversial section of the epistle. In my analysis of this text, I relied upon Second Temple parallels to demonstrate that authors used Deut. 27–29 and Lev. 18:5 in conjunction to speak about Israel's corporate failure to do the Law and their experience of the Deuteronomic curses as a result. Particularly important was the use of Deut. 27–29 and Lev. 18:5 in the Damascus Document. In the Damascus Document the author argued that while the rest of the Israel remained under the covenant curses for failing to do the Law and live, his community was no longer under the curse. In contrast to the rest of the nation, the Qumranites were experiencing the beginning of the final realization of God's promises. I contended that Paul's argument in Gal. 3:10-14 was similar: attempting to be justified through doing the works of the Law entailed returning to the covenant curses.

Our focus on the curse in Galatians led to an analysis of the nature of the covenant curses outlined in Deut. 27–29. We demonstrated that a central feature of the covenant curses was the loss of the inheritance. Building on my insight about the inheritance and the curse, I argued that it was precisely because Jesus's death ended the curse that it could be described as messianic. His curse-ending death was messianic because the covenant curses stood in the way of the final realization of God's promises to Abraham, especially the promised inheritance. Furthermore, we showed that Paul's interpretation of Jesus's death in Gal. 1:4 and 3:13 drew upon the narrative of the Isaianic servant (Isa. 52–54). In that narrative, the servant's death ended the curse and Israel's slavery. Furthermore as a reward for his death for sins, God gave the servant an inheritance that he shared with others (Isa. 53:12 LXX). This idea of an inheritance given and shared corresponded quite nicely to Paul's claim that inheritance belonged to the Messiah (3:16) and that the Galatians were heirs in him (Gal. 3:26-29).

In our analysis of 3:14, I argued that the promised Spirit did not fully realize the inheritance. Instead, it marked out those who would inherit in the future. Important in this regard was Paul's emphasis on the Spirit giving birth to the children of Abraham (Gal. 4:29). This emphasis on the Spirit's role at the beginning of the Christian life showed that the Spirit was associated with the status of being an heir. It was not the heir's full inheritance.

6.4. *The Messianic Seed, His Inheritance, and the Kingdom in Galatians 3:15–4:7 and 5:21*

The examination of Gal. 3:15–4:7 and 5:21 finally allowed us to focus on the heir and inheritance language that dominated this portion of the epistle. First, we analyzed Gal. 3:15-19. This section was vital to our proposal. In Gal. 3:15-19 Paul argued that the promises did not belong to corporate Israel, but to the singular messianic seed. We showed that this messianic interpretation of seed was based upon Paul's reading of Gen. 17:1-21 and its focus on kingship arising from Abraham's seed. Paul linked this predication of kings coming from the Abrahamic seed to the seed of David predicted in 2 Sam. 7:12-14. But this link between the Davidic and Abrahamic seed also had ramifications for how we understand the inheritance. If Paul's reading of seed was messianic, then we have good reason for believing that his reading of inheritance was messianic as well. Here the Psalms were instructive. According to Ps. 2:7-8, the inheritance given to the Son was the peoples and territories of the world.

The messianic reading of inheritance was based upon the fact that 2 Sam. 7:12-14 did not merely predict the rise of the David's offspring, it also spoke to the establishment of his kingdom. The kingdom was what gave his rise its importance; otherwise it was meaningless. Furthermore, this link between the arrival of the Davidic Messiah and the establishment of his kingdom was a central feature of Second Temple presentations of Davidic Messiahs. Therefore, we were justified in claiming that the inheritance that belonged to Jesus as the seed of Abraham and David was the inheritance promised to him as Messiah.

The analysis of Gal. 3:18-19 supported this messianic reading of inheritance by showing that Paul relied upon Gen. 49:10 when he argued that the inheritance belonged to the messianic seed. The use of Gen. 49:10 and 2 Sam. 7:12-14 in the midst of an argument about who was the rightful heir to the Abrahamic promises gave us strong warrant for maintaining that Paul linked the final realization of the Abrahamic land promise to the rise and rule of the Abrahamic and Davidic Seed.

I used Gal. 3:26-29 to support the messianic reading of seed and inheritance by demonstrating that Paul referred to the Galatians as heirs in waiting for the inheritance. This focus on who was and was not an heir shed fresh light on Gal. 3:28. We observed that Jewish inheritance law best explained his proclamation that there was no Jew or Gentile, slave or free, male and female in Christ. Paul's point was that the Law advocated by his opponents placed boundaries around who could and could not be deemed an heir to the inheritance.

We concluded our analysis of Galatians by a consideration of Gal. 4:1-7 and 5:21. Three insights stood out as significant. First, I showed that the use of κύριος πάντων in 4:1-2 to describe the heir was rooted in the belief that the Jewish people were heirs to the world. This heirship to the world was reaffirmed for all those who believe. Second, the language of adoption itself evoked the image of a wealthy father who passed his estate to his son. Since believers' adoption was rooted in their relationship to God's divine and messianic Son, it is accurate to say that they share in what belongs to him. This insight brought us back to Gal. 3:16-19, where Paul asserted that the inheritance belonged to Christ the messianic seed. The question, then, was: What did the Father give to the Son, which he in turn shared with those who believe? The most viable answer to that question is the worldwide kingdom given to the messianic and divine Son.

We concluded our exegetical study of Galatians with a brief analysis of Gal. 5:21. We argued that Paul's kingdom language was in keeping with the future orientation of his heir language throughout the letter. There is no good reason to suggest that the "traditional" language that Paul used in Gal. 5:21 meant that he would be unconcerned with contradicting his language about heirs and the inheritance that he used earlier in the letter. Stated differently, in both Gal. 3:15–4:7 and 5:21 the inheritance was not fully realized. According to Paul, the believer would receive his full inheritance when he or she shared in the kingdom of the Son.

6.5. *Implications of this Study*

6.5.1. *Pauline, Second Temple, and Early Christian Messianism*

Recent scholarship on Second Temple and Pauline messianism has focused on two themes: (1) the importance of messianic titles such as *Christos*, Son, and Lord; and (2) the incoherence of Second Temple Jewish messianic portrayals. In response to the first trend, Dahl argued a generation ago that the importance of messiahship in Paul could not be reduced to the linguistic question of the meaning of *Christos*. Instead, the real question was what impact did Jesus's status as Messiah have on Paul's thought? We have argued that Jesus's messiahship shed light on Paul's understanding of the inheritance.

Therefore, this study has shown that rather than focusing on the importance of Pauline titles, we should place Paul's claims about Jesus in conversation with other Second Temple claims about royal and messianic figures. These conceptual studies might allow us to discern more accurately where Paul and early Christian messianism diverged from other Second Temple presentations. The point about diversity has been well made, but it is possible that this insight has been overemphasized in New Testament scholarship. Maybe now is the time for a return to a more flexible reading of the evidence in which we prioritize trends and themes over lexemes and exact correspondences.

Along those lines it might be time to move beyond arguing about whether or not said individual is "messianic" and instead bring together the rather disparate set of characters of the Second Temple period under the designation "royal." If they are vying for authority over the people of God it is possible to have some conversation about points of correspondence and divergence. In our day we can speak about capitalism, socialism, and communion under the broad category of economics. We can also compare and contrast of divergent systems of modern government for points of continuity and discontinuity. I fail to see why this can't be done for our analysis of the various royal figures of the Second Temple and their accomplishments, real or imagined. This might lead to fresh insights into why one group looked to a king, another a ruling high priest, and another a divine or angelic character. This conversation might be pursued in a spirit that allows for Second Temple literary and theological creativity instead of assuming that every portrayal can be reduced to a commentary on their circumstances. These authors had agency.

This much remains clear: Paul and the early Christians stood alone in arguing that the Messiah would bring about the final realization of the land promises through his suffering and death. Furthermore, no other writers had such a robust affirmation of the place of Gentiles, although *Pss. Sol.* 17 and *2 Baruch* hint in that direction. Despite these differences, Paul and his contemporaries who wrote about messiahs looked to them to realize the promise of a place for God's people.

Finally, much reconstruction of early Christian relies upon a parting of ways between early Jewish Christian messianism and the Pauline communities that had little time for a Messiah figure. This supposed contrast has justified the search for fragments of early Christian confessions in Paul's writings. The purpose of locating these fragments has often been to dismiss them as not representative of Paul's thought. However, if Paul himself had a place in his own theology for a kingship of Jesus that fulfills God's promises, then we need to rethink our interpretation of these fragments, assuming that we can identify them. Maybe instead of being dismissed, Paul's use of these fragments are evidence of the ongoing importance of Jewish Christian ideas in this own thought and in that of his community. Is it possible that, rather than thinking of a sharp division between Jewish Christian and Pauline communities, we need to think more in terms of a spectrum. Disagreement about the role of the Law in the life of Gentile believers need not signify the rejection of all things Jewish in Pauline communities. That mistake has been made often enough and should be retired.

6.5.2. *Paul's Interpretation of the Land Promise as Worldwide Kingdom*

Most scholars assumed that in Galatians and elsewhere Paul showed little concern for the Abrahamic land promise. The perceived lack of concern has been reflected in the dearth of studies on the topic. This dearth has been explained by Paul's limited discussion of the kingdom in his writings. But we have yet to articulate a standard for mentions that would warrant studies. How many letters do we need?

Hopefully, this work fosters a reconsideration of inheritance as kingdom in Galatians. Furthermore, it may be time to develop a robust understanding of kingdom in Paul that goes beyond the word-concept fallacy to include texts such as Rom. 4:13; 8:17-35; 15:7-13, and 1 Cor. 15:24-28 alongside our analysis of sharing in the inheritance in Galatians. Paul also repeatedly talks about Jesus's reign over all things. How might we include the concept of Jesus's present and impending reign in conversations about kingdom and land? In that vein, we might ask ourselves how we managed to separate Jesus's reign above all things described in places like Phil. 2:5-11 from discussions about the land and the kingdom. Once we free ourselves from the straightjackets put in place by questions of a previous generation of scholarship it, might become clear that the kingship of Jesus and therefore his kingdom is a central aspect of this theology.

6.5.3. *Paul's Heir language and the Spirit*

Many have argued that in Galatians the inheritance was fully realized, but in Paul's other letters the Spirit only began the inheritance. For example, the Spirit was the ἀρραβών of the inheritance in 2 Cor. 5:5. Although Paul did not use ἀρραβών language in Rom. 8:17-35, the believer was also clearly an heir in waiting. This book has shown that in Galatians the Spirit also began, but did not fully realize, the inheritance. This consistency suggests that Paul's understanding of the role of the Spirit remained unchanged despite his shifting rhetorical contexts. The Spirit was the initial experience of the transformation of people and creation until the believer received the inheritance in full at the resurrection. This insight into Paul's consistent depiction of the Spirit across his letters might have an impact on the interpretation of Ephesians. Although the reasons for denying Pauline authorship of Ephesians are complex, one feature of the argument is the differences in fundamental theological ideas between Ephesians and the undisputed corpus. However, the depiction of the Spirit as the beginning of the inheritance in Galatians, Romans, 2 Corinthians, and Ephesians is a point of agreement that might inspire a reconsideration of the evidence.

Finally, I compared the Spirit as the beginning of the inheritance to the Greco-Roman concept of the peculium. To my knowledge this has not been a feature of much discussion of the Spirit and inheritance in Paul. Is this analogy apt? Would a deeper exploration of this concept of the peculium help explain the rights and privileges of heirs in Paul's thought? What other rights and privileges given to heirs in waiting in the Greco-Roman world might shed light into Paul's discussion of heirs in Galatians and Romans?

6.5.4. *Kingdom, Multi-ethnicity, and Value*

Space precludes a full discussion of Paul's concept of the kingdom as inheritance in light of Gal. 3:28 and his wider concern for Jew–Gentile unity. This much can be said here. The Roman empire sought to unify diverse peoples under the rule of the emperor. Propagandists of the empire spoke of the peace and prosperity that Rome brought to the world. However, there were clear differences in the rights and privileges given to citizens and non-citizens. There were clear differences in rights given to men and women and of course slave and free. The "everybody" of Rome had its limits. If Gal. 3:28 does indeed address the issue of who has a right to *inherit* in the Messiah's kingdom, then Paul's words about the right to be named an heir also shows who is valued as a citizen in the Jesus's kingdom. This equality across gender, ethnicity, and class stood in contrast to Roman empire that valued certain groups. There are fresh avenues available, then, of comparing Paul's gospel with that of the empire, especially as it pertains to who is valued and welcomed.

Much of the discussion of Gal. 3:28 has already affirmed equality across race, class, and gender. It has often done so at the expense of a coherent connection to the context of the argument of Galatians. What does Paul's ongoing polemic against keeping the Law as a requirement for membership in the people of God have to do with the equality of men, women, Jew, Gentile, slave, and free? The answer to this problem has been hiding in plain sight. Instead of being less connected to the context of Galatians, we needed to be more connected. We needed to take Paul's heir and inheritance language seriously. The Law placed limits on the inheritance rights of certain groups and for that reason could not be the means by which one was made an heir. Future studies might want to take a closer analysis of inheritance law and practice in biblical and Second Temple texts to bring texts those into conversation with Paul's inheritance language in Galatians and elsewhere.

It is possible, then, that part of Paul's concern for Jew–Gentile unity was that it spoke to the type of worldwide kingdom of equals brought into being by the death and resurrection of the Messiah Jesus. The very diversity of the church might, for Paul, testify to the universal extent of the Messiah's reign, a physical manifestation of the good news for all. Some Second Temple messianic texts hint at benefits that would accrue to the Gentiles, but these remarks are often fleeting. Paul's depiction of the messianic kingdom stands out in that it places the Gentiles (alongside the Jews) at the center of his picture. If this unity across ethnicity, class, and gender is indeed tied to the kingdom, then justification, the means by which Jews and Gentiles are brought into the one family of God, becomes a kingdom doctrine, a point of entry. An exploration of all the links between justification, kingdom, and multi-ethnicity, however, would take us far beyond the bounds of this project.

BIBLIOGRAPHY

Primary Sources

Aland, Kurt, Barbara Aland, Johannes Karavidopoulos, Carlo M. Martini, and Bruce M. Metzger. eds. 2012. *Novum Testamentum Graece 28th ed.* Stuttgart: Deutsche Bibelgesellschaft.
Charlesworth, James H., and Loren T. Stuckenbruck. 1994. "Blessings (1QSb)." Pages 119–31 in *The Dead Sea Scrolls Hebrew, Aramaic, and Greek Texts with English Translations: Rule of Community and Related Documents.* The Princeton Theological Seminary Dead Sea Scrolls Project 1. Louisville: Westminster John Knox.
Demosthenes. *Demosthenes with an English Translation.* 1926. Translated by C.A. Vince and J.H. Vince. Cambridge: Harvard University Press.
Elliger, Karl, Wilhelm Rudolph, and Adrian Schenker eds. 1997. *Biblica Hebraica Stuttgartensia 5th ed.* Stuttgart: Deutsche Bibelgesellschaft.
García Martínez, Florentino, and Eibert J.C. Tigchelaar, eds. 1997. *The Dead Sea Scrolls Study Edition: 1Q1–4Q273.* Vol. 1. Leiden: Brill.
———. 1997. *The Dead Sea Scrolls Study Edition: Q4274–11Q31.* Vol. 2. Leiden: Brill.
Grossfeld, Benard. 1990. *Targum Onqelos to Genesis Translated with Apparatus and Notes.* The Aramaic Bible 6. Collegeville: Liturgical Press.
Josephus, Flavius. 1987. *The Works of Flavius Josephus, Complete and Unabridged.* Translated by William Whiston. New Updated ed. Peabody: Hendrickson.
Klijn, A.F.J. "2 (Syriac Apocalypse of) Baruch: A New Translation and Introduction." 1983. Pages 615–53 in *The Old Testament Pseudepigrapha.* Edited by James H. Charlesworth. London: Yale University Press.
McNamara, Martin. 1992. *Targum Neofiti 1: Genesis Translated with Apparatus and Notes.* The Aramaic Bible 1A. Collegeville: Liturgical Press.
Metzger, Bruce M. 1983. "The Fourth Book of Ezra: A New Translation and Introduction." Pages 517–60 in *The Old Testament Pseudepigrapha Volume 1: Apocalyptic Literature and Testaments.* Edited by James H. Charlesworth. New Haven: Yale University Press.
Rahlfs, Alfred, and Robert Hanhart eds. 2006. *Septuaginta.* New ed. Stuttgart: Deutsche Bibelgesellschaft.
Wise, Michael O., Martin G. Abegg Jr., and Michael Cook. 1996. *The Dead Sea Scrolls: A New Translation.* New York: HarperCollins.

Secondary Sources

Abasciano, Brian J. 2007. "Diamonds in the Rough: A Reply to Christopher Stanley concerning the Reader Competency of Paul's Original Audiences." *NovT* 49: 153–83.

Abegg, Martin G. 2003. "1QSb and the Elusive High Priest." Pages 3–16 in *Emanuel: Studies in Hebrew Bible, Septuagint, and Dead Sea Scrolls in Honor of Emanuel Tov*. Leiden: Brill.

Alexander, T. Desmond. 1997. "Further Observations on the Term 'Seed' in Genesis." *TynBul* 48: 363–67.

Allen, Leslie C. 1990. *Ezekiel 20–48*. WBC 29. Dallas: Word Books.

Atkinson, Kenneth. 2001. *An Intertextual Study of the Psalms of Solomon: Pseudepigrapha*. Studies in the Bible and Early Christianity 49. Lewiston: Edwin Mellen Press.

———. 2004. *I Cried to the Lord: A Study of the Psalms of Solomon's Historical Background and its Social Setting*. Edited by John J. Collins. JSJSup 84. Leiden: Brill.

Babota, Vasile. 2014. *The Institution of the Hasmonean High Priesthood*. JSJSup 165. Leiden: Brill.

Bachmann, Veronika. 2014. "More than the Present: Perspectives on World History in 4 Ezra and the Book of the Watchers." Pages 3–21 in *Interpreting 4 Ezra and 2 Baruch: International Studies*. Edited by Gabriele Boccaccini and Jason Zurawski. Library of Second Temple Studies 87. New York: Bloomsbury T&T Clark.

Baltzer, Klaus. 2001. *Deutero-Isaiah: A Commentary on Isaiah 40–55*. Translated by Margaret Kohl. Hermeneia 23C. Minneapolis: Fortress.

Barclay, John M.G. 1996. *Jews in the Mediterranean Diaspora: from Alexander to Trajan (323 BCE – 117 CE)*. Edinburgh: T. & T. Clark.

———. 1988. *Obeying the Truth: Paul's Ethics in Galatians*. Vancouver: Regent College Publishing.

———. 2015a. "Paul and the Faithfulness of God." *Scottish Journal of Theology* 68: 235–43.

———. 2015b. *Paul and the Gift*. Grand Rapids: Eerdmans.

Barr, James. 1961. *The Semantics of Biblical Language*. London: Oxford University Press.

Bauckham, Richard. 1995. "The Messianic Interpretation of Isa. 10:34 in the Dead Sea Scrolls, 2 Baruch and the Preaching of John the Baptist." *DSD* 2: 202–16.

———. 1998. *God Crucified: Monotheism and Christology in the New Testament*. Grand Rapids: Eerdmans.

Baur, Ferdinand Christian. 1876. *Paul, the Apostle of Jesus Christ: His Life and Work, His Epistles and His Doctrine*. Vol. 1. Translated by Eduard Zeller. Second ed. Edinburgh: Williams & Norgate.

Beale, G.K. 2011. *A New Testament Biblical Theology: The Unfolding of the Old Testament in the New*. Grand Rapids: Baker Academic.

Becker, Jürgen. 1998. "Der Brief an die Galater." Pages 9–106 in *Die Briefe an die Galater, Epheser und Kolosser: Ubersetzt und Erlkärt*. Edited by Jürgen Becker and Ulrich Luz. Das Neue Testament Deutsch 8/1. Göttingen: Vandenhoeck & Ruprecht.

Benson, Michael Eric. 1996. "Hasmoneans, Herodians and Davidic Descent: King and Kingship in Post-Biblical Jewish Literature." New York University.

Berrin, Shani. 2005. "Qumran Pesharim." Pages 110–33 in *Biblical Interpretation at Qumran*. Edited by Matthias Henze. Grand Rapids: Eerdmans.

Berthelot, Katell. 2007. "The Biblical Conquest of the Promised Land and the Hasmonean Wars according to 1 and 2 Maccabees." Pages 44–60 in *The Books of Maccabees*. Edited by Géza Xeravits. Leiden: Brill.

Betz, Hans Dieter. 1979. *Galatians: A Commentary on Paul's Letter to the Churches in Galatia*. Hermeneia. Philadelphia: Fortress.

Blenkinsopp, Joseph. 2000. *Isaiah 40–55: A New Translation with Introduction and Commentary*. Edited by William Foxwell Albright and David Noel Freedman. AB 19A. New York: Doubleday.

———. 2006. *Opening the Sealed Book: Interpretations of the Book of Isaiah in Late Antiquity*. Grand Rapids: Eerdmans.

Block, Daniel Isaac. 1997. *The Book of Ezekiel*. 2 vols. NICOT. Grand Rapids: Eerdmans.

Boccaccini, Gabriele. 1998. *Beyond the Essene Hypothesis: The Parting of the Ways between Qumran and Enochic Judaism*. Grand Rapids: Eerdmans.

Bogaert, Pierre. 1969. *L'Apocalypse Syriaque de Baruch: Introduction, Traduction du Syriaque et Commentaire*. Vol. 2. Paris: Editions du Cerf.

Bousset, Wilhelm. 1970. *Kyrios Christos: A History of the Belief in Christ from the Beginnings of Christianity to Irenaeus*. Reprint of 1913. Nashville: Abingdon.

Brayford, Susan. 2007. *Genesis*. Septuagint Commentary Series. Leiden: Brill.

Bromiley, Geoffrey W. 1995. *The International Standard Bible Encyclopedia: Fully Revised and Illustrated*. 4 vols. Grand Rapids: Eerdmans.

Brondos, David A. 2001. "The Cross and the Curse: Galatians 3.13 and Paul's Doctrine of Redemption." *JSNT* 81: 3–32.

Brooke, George J. 1985. *Exegesis at Qumran: 4QFlorilegium in Its Jewish Context*. JSPSup 29. Sheffield: JSOT.

———. 1994. "The Deuteronomic Character of 4Q252." Pages 121–35 in *Pursuing the Text: Studies in Honor of Ben Zion Wacholder on the Occasion of his Seventieth Birthday*. Edited by John C. Reeves and John Kampen. Sheffield: Sheffield Academic.

———. 2006. "Biblical Interpretation at Qumran." Pages 287–319 in *The Bible and the Dead Sea Scrolls*. Vol. 1, *Scripture and the Scriptures and the Scrolls*. Edited by James H. Charlesworth. The Second Princeton Symposium on Judaism and Christian Origins. Waco: Baylor University Press.

Brown, Colin. 1986. *Dictionary of New Testament Theology*. Grand Rapids: Zondervan.

———. 2005. "Thematic Commentaries on Prophetic Scriptures." Pages 134–57 in *Biblical Interpretation at Qumran*. Edited by Matthias Henze. Grand Rapids: Eerdmans.

Bruce, F.F. 1982. *The Epistle to the Galatians: A Commentary on the Greek Text*. NIGTC. Grand Rapids: Eerdmans.

Brueggemann, Walter. 1968. "Isaiah 55 and Deuteronomic Theology." *ZAW* 80: 191–203.

Burton, Ernest De Witt. 1980 [1921]. *A Critical and Exegetical Commentary on the Epistle to the Galatians*. ICC 36. Reprint. Edinburgh: T. & T. Clark.

Callaway, Phillip R. 1988. *The History of the Qumran Community*. Edited by James H. Charlesworth. JSPSup 3. Sheffield: JSOT.

Campbell, Jonathan G. 1995. *The Use of Scripture in the Damascus Document 1–8, 19–20*. Berlin: de Gruyter.

———. 2004. *The Exegetical Texts*. Companion to the Scrolls 4. London: T&T Clark.

Caneday, Ardel B. 1989. "'Redeemed from the Curse of the Law': The Use of Deut 21:22–23 in Gal 3:13." *TJ* 10: 185–209.

Capes, David B. 1992. *Old Testament Yahweh Texts in Paul's Christology*. WUNT II/47. Tübingen: J.C.B. Mohr.

Carson, Donald A. 1990. "The Cross and the Spirit: A Study in the Argument and Theology of Galatians." *TJ* 11: 239–42.

Cerfaux, Lucien. 1962. *Christ in the Theology of St. Paul*. New York: Herder & Herder.

Charles, R.H. 1896. *The Apocalypse of Baruch: Translated from the Syriac*. London: A. & C. Black.
Charlesworth, James H. 1987. "From Jewish Messianology to Christian Christology." Pages 225–64 in *Judaisms and Their Messiahs at the Turn of the Christian Era*. Edited by Jacob Neusner, William Scott Green, and Ernest S. Frerichs. Cambridge: Cambridge University Press.
———. 2002. *The Pesharim and Qumran History: Chaos of Consensus*. Grand Rapids: Eerdmans.
Chester, Andrew. 2007. *Messiah and Exaltation: Jewish Messianic and Visionary Traditions and New Testament Christology*. WUNT 207. Tübingen: Mohr Siebeck.
Childs, Brevard S. 2001. *Isaiah: A Commentary*. OTL. Louisville: Westminster John Knox.
Christensen, Duane L. 2002. *Deuteronomy 21:10–34:12*. WBC 6B. Waco: Word Books.
Ciampa, Roy E. 1998. *The Presence and Function of Scripture in Galatians 1 and 2*. WUNT II/102. Tübingen: Mohr Siebeck.
———. 2007. "Deuteronomy in Galatians and Romans." Pages 99–117 in *Deuteronomy in the New Testament: The New Testament and the Scriptures of Israel*. Edited by Steve Moyise and Maarten J.J. Menken. LNTS 358. New York: T&T Clark International.
Ciampa, Roy E., and Brian S. Rosner. 2010. *The First Letter to the Corinthians*. PNTC. Grand Rapids: Eerdmans.
Collins, Adela Yarbro, and John J. Collins. 2008. *King and Messiah as Son of God: Divine, Human, and Angelic Messianic Figures in Biblical and Related Literature*. Grand Rapids: Eerdmans.
Collins, C. John. 2003. "Galatians 3:16: What Kind of Exegete Was Paul?" *TynBul* 54: 75–86.
Collins, John J. 1992. "The Son of Man in First-Century Judaism." *NTS* 3: 448–66.
———. 2010. *The Scepter and the Star: Messianism in Light of the Dead Sea Scrolls*. 2nd ed. Grand Rapids: Eerdmans.
Conzelmann, Hans. 1975. *1 Corinthians: A Commentary on the First Epistle to the Corinthians*. Translated by James W. Leitch. Hermeneia. Philadelphia: Fortress.
Cosgrove, Charles H. 1988. *The Cross and the Spirit: A Study in the Argument and Theology of Galatians*. Macon: Mercer University Press.
Dahl, Nils Alstrup. 1974. *Crucified Messiah and Other Essays*. Minneapolis: Augsburg.
———. 1977. *Studies in Paul: Theology for the Early Christian Mission*. Minneapolis: Augsburg.
Darr, Katheryn Pfisterer. 2001. "The Book of Ezekiel." Pages 1075–1610 in *Introduction to Prophetic Literature; Lamentations–Ezekiel*. Vol. 6 of *NIB*. Nashville: Abingdon.
Das, A. Andrew. 2001. *Paul, the Law, and the Covenant*. Peabody: Hendrickson.
———. 2014. *Galatians*. Concordia Commentary. Saint Louis: Concordia Publishing House.
Daube, David. 1944. "The Interpretation of a Generic Singular in Galatians 3:16." *JQR* 35: 227–30.
Davenport, Gene L. 1980. "The 'Anointed of the Lord' in Psalms of Solomon 17." Pages 67–92 in *Ideal Figures in Ancient Judaism*. Edited by John Joseph Collins and George W.E. Nickelsburg. Chico: Scholars Press.
Davies, W.D. 1979. *The Gospel and the Land: Early Christianity and Jewish Territorial Doctrine*. Berkeley: University of California.
———. 1980 [1948] *Paul and Rabbinic Judaism: Some Rabbinic Elements in Pauline Theology*. Reprint of 4th ed. Philadelphia: Fortress.

de Boer, Martinus C. 2011. *Galatians: A Commentary*. NTL. Louisville: Westminster John Knox.
Denton, D.R. 1982. "Inheritance in Paul and Ephesians." *Evangelical Quarterly* 54: 157–62.
Diffey, Daniel S. 2011. "The Royal Promise in Genesis: The Often Underestimated Importance of Genesis 17:6, 17:16 and 35:11." *TynBul* 62: 313–16.
Dimant, Devorah. 1984. "Qumran Sectarian Literature." Pages 483–550 in *Jewish Writing of the Second Temple Period: Apocrypha, Pseudepigrapha, Qumran Sectarian Writings, Philo, Josephus*. Edited by Michael E. Stone. Philadelphia: Fortress.
———. 2000. "The Library of Qumran: Its Content and Character." Pages 170–77 in *The Dead Sea Scrolls: Fifty Years After Their Discovery: Proceedings of the Jerusalem Congress, July 20–25, 1997*. Edited by Lawrence H. Schiffman, Emanuel Tov, James C. VanderKam, and Galen Marquis. Jerusalem: Israel Exploration Society.
Docherty, Susan. 2014. *The Jewish Pseudepigrapha: An Introduction to the Literature of the Second Temple Period*. London: SPCK.
Doering, Lutz. 2013. "The Epistle of Baruch and its Role in 2 Baruch." Pages 151–74 in *Fourth Ezra and Second Baruch: Reconstruction After the Fall*. Edited by Matthias Henze and Gabriele Boccaccini. JSJSup 164. Leiden: Brill.
Donaldson, Terry L. 1981. "Levitical Messianology in Late Judaism: Origins, Development and Decline." *JETS* 24: 193–207.
Doran, Robert. 1996. "The First Book of Maccabees." Pages 1–178 in *The First Book of Maccabees; The Second Book of Maccabees; Introduction to Hebrew Poetry; The Book of Job; The Book of Psalms*. Edited by Leander E. Keck. Vol. 4 of *NIB*. Nashville: Abingdon.
Duling, Dennis C. 1973. "Promises to David and their entrance into Christianity: Nailing Down a Likely Hypothesis." *NTS* 20: 55–77.
Duncan, George S. 1934. *The Epistle to the Galatians*. Moffatt New Testament Commentary. London: Hodder and Stoughton.
Dunn, James D.G. 1970 *Baptism in the Holy Spirit: A Re-examination of the New Testament Teaching on the Gift of the Spirit in Relation to Pentecostalism Today*. SBT 15. 2nd ed. London: SCM.
———. 1993. *The Epistle to the Galatians*. Edited by Henry Chadwick. BNTC. Peabody: Hendrickson.
———. 2008. *The New Perspective on Paul*. Rev. ed. Grand Rapid: Eerdmans.
Eastman, Susan Grove. 2001. "The Evil Eye and the Curse of the Law: Galatians 3.1 Revisited." *JSNT* 83: 69–87.
Egger-Wenzel, Renate. 2006. "The Testament of Mattathias to his Sons in 1 Macc 2:49–70: A Keyword Composition with the Aim of Justification." Pages 141–49 in *History and Identity: How Israel's Later Authors Viewed Its Earlier History*. Edited by Nãauria Calduch-Benages and Jan Liesen. Berlin: de Gruyter.
Eisenman, Robert H., and Michael Owen Wise. 1992. "Biblical Interpretation." Pages 77–105 in *The Dead Sea Scrolls Uncovered: The First Complete Translation and Interpretation of 50 Key Documents Withheld for Over 35 Years*. Edited by Robert H. Eisenman and Michael Wise. Shaftesbury: Element.
Elliott, Neil. 2000. "Paul and the Politics of Empire." Pages 17–39 in *Paul and Politics: Ekklesia, Israel, Imperium, and Interpretation*. Edited by Richard A. Horsley. Harrisburg: Trinity Press International.
Embry, Brad. 2002. "The Psalms of Solomon and the New Testament: Intertextuality and the Need for a Re-Evaluation." *JSP* 13: 99–136.

Evans, Craig A. 2003. "The Messiah and the Dead Sea Scrolls." Pages 85–102 in *Israel's Messiah in the Bible and the Dead Sea Scrolls*. Edited by Richard S. Hess and M. Daniel Carroll R. Grand Rapids: Baker.

Fee, Gordon D. 2011. *Galatians*. Edited by John Christopher Thomas. Pentecostal Commentary Series. Blandford Forum: Deo Publishing.

Fensham, F. Charles. 1982. *The Books of Ezra and Nehemiah*. NICOT. Grand Rapids: Eerdmans.

Ferch, Arthur J. 1977. "The Two Aeons and the Messiah in Pseudo-Philo, 4 Ezra, and 2 Baruch." *Andrews University Seminary Studies* 15: 135–51.

Fishbane, Michael. 1988. "Use, Authority and Interpretation of Mikra at Qumran." Pages 339–78 in *Mikra: Text, Translation, Reading and Interpretation of the Hebrew Bible in Ancient Judaism and Early Christianity*. Edited by Martin Jan Mulder. Philadelphia: Fortress.

Fletcher-Louis, Crispin. 2015. *Jesus Monotheism: Christological Origins: The Emerging Consensus and Beyond*. Vol. 1. Eugene: Cascade Books.

Forman, Mark. 2011. *The Politics of Inheritance in Romans*. SNTSMS 148. Cambridge: Cambridge University Press.

Foster, P. 2005. "Echoes without Resistance: Critiquing Certain Aspects of Recent Scholarly Trends in the Study of the Jewish Scriptures in the New Testament." *JSNT* 38: 96–111.

Fuks, Alexander. 1961. "Aspects of the Jewish Revolt in A.D. 115-117." *JRS* 51: 98–104.

Fung, Ronald Y.K. 1988. *The Epistle to the Galatians*. NICNT. Grand Rapids: Eerdmans.

García Martínez, Florentino. 1995. "Messianic Hopes in the Qumran Writings." Pages 159–86 in *The People of the Dead Sea Scrolls: Their Writings, Beliefs and Practices*. Edited by Florentino García Martínez, Julio Trebolle Barrera, and Wilfred G. E. Watson. Leiden: Brill.

Garlington, Don B. 2007, *An Exposition of Galatians: A Reading from the New Perspective*. 3rd ed. Eugene: Wipf & Stock.

George, Timothy. 1994. *Galatians*. NAC 30. Nashville: Broadman & Holman.

Golb, Norman. 1995. *Who Wrote the Dead Sea Scrolls: The Search for the Secret of Qumran*. New York: Touchstone.

Goldingay, John E. 1989. *Daniel*. WBC 30. Grand Rapids: Zondervan.

Goldstein, Jonathan A. 1976. *1 Maccabees: A New Translation with Introduction and Commentary*. New York: Doubleday.

Goodrich, John K. 2010. "Guardians, Not Taskmasters: The Cultural Resonances of Paul's Metaphor in Galatians 4.1–2." *JSNT* 32: 251–84.

———. 2013. "'As long as the heir is a child': The Rhetoric of Inheritance in Galatians 4:1–2 and P.Ryl. 2.153." *NovT* 55: 61–76.

Green, William Scott. 1987. "Introduction: Messiah in Judaism: Rethinking the Question." Pages 1–14 in *Judaisms and their Messiahs at the turn of the Christian Era*. Edited by Jacob Neusner, William Scott Green, and Ernest S. Frerichs. Cambridge: Cambridge University Press.

Grindheim, Sigurd. 2007. "Apostate Turned Prophet: Paul's Prophetic Self-Understanding and Prophetic Hermeneutic with Special Reference to Galatians 3.10–12." *NTS* 53: 545–65.

Hafemann, Scott J. 1997. "Paul and the Exile of Israel in Galatians 3-4." Pages 329–72 in *Exile: Old Testament, Jewish, and Christian Conceptions*. Edited by James M. Scott. JSJSup 56. Leiden: Brill.

Hahn, Scott W. 2009. *Kinship by Covenant: A Canonical Approach to the Fulfillment of God's Saving Promises*. ABRL. New Haven: Yale University Press.

Hamilton, Victor P. 1995. *The Book of Genesis 18–50*. NICOT. Grand Rapids: Eerdmans.

Hammer, Paul L. 1960. "Comparison of klēronomia in Paul and Ephesians." *JBL* 79: 267–72.

———. 1992. "Inheritance (NT)." Pages 415–17 in vol. 3 of *ABD*. Edited by D.N. Freedman. 6 vols. New York: Doubleday.

Hardin, Justin K. 2008. *Galatians and the Imperial Cult: A Critical Analysis of the First-Century Social Context of Paul's Letter*. WUNT 237. Tübingen: Mohr Siebeck.

Harmon, Matthew S. 2010. *She Must and Shall Go Free: Paul's Isaianic Gospel in Galatians*. BZNW168. New York: de Gruyter.

———. 2016. "When Return from Exile is More than a Return: Paul's Use of the Isaianic Exile and Return Motif in Galatians." Paper presented at SBL. San Antonio, TX, 18 November.

Harrington, Daniel J. 2003. "The 'Holy land' in Pseudo-Philo, 4 Ezra, and 2 Baruch." Pages 661–72 in *Emanuel: Studies in Hebrew Bible, Septuagint and Dead Sea Scrolls in Honor of Emanuel Tov*. Edited by Shalom M. Paul, Robert A. Kraft, Lawrence H. Schiffman, and Weston W. Fields. Leiden: Brill.

———. 2012. *First and Second Maccabees*. Edited by Daniel Durken. New Collegeville Bible Commentary 12. Collegeville: Liturgical Press.

Harris, J.R. 1895. "A New Patristic Fragment." *The Expositor* (5th Series) 1: 448–55.

Hays, Richard B. 1989. *Echoes of Scripture in the Letters of Paul*. New ed. New Haven: Yale University Press.

———. 2002. *The Faith of Jesus Christ: The Narrative Substructure of Galatians 3:1–4:11*. 2nd ed. Grand Rapids: Eerdmans.

———. 2000. "The Letter to the Galatians." Pages 181–48 in *2 Corinthians, Galatians, Ephesians, Philippians, Colossians, 1 & 2 Thessalonians, 1 & 2 Timothy, Titus, Philemon*. Edited by Leander E. Keck. Vol. 11 of *NIB*. Nashville: Abingdon.

———. 2014. "Apocalyptic *Poiēsis* in Galatians." Pages 200-19 in *Galatians and Christian Theology: Justification, the Gospel, and Ethics in Paul's Letter*. Edited by Mark W. Elliott, Scott J. Hafemann, and N.T. Wright. Grand Rapids: Baker Academic.

Hengel, Martin. 1976. *The Son of God: The Origin of Christology and the History of Jewish Hellenistic Religion*. Eugene: Wipf & Stock.

———. 1981. *The Atonement: The Origins of the Doctrine in the New Testament*. Eugene: Wipf & Stock.

Henze, Matthias. 2011. *Jewish Apocalypticism in Late First Century Israel: Reading Second Baruch in Context*. Texts and Studies in Ancient Judaism 142. Tübingen: Mohr Siebeck.

Hermisson, Hans-Jürgen. 2004. "The Fourth Servant Song in the Context of Second Isaiah." Pages 16–47 in *The Suffering Servant: Isaiah 53 in Jewish and Christian Sources*. Edited by Bernd Janowski and Peter Stuhlmacher. Grand Rapids: Eerdmans.

Hester, James D. 1968. *Paul's Concept of Inheritance: A Contribution to the Understanding of Heilsgeschichte*. Scottish Journal of Theology Occasional Papers 14. Edinburgh: Oliver & Boyd.

Hezser, Catherine. 2005. *Jewish Slavery in Antiquity*. Oxford: Oxford University Press.

Hieke, Thomas. 2007. "The Role of 'Scripture' in the Last Words of Mattathias (1 Macc 2:49–70)." Pages 61–74 in *The Books of Maccabees*. Edited by Géza Xeravits. Leiden: Brill.

Hobbins, John F. 1998. "The Summing up of History in 2 Baruch." *JQR* 89: 45–79.

Hogan, Karina Martin. 2008. *Theologies in Conflict in 4 Ezra: Wisdom, Debate, and Apocalyptic Solution.* JSJSup, 164. Boston: Brill.
Hooker, Morna D. 2002. "Heirs of Abraham: The Gentiles' Role in Israel's Story." Pages 85–96 in *Narrative Dynamics in Paul: A Critical Assessment.* Edited by Bruce W. Longenecker. Louisville: Westminster John Knox.
Horsley, Richard A. 1997. "General Introduction." Pages 1–8 in *Paul and Empire: Religion and Power in Roman Imperial Society.* Edited by Richard A. Horsley. Harrisburg: Continuum.
Horsley, Richard A., ed. 2000. *Paul and Politics: Ekkleisa, Israel, Imperium, and Interpretation.* Harrisburg: Trinity Press International.
Hossfeld, Frank-Lothar, and Erich Zenger. 2005. *A Commentary on Psalms 51–100.* Translated by Linda M. Maloney. Hermeneia 19B. Minneapolis: Fortress.
Hull, Michael F. 2005. *Baptism on Account of the Dead (1 Cor 15:29): An Act of Faith in the Resurrection.* AcBib 22. Atlanta: Society of Biblical Literature.
Hunn, Debbie. 2016. "Galatians 3:6–9: Abraham's Fatherhood and Paul's Conclusions." *CBQ* 78: 500–14.
Hurtado, Larry W. 2003. *Lord Jesus Christ: Devotion to Jesus in Earliest Christianity.* Grand Rapids: Eerdmans.
Janse, Sam. 2009. *You Are My Son: The Reception History of Psalm 2 in Early Judaism and the Early Church.* CBET 51. Leuven: Peeters.
Jassen, Alex P. 2011. "Reading 4QPesher Isaiah A (4Q161) Forty Years After DJD V." Pages 57–90 in *The Mermaid and the Partridge: Essays from the Copenhagen Conference on Revising Texts from Cave Four.* Edited by George J. Brooke and Jesper Høgenhaven. STDJ 96. Leiden: Brill.
Jervell, Jacob. 1998. *Die Apostlegeschichte Übersetzt und erklärt.* KEK 3. Göttingen: Vandenhoeck & Ruprecht.
Jervis, L. Ann. 1991. *The Purpose of Romans: A Comparative Letter Structure Investigation.* Sheffield: Sheffield Academic.
———. 1999. *Galatians.* Understanding the Bible Commentary Series. Grand Rapids: Baker.
Jipp, Joshua W. 2015. *Christ Is King: Paul's Royal Ideology.* Minneapolis: Fortress.
Jobes, Karen H. 1993. "Jerusalem, Our Mother: Metalepsis and Intertextuality in Galatians 4:21–31." *WTJ* 55: 299–320.
Johnson Hodge, Caroline. 2007. *If Sons, Then Heirs: A Study of Kinship and Ethnicity in the Letters of Paul.* New York: Oxford University Press.
Juel, Donald. 1992. *Messianic Exegesis: Christological Interpretation of the Old Testament in Early Christianity.* 1st Paperback ed. Philadelphia: Fortress.
Kartzow, Marianne Bjelland. 2010. "Asking the Other Question: An Intersectional Approach to Galatians 3:28 and the Colossian Household Codes." *BibInt* 18: 364–89.
Keesmaat, Sylvia C. 1999. *Paul and his Story (Re)Interpreting the Exodus Tradition.* JSNTSup 181. Sheffield: Sheffield Academic.
Keiser, Thomas A. 2005. "The Song of Moses a Basis for Isaiah's Prophecy." *VT* 55: 486–500.
Keown, Gerald L., Pamela J. Scalise, and Thomas G. Smothers. 1995. *Jeremiah 26–52.* WBC 27. Waco: Word Books.
Kim, Seyoon. 2002. *Paul and the New Perspective: Second Thoughts on the Origin of Paul's Gospel.* Grand Rapids: Eerdmans.
Klausner, Joseph. 1955. *The Messianic Idea in Israel: From its Beginning to the Completion of the Mishnah.* Translated by W.F. Stinespring. New York: Macmillan.

Klein, Ralph W. 1972. "Aspects of Intertestamental Messianism." *CTM* 43: 507–17.
Knibb, Michael A. 1995. "Messianism in the Pseudepigrapha in the Light of the Scrolls." *DSD* 2: 165–84.
Knöppler, Thomas. 2001. *Sühne im Neuen Testament: Studien zum urchstrictlichen Verständis der Heilsbedeutung des Todes Jesu*. WMANT 88. Neukirchen-Vluyn: Neukirchener.
Kramer, Werner S. 1966. *Christ, Lord, Son of God*. SBT 50. London: SCM.
Kwon, Yon-Gyong. 2004. *Eschatology in Galatians: Rethinking Paul's Response to the Crisis in Galatia*. WUNT II/183. Tübingen: Mohr Siebeck.
Lambrecht, Jan. 1994. "Curse and Blessing: A Study of Galatians 3:10–14." Pages 271–98 in *Pauline Studies*. Edited by Jan Lambrecht. BETL 140. Leuven: Leuven University Press.
Lange, Armin. 2002. "The Status of Biblical Texts in the Qumran Corpus and the Canonical Process." Pages 21–30 in *The Bible as Book: The Hebrew Bible and the Judean Desert Discoveries*. Edited by Edward D. Herbet and Emanuel Tov. London: The British Library.
Lategan, Bernard C. 2012. "Reconsidering the Origin and Function of Galatians 3:28." *Neot* 46: 274–86.
Lee, Aquila H.I. 2016. "Messianism and Messiah in Paul: Christ as Jesus?" Pages 372–92 in *God and the Faithfulness of Paul: A Critical Examination of the Pauline Theology of N.T. Wright*. Edited by Christoph Heilig, J. Thomas Hewitt, and Michael F. Bird. WUNT II/413. Tübingen: Mohr Siebeck.
Lee, Chee Chiew. 2013. *The Blessing of Abraham, The Spirit, and Justification in Galatians: Their Relationship and Significance for Understanding Paul's Theology*. Eugene: Pickwick.
Lessing, R. Reed. 2011. *Isaiah 40–55*. Concordia Commentary. Saint Louis: Concordia.
Lichtenberger, Hermann. 1998. "Messianic Expectations and Messianic Figures in the Second Temple Period." Pages 9–20 in *Qumran-Messianism: Studies on the Messianic Expectations in the Dead Sea Scrolls*. Edited by James H. Charlesworth, Hermann Lichtenberger, and Gerbern S. Oegema. Tubingen: Mohr Siebeck.
Lied, Liv Ingebord. 2008. *The Other Lands of Israel: Imaginations of the Land in 2 Baruch*. Edited by John J. Collins. JSJSup 129. Leiden: Brill.
———. 2011. "Recent Scholarship on 2 Baruch 2000–2009." *CurBS* 9: 238–76.
Lieu, Judith. 1994. "Circumcision, Women and Salvation." *NTS* 40: 358–70.
Lightfoot, J.B. 1902. *St. Paul's Epistle to Galatians*. Reprint of 1874. London: Macmillan.
Lincicum, David. 2010. *Paul and the Early Jewish Encounter with Deuteronomy*. WUNT II/284. Tübingen: Mohr Siebeck.
Longenecker, Bruce W. 1991. *Eschatology and the Covenant: A Comparison of 4 Ezra and Romans 1–11*. JSNTSup 57. Sheffield: JSOT.
———. 1998. *The Triumph of Abraham's God: The Transformation of Identity in Galatians*. Nashville: Abingdon.
———. 2002. "Sharing in Spiritual Blessings? The Stories of Israel in Galatians and Romans." Pages 58–84 in *Narrative Dynamics in Paul: A Critical Assessment*. Edited by Bruce W. Longenecker. Louisville: Westminster John Knox.
———. ed. 2002. *Narrative Dynamics in Paul: A Critical Assessment*. Louisville: Westminster John Knox.
Longenecker, Richard N. 1990. *Galatians*. WBC 41. Repr. ed. Waco: Word Books.
Lundbom, Jack R. 2004. *Jeremiah 21–36*. AB 21B. New York: Doubleday.

Lyons, George. 1991. "The Cross and the Spirit: A Study in the Argument and Theology of Galatians." *JBL* 110: 171–73.

Maier, Johann. 1996. "Early Jewish Biblical Interpretation in the Qumran Literature." Pages 108–29 in *Hebrew Bible/Old Testament, The History of Its Interpretation from the Beginnings to the Middle Ages (Until 1300): Part I Antiquity*. Edited by Magne Sæbø and Menahem Haran. Göttingen: Vandenhoeck & Ruprecht.

Martin, Oren R. 2015. *Bound for the Promised Land: The Land Promise in God's Redemptive Plan*. NSBT 34. Downers Grove: IVP Academic.

Martin, Troy W. 2003. "The Covenant of Circumcision (Genesis 17:9–14) and the Situational Antithesis in Galatians 3:28." *JBL* 122: 111–25.

Martyn, J. Louis. 1997. *Galatians: A New Translation with Introduction and Commentary*. Edited by William F. Albright and David Noel Freedman. AB 33A. New Haven: Yale University Press.

Matera, Frank J. 1992. *Galatians*. Edited by Daniel J. Harrington. SP 9. Collegeville: Liturgical Press.

McCann Jr., J. Clinton. 1996. "The Book of Psalms." Pages 641–1282 in *1 Maccabees–Psalms*. Edited by Leander E. Keck. Vol. 4 of *NIB*. Nashville: Abingdon.

Meeks, Wayne A. 1974. "The Image of the Androgyne: Some Uses of a Symbol in Earliest Christianity." *HR* 13: 165–208.

Miller, Ed L. 2002. "Is Galatians 3:28 the Great Egalitarian Text?" *ExpTim* 114: 9–11.

Moo, Douglas J. 2013. *Galatians*. BECNT. Grand Rapids: Baker Academic.

Moo, Jonathan. 2011. *Creation, Nature and Hope in 4 Ezra*. FRLANT 237. Göttingen: Vandenhoeck & Ruprecht.

Morales, Rodrigo J. 2010. *The Spirit and the Restoration of Israel: New Exodus and New Creation Motifs in Galatians*. WUNT II/282. Tübingen: Mohr Siebeck.

Motyer, J. Alec. 1993. *The Prophecy of Isaiah: An Introduction and Commentary*. Downers Grove: IVP Academic.

Mußner, Franz. 1974. *Der Galaterbrief*. HthKNT 9. Freidurg: Herder.

Nanos, Mark D. 2003. "The Social Context and Message of Galatians in View of Paul's Evil Eye Warning." Available from http://www.marknanos.com/evileyewarning-6-20-03.pdf.

Nelson, Richard D. 2002. *Deuteronomy: A Commentary*. OTL. Louisville: Westminster John Knox.

Neusner, Jacob, William Scott Green, and Ernest S. Frerichs eds. 1987. *Judaisms and Their Messiahs at the Turn of the Christian Era*. Cambridge: Cambridge University Press.

North, Christopher. 1964. *The Second Isaiah: Introduction, Translation and Commentary to Chapters XL–LV*. Oxford: Clarendon.

Novakovic, Lidija. 2014. *Raised from the Dead According to Scripture: The Role of Israel's Scripture in the Early Christian Interpretations of Jesus' Resurrection*. Jewish and Christian Texts in Contexts and Related Studies 12. London: Bloomsbury T&T Clark.

Novenson, Matthew V. 2012. *Christ Among the Messiahs: Christ Language in Paul and Messiah Language in Ancient Judaism*. Oxford: Oxford University Press.

———. 2016. Review of John M.G. Barclay, *Paul and the Gift*. *Review of Biblical Literature*. http://www.bookreviews.org.

Oakes, Peter. 2015. *Galatians*. Paideia. Baker Academic: Grand Rapids.

Oegema, Gerbern S. 1998a. *The Anointed and His People: Messianic Expectations from the Maccabees to the Bar Kochba*. JSPSup 27. Sheffield: Sheffield Academic.

———. 1998b. "Messianic Expectations in the Qumran Writings: Theses on their Development." Pages 53–82 in *Qumran-Messianism: Studies on the Messianic Expectations in the Dead Sea Scrolls*. Edited by James H. Charlesworth, Hermann Lichtenberger, and Gerbern S. Oegema. Tubingen: Mohr Siebeck.

Oepke, Albrecht. 1973. *Der Brief des Paulus an die Galater*. 2 ed. Theologischer HKNT 9. Berlin: Evangelische Verlagsanstalt.

Olley, John W. 1987. "'The many': How Is Isa 53:12a to Be Understood." *Bib* 68: 330–56.

Oswalt, John. 1998. *The Book of Isaiah, Chapters 40–66*. NICOT. Grand Rapids: Eerdmans.

Pate, C. Marvin. 2000. *Communities of the Last Days: The Dead Sea Scrolls, the New Testament & the Story of Israel*. Downers Grove: InterVarsity Press.

Paulsen, Henning. 1980. "Einheit und Freiheit der Söhne Gottes - Gal 3:26–29." *ZNW* 71: 74–95.

Peppard, Michael. 2011. *The Son of God in the Roman World: Divine Sonship in its Social and Political Context*. Oxford: Oxford University Press.

Perkins, Pheme. 2012. *First Corinthians*. Paideia. Grand Rapids: Baker Academic.

Pomykala, Kenneth E. 1995. *The Davidic Tradition in Early Judaism: Its History and Significance For Messianism*. Edited by William Adler. SBL Judaism and Its Literature 7. Atlanta: Scholars Press.

Pyne, Robert A. 1995. "The 'Seed,' the Spirit, and the Blessing of Abraham." *BSac* 152: 211–22.

Rabens, Volker. 2012. "Power from in Between: The Relational Experience of the Holy Spirit and Spiritual Gifts in Paul's Churches." Pages 138–55 in *The Spirit and Christ in the New Testament and Christian theology: Essays in Honor of Max Turner*. Edited by Max Turner, I. Howard Marshall, Volker Rabens, and Cornelis Bennema. Grand Rapids: Eerdmans.

Ridderbos, Herman N. 1953. *The Epistle of Paul to the Churches of Galatia*. Edited by N.B. Stonehouse. NICNT. Grand Rapids: Eerdmans.

Robertson, O. Palmer. 1990. *The Books of Nahum, Habakkuk, and Zephaniah*. NICOT. Grand Rapids: Eerdmans.

Rusam, Dietrich. 1992. "Neue Belege zu den stoicheia tou kosmou (Gal 4,3.9, Kol 2,8.20)." *ZNW* 83: 119–25.

Saller, Richard P. 1994. *Patriarchy, Property, and Death in the Roman Family*. Cambridge Studies in Population, Economy and Society in Past Time 25. Cambridge: Cambridge University Press.

Sanders, E.P. 1977. *Paul and Palestinian Judaism*. London: SCM.

———. 1983. *Paul, the Law, and the Jewish People*. London: SCM.

———. 1992. *Judaism: Practice and Belief, 63 BCE–66 CE*. London: SCM.

Sandmel, Samuel. 1962. "Parallelomania." *JBL* 81: 1–13.

Saukkonen, Juhana Markus. 2009. "Selection, Election, and Rejection: Interpretation of Genesis in 4Q252." Pages 63–81 in *Northern Lights on the Dead Sea Scrolls Proceedings of the Nordic Qumran Network 2003–2006*. Edited by Anders Klostergaard Petersen et. al. Leiden: Brill.

Schlier, Heinrich. 1965. *Der Brief an die Galater*. 13 ed. KEK 7. Göttingen: Vandenhoeck & Ruprecht.

Schnelle, Udo. 2014. *Paulus: Leben und Denken*. 2nd ed. Berlin: de Gruyter.
Schreiner, Thomas R. 2010. *Galatians*. Edited by Clifton E. Arnold. Zondervan Exegetical Commentary on the New Testament. Grand Rapids: Zondervan.
Schröter, Jens. 2013. *From Jesus to the New Testament: Early Christian Theology and the Origin of the New Testament Canon*. Waco: Baylor University Press.
Schüssler Fiorenza, Elisabeth. 1983. *In Memory of Her: A Feminist Theological Reconstruction of Christian Origins*. New York: Crossroad.
Schwartz, Daniel R. 1981. "The Messianic Departure from Judah (4Q Patriarchal Blessings)." *TZ* 37: 257–66.
———. 1992. *Studies in the Jewish Background of Christianity*. WUNT 60. Tübingen: Mohr-Siebeck.
Schweitzer, Albert. *The Mysticism of Paul the Apostle*. 1998 [1931]. Reprint. Johns Hopkins paperback ed. Baltimore: The Johns Hopkins University Press.
Scott, James M. 1992. *Adoption as Sons of God: An Exegetical Investigation into the Background of yiothesia in the Pauline Corpus*. WUNT II/48. Tübingen: J.C.B. Mohr (Paul Siebeck).
———. 1993. "Paul's Use of Deuteronomic Tradition." *JBL* 112: 645–65.
———. 1995. *Paul and the Nations: The Old Testament and Jewish Background of Paul's Mission to the Nations with Special Reference to the Destination of Galatians*. WUNT 84. Tübingen: J.C.B. Mohr (Paul Siebeck).
Sharp, Daniel B. 2014. "Vicarious Baptism for the Dead: 1 Corinthians 15:29." *Studies in the Bible and Antiquity* 6: 36–66.
Smith, Ralph L. 1984. *Micah–Malachi*. WBC 32. Waco: Word Books.
Soards, Marion L., and Darrell J. Pursiful. 2015. *Galatians*. SHBC. Macon: Smyth & Helwys.
Spicq, Ceslas. 1994. *Theological Lexicon of the New Testament*. Translated by James D. Ernest. 3 vols. Peabody: Hendrickson.
Sprinkle, Preston. 2008. *Law and Life: The Interpretation of Leviticus 18:5 in Early Judaism and in Paul*. WUNT 241. Tübingen: Mohr Siebeck.
Stanley, Christopher D. 1990. "'Under a Curse': A Fresh Reading of Galatians 3.10–14." *NTS* 36: 481–511.
Stegemann, Hartmut. 1996. "Some Remarks to '1Qsa' to '1Qsb', and to Qumran Messianism." *RevQ* 17: 479–505.
Steudel, Annette. 1994. *Der Midrasch zur Eschatologie aus der Qumrangemeinde (4QMidrEschata,b): materielle Rekonstruktion, Textbestand, Gattung und traditionsgeschichtliche Einordnung des durch 4Q174 („Florilegium") und 4Q177 („Catena A") repräsentierten Werkes aus den Qumranfunden*. Studies on the Texts of the Desert of Judah 13. Leiden: Brill.
Stewart, Alexander E. 2013. "Narrative World, Rhetorical Logic, and the Voice of the Author in 4 Ezra." *JBL* 132: 373–91.
Stone, Michael E. 1987. "The Question of the Messiah in 4 Ezra." Pages 209–24 in *Judaisms and Their Messiahs at the Turn of the Christian Era*. Edited by Jacob Neusner, William Scott Green, and Ernest S. Frerichs. Cambridge: Cambridge University Press.
———. 1990. *Fourth Ezra: A Commentary on the Book of Fourth Ezra*. Hermeneia. Minneapolis: Fortress.
Tamási, Ralázs. 2013. "Baruch as a prophet in 2 Baruch." Pages 195–220 in *Fourth Ezra and Second Baruch: Reconstruction after the Fall*. Edited by Matthias Henze and Gabriele Boccaccini. JSJSup 164. Leiden: Brill.

Thiessen, Matthew. 2016. *Paul and the Gentile Problem*. New York: Oxford University Press.
Thiselton, Anthony C. 2000. *The First Epistle to the Corinthians: A Commentary on the Greek Text*. NIGTC. Grand Rapids: Eerdmans.
Tooman, William A. 2011. *Gog of Magog: Reuse of Scripture and Compositional Technique in Ezekiel 38–39*. FAT 2/32. Tübingen: Mohr Siebeck.
Trick, Bradley. 2016. *Abrahamic Descent, Testamentary Adoption, and the Law in Galatians: Differentiating Abraham's Sons, Seed, and Children of Promise*. NovTSup 169. Leiden: Brill.
Tromp, Johannes. 1993. "The Sinners and the Lawless in Psalm of Solomon 17." *NovT* 35: 344–61.
Uzukwu, Gesila Nneka. 2010. "Gal 3,28 and its Alleged Relationship to Rabbinic Writings." *Bib* 91: 370–92.
———. 2015. *The Unity of Male and Female in Jesus Christ: An Exegetical Study of Galatians 3.28c in Light of Paul's Theology of Promise*. International Studies in Christian Origins 531. London: Bloomsbury.
Vermès, Géza. 1981. "The Essenes and History." *JSS* 32: 18–31.
———. 1989a. "Biblical Interpretation at Qumran." *ErIsr* 20: 184–91.
———. 1989b. "Biblical Proof-Texts in Qumran Literature." *JSS* 34: 493–508.
Wall, Robert W. 2002. "The Acts of the Apostles." Pages 4–369 in *The Acts of the Apostles—The First Letter to the Corinthians* Vol. 10B of *NIB*. Nashville: Abingdon.
Warren, Nathanael. 2014. "Adoption-alienation in Ez 47,22.23 and in the Ancient Near East." *ZAW* 126: 421–4.
Watson, Francis. 2004. *Paul and the Hermeneutics of Faith*. London: T&T Clark.
Watts, Rikki E. 1999. "'For I am not ashamed of the Gospel': Romans 1:16–17 and Habakkuk 2:4." Pages 3–25 in *Romans and the People of God: Essays in Honor of Gordon D. Fee on the Occasion of His 65th Birthday*. Edited by Sven K. Soderlund and N.T. Wright. Grand Rapids: Eerdmans.
Westermann, Claus. 1969. *Isaiah 40–66: A Commentary*. OTL. Philadelphia: Westminster.
Wevers, John William. 1995. *Notes on the Greek text of Deuteronomy*. Edited by Bernard A. Taylor. SBL Septuagint and Cognate Studies 39. Atlanta: Scholars Press.
Whitters, Mark F. 2003. *The Epistle of Second Baruch: A Study in Form and Message*. JSPSup 42. London: Sheffield Academic.
Wilcox, Max. 1979. "The Promise of the 'Seed' in the New Testament and the Targumim." *JSNT* 5: 2–20.
Wilder, William N. 2001. *Echoes of the Exodus Narrative in the Context and Background of Galatians 5:18*. Edited by Hemchand Gossai. StBibLit 23. New York: Peter Lang.
Williams, Sam K. 1988. "Promise in Galatians: A Reading of Paul's Reading of Scripture." *JBL* 107: 709–20.
———. 1997. *Galatians*. ANTC. Nashville: Abingdon.
Willitts, Joel. 2003. "Context Matters: Paul's Use of Leviticus 18:5 in Galatians 3:12." *TynBul* 54: 105–22.
———. 2006. "The Remnant of Israel in 4QpIsaiah[a] (4Q161) and the Dead Sea scrolls." *JJS* 57: 11–25.
———. 2012a. "Davidic Messianism in Galatians." *JSPL* 2: 143–62.
———. 2012b. "Matthew and Psalms of Solomon's Messianism: A Comparative Study in First-Century Messianology." *BBR* 221: 27–50.

Wilson, Todd A. 2004. "Wilderness Apostasy and Paul's Portrayal of the Crisis in Galatians." *NTS* 50: 550–71.
———. 2007. *The Curse of the Law and the Crisis in Galatia: Reassessing the Purpose of Galatians*. WUNT II/225. Mohr Siebeck.
Winninge, Mikael. 1995. *Sinners and the Righteous: A Comparative Study of the Psalms of Solomon and Paul's Letters*. CBNTS 26. Stockholm: Almqvist & Wiksell.
Witherington, Ben. 1981. "Rite and Rights for Women – Galatians 3:28." *NTS* 27: 593–604.
———. 2004. *Grace in Galatia: A Commentary on St. Paul's Letter to the Galatians*. Reprint of 1998. London: T&T Clark.
Wolter, Michael. 2011. *Paulus: ein Grundriss seiner Theologie*. Neukirchen-Vluyn: Neukirchener.
Wright, N.T. 1992a. *The Climax of the Covenant: Christ and the Law in Pauline theology*. 1st Fortress ed. Minneapolis: Fortress.
———. 1992b. *The New Testament and the People of God*. Christian Origins and the Question of God. Minneapolis: Fortress.
———. 2002. "The Letter to the Romans." Pages 395–772 in *The Acts of the Apostles– The First Letter to the Corinthians*. Edited by Leander E. Keck. Vol. 10 of *NIB*. Nashville: Abingdon.
———. 2003. *The Resurrection of the Son of God*. Christian Origins and the Question of God 3. London: SPCK.
———. 2013. *Paul and the Faithfulness of God*. Minneapolis: Fortress.
———. 2015a. *Paul and His Recent Interpreters*. London: SPCK.
———. 2015b. *The Paul Debate: Critical Questions for Understanding the Apostle*. Waco: Baylor University Press.
Xeravits, Géza G. 2003. *King, Priest, Prophet: Positive Eschatological Protagonists of the Qumran Community*. Edited by F. García Martínez. STDJ XLVII. Leiden: Brill.
Zimmerli, Walther. 1979. *Ezekiel*. Translated by Ronald E. Clements. BKAT XIII/1+2. Neukirchen-Vluyn: Neukirchener.
Zimmermann, Johannes. 1998. *Messianische Texte aus Qumran, Königliche, priesterliche und prophetische Messiasvorstellungen in den Schriftfunden von Qumran*. WUNT II/104. Tubingen: Mohr Siebeck.

Index of References

Hebrew Bible/Old Testament

Genesis
Ref	Page
1.27	168
12.1-3	3, 60
12.3	20, 108, 110-14, 127, 136, 137, 195, 196
12.7	136
12.15	114
13.14-18	63
13.15	15
15	14, 18, 23, 24, 109
15.1-21	3, 64, 109
15.1-5	23
15.2-6	52
15.6	14, 108, 109, 127
15.7-21	14
15.8	136
15.17-21	110
15.18	113
17	18, 145
17.1-21	145, 149-53, 158, 197
17.5	152
17.6-7	151
17.6	152
17.7-10	149, 150
17.7-8	15, 149
17.7	149
17.8	13, 147-50, 152, 153, 157
17.15-19	149, 150
17.16-19	152
17.19	149, 152
18.1	64
18.18	113
21.6-14	139
22	24
22.16-18	90
22.17-18	147
22.17	25, 136
22.18-20	147
22.18	112, 113, 146, 147
24.17	97
26.3-4	25
26.4	113
26.14	113
27.28-29	60
27.28	60
28.1-4	138
28.4	138
28.5	138
28.13	158
28.14	134
35.9-11	149
35.10-11	152
41.49	90
49.9-10	70, 97
49.9	97
49.10	67, 84, 86, 88, 97, 145, 154, 155, 157, 158, 194, 197
49.10 MT	156

Exodus
Ref	Page
2.24	149
6.8	149
12.44	168
13.11	3
15.9	132
15.17-18	83
15.17	82, 83
18.21	86
18.25	86
21.1-3	168
21.6	168
22.21	167
32.13	149

Leviticus
Ref	Page
18.5	115, 118-23, 126, 128, 196
25.44-46	168
26.42	149

Numbers
Ref	Page
24.17	92
26.1-4	131, 132
27.1-11	169
31.4	86
31.48	86
36.6-9	52

Deuteronomy
Ref	Page
3.18-20	52
4.26-28	181
9.5	150
21.23	134, 135
23.21	135
25.58	116
26.1	124
27–30	116, 117
27–29	22, 24, 27, 103, 106, 115, 117, 119, 121-23, 126, 128, 130, 135, 181, 196
27–28	130

Deuteronomy (cont.)		2 Samuel			136, 148,
27.15-26	116	6	4		152, 153,
27.26	115-18,	7	79		157, 197
	120, 134	7.10-14	79, 83, 84	7.12-14	197
28.22	130	7.10-11	82, 83	8	37
28.27-28	130	7.10	83	8.4-6	8
28.35	130	7.12-14	36, 37, 80,	8.6	162, 189
28.47-48	122		84, 145,	43	50, 51
28.49	126		150, 152,	43.1-3 LXX	51
28.53-61	102-104,		194, 197	43.4	51
	195	7.12	23, 80, 86,	43.5	50
28.58	104, 115,		101, 129	43.6	51
	117	7.14	39, 150,	43.9-16	51
28.59-61	130, 131		152, 174,	43.17-22	51
28.59	130		175, 186,	43.26	51
28.61	117, 130,		187	44 MT	50
	131	20.1	38	71	114
28.64	119, 178,	23.5	87	71 LXX	113, 114
	181			71.8-11 LXX	114
29.18-19	120	1 Kings		71.8	113
29.19-28	120	4.11	73	71.17	112, 113,
29.19	115-17,	4.24-25	73		196
	134	4.25	73	71.17 LXX	108, 112,
29.20	117	6–7	4		113
29.26	117			72	97
29.58-63 LXX	124	1 Chronicles		72 MT	114
30.1-3	53	17.10-14	150	72.1-4	73
30.6	140			72.8-17	159
30.10	117	Nehemiah		72.8-16	153
30.11-20	125	9	122, 123	72.8-11	97
30.11-19	139	9.1-37	118	72.11	96, 97
30.18	124	9.28-37	122	72.17	147
32	130	9.29-38	122	89	37, 153
32.5	106	9.29-37	119	89.2-4	153
33	79	9.29	122	89.3-4	87, 150
		9.35-37	122	89.4	95, 153
Joshua				89.20-29	87
8.2	132	Psalms		89.25-27	153
11.4	90	1.1	79	89.26-29	87, 88
11.14	132	2	37, 70	89.27-29	88
22.8	132	2.1-8	70	110	34, 37
		2.1	79	110.1	162
Judges		2.5-7	69	132.11-12	87
7.12	90	2.7-9	67		
		2.7-8	2, 25, 38,	Isaiah	
1 Samuel			101, 112,	9	49
30.16	132		113, 129,	9.1-7	59

9.1-6	7, 61	53.11-12	131	21.27 MT	156
9.4-7	73	53.11	133	21.32	156, 157
9.4	72	53.12	128, 129, 131-34	21.32 MT	156
10.20–11.5	88			22.15	119
10.20-21	89	53.12 LXX	128, 129	27.1-14	125
10.21-22	89, 90, 94	53.12–54.4	134, 135	34.24-27	73
10.22-23	89	54.1-4	128, 134	36.25	125
10.24-27	89-91	54.1	134	36.26-28	21
10.25-27	72	54.3	134	36.26-27	140
10.28-32	89, 92	55.3	87	36.35	140
10.32	93	56.1-3	167	37	106
10.33-34	89	65.17-25	125	37.1-28	139
11	49, 96			37.4-14	106
11.1-5	89, 93, 94, 96, 97, 194	*Jeremiah*		37.11-14	3
		16.11-13	181	47.21-23	167
11.1	15, 151	23	84	47.21	50, 52
11.2-5	96	23.3-6	81, 82	47.22	167
11.2-3	21	23.5	80, 84		
11.2	96	30.8-9 MT	54	*Daniel*	
11.4	96	30.8-9	72, 73	7	68
11.6-8	59, 61	33.14-26	81, 84, 88	7.1-14	70
11.10	188	33.14-17	85	7.9-14	125
11.11-16	3	33.15	80, 84, 85	7.13-14	70
32.14-16	106, 107	33.17-25	85	9.1-2	125
32.14	107	33.17	85	12	125
32.15	106, 107	33.25-26	85	12.1-3	125
40–55	130	37.8 LXX	50, 53		
44.3	138	37.8-9	54	*Hosea*	
51.1-18	112			11.1	175
51.1-8	112	*Ezekiel*			
52–54	131, 196	11.17	119	*Joel*	
52.1-12	130	12.15	119	2.28-29	106
52.1	130	20	118, 119, 121-23		
52.3	133			*Amos*	
52.10-12	132-34	20.4-8	121	9.11-15	83
52.12	130	20.7-8	120	9.11-14	83
52.13–53.12	130	20.8-10	119	9.11	81, 83
52.13–52.13	128	20.11	119		
53	128, 133	20.13	119, 121	*Habakkuk*	
53.1-11	134	20.21	119	1.4	126
53.1	105	20.23	119	1.6-9	126
53.3-4	134	20.28	121	1.12	126
53.3	131	20.32	119	2.1-4	126, 127
53.4-5	131	20.33-37	91	2.3-4	129
53.4	130	20.35	91	2.4	115, 118, 123, 126, 127
53.5	131	20.42	91		
53.10-12	129	21.27	156		

Zechariah		Acts		1 Corinthians	
3.8-10	80	1.6	191	3.21-23	44
6.12	80	2.31-32	111	3.21-22	173
		2.40	106	4.8-9	44
Tobit		10.36	172	4.8	14
3.7-14	169			4.18	140
3.14-15	169	Romans		4.20	188
		1.2-4	111, 113	6.2-3	44
Wisdom of Solomon		1.3-4	14, 15,	6.9-11	44, 160,
13	181		112, 148		161, 188
13.1-10	181	1.4	26	6.9	9, 188
13.1-2	181	2.28-29	140	6.10	161
13.10	181	3.6	180	6.11	161
		4	18	10.1-5	161, 162,
1 Maccabees		4.13	1, 9, 18,		188
2.49-70	47, 71-73		27, 33,	10.17-22	188
13–14	70, 71, 75,		139, 141,	11.23-32	188
	193		200	11.23-26	188
13.41-42	70, 72,	5.12	180	12.4-11	188
	73	5.17	44	12.13-14	160, 188
13.41	47	6.1-11	160, 162,	12.13	164, 166
14	75		188	13.8-13	7
14.4-14	47, 73,	8.3	166	15	8
	74	8.14-26	42	15.3-8	7, 8
14.4-6	73	8.17-35	200	15.18-22	9
14.5-7	74	8.17-32	141	15.20-29	161
14.6-14	29	8.17	14, 140	15.20-28	44, 161,
14.10	74	8.20-24	139		162, 188
14.11-12	73	8.20-21	7	15.22-28	6
14.13	74	8.23	101	15.24-28	15, 189,
14.14	73, 74	8.29	166		200
14.15	74	9.4	8	15.24-26	35
14.16-49	70	10.12	172	15.24	8, 188, 191
		10.14-17	105	15.25-30	160, 161
NEW TESTAMENT		10.17	105	15.25-27	8, 162
Matthew		11.12	180	15.25	140
1.1	159	12.3-8	188	15.49	166
20.8	172, 173,	14.17	188	15.50-58	44
	176	15.2	15	15.50	8, 9, 188
		15.7-15	159	15.53-55	7
Luke		15.7-13	200		
1.68	159	15.8-13	139	2 Corinthians	
1.76-74	159	15.8-12	9, 113	1.21-22	44
8.3	176	15.12	10, 15, 188	1.22	101
12.43	172, 173			5.5	101, 200
				6.14–7.1	175

Galatians
1.1–2.21   105
1.4   128, 133, 134, 196
1.15-16   185
1.16   183
2.20   112, 183
3   13, 18, 159
3.1–4.11   10, 136
3.1–4.7   2, 5, 14, 40, 49, 193
3.1-29   170
3.1-18   11
3.1-14   100, 101, 143, 195
3.1-5   10, 23, 102, 105, 106, 108, 161, 190, 195
3.1-4   26
3.1   102-104, 106
3.2-5   101-106, 115, 140, 195
3.2   10
3.5   10
3.6-14   11, 105
3.6-9   101, 107-109, 159, 195
3.6-7   108
3.6   1, 109
3.7-9   109
3.7   109
3.8-14   12, 14
3.8-9   110
3.8   10, 101, 110-12, 137, 141
3.9   114
3.10-14   19, 20, 22, 25, 101, 106, 111, 112, 115, 117, 122, 123, 131, 159, 179-81, 185, 196
3.10-12   115, 119, 120, 122-24, 127, 128, 133
3.10   104, 115-18, 120, 123, 134, 135
3.11-12   118
3.11   123, 126, 127, 129
3.12   118, 123, 134
3.13   44, 104, 115, 124, 128, 131, 133, 134, 196
3.14   1, 6, 10-12, 15, 101, 103, 106, 115, 133, 136-38, 141, 161, 190, 192, 195, 196
3.15–4.7   101, 143-45, 171, 197, 198
3.15-29   12, 164, 179
3.15-19   138, 144, 145, 158, 159, 190, 197
3.15-18   1, 11, 12, 14, 117, 139, 146, 147, 153, 154, 192
3.15   146, 148
3.16-19   103, 198
3.16   2, 11-13, 15-17, 23, 25, 27, 44, 98, 101, 109, 110, 112, 113, 128, 129, 133-36, 141, 146-48, 150-52, 154, 155, 157, 158, 187, 192, 194
3.17   127
3.18-19   155, 157, 197
3.18   9-12, 44, 136, 154, 155, 190
3.19-25   159
3.19   12, 15, 27, 28, 67, 112, 134, 145, 154-57, 180, 187, 194
3.21-22   124
3.24-25   176, 177
3.26–4.11 28
3.26-29   1, 11, 12, 15, 19, 44, 98, 101, 102, 107, 109, 110, 124, 134-36, 144, 147, 159, 163, 170, 190, 196, 197
3.26-27   160
3.27   188
3.28-29   160, 162

Galatians (cont.)		4.28-31	12	Pseudepigrapha	
3.28	160, 163-66, 168, 170, 197, 201	4.29	196	2 Baruch	
		4.30-31	1	10–77	56
		5.1	124, 131, 134, 179	10.1-2	56
				25.2-4	57
3.29	16, 99, 109, 159, 160, 191	5.3	116	29–30	47, 57, 61, 64
		5.5	110, 139		
		5.16-21	107	29.2-6	60
3.8.9	1	5.21	5, 6, 9, 28, 44, 110, 115, 141, 144, 145, 159, 170, 171, 183, 188-90, 193, 197, 198	29.2	58
4	13			30.1-2	62
4.1-11	107, 134			35–40	47, 57, 64
4.1-7	9, 18, 36, 40, 44, 144, 159, 170, 172, 177, 182, 187, 190, 192, 198			36–40	57
				36.4-6	58
				37.1	59
				39.7–40.2	58
				40	59
				40.1-2	59
		5.22-24	189	47.1	63
4.1-2	13, 18, 171-78, 187, 198	6.13	116	53–74	61
		6.14-16	9	55.1	63
		6.16	42	57.1-3	62
4.3-7	171, 174-78			71.1-6	60
		Ephesians		72–74	47, 57, 64
4.3-5	187	1.14	101	72.1-4	61
4.3	22, 178, 180, 182, 185	4.7-16	188	73	59, 61
		5.5	188	73.1-6	49, 59, 61
		6.1	165	74.1-2	61
4.4-7	44, 102, 111, 112, 124, 131, 134, 179, 180, 182, 190			78–87	56
		Philippians		78.3-6	63
		2.5-11	166, 200	78.18	63
		2.6-11	15, 44	78.28	63
		2.9-11	140		
				4 Ezra	
4.4-5	44, 182	Colossians		1–2	64
4.5	140, 179, 187	1.13	188	3–14	64
		1.15-20	44, 166	3.1–5.20	65
4.6-7	178	3.11	164	3.12-14	112
4.7	1, 16, 99, 169	3.20	165	4.9	65
		3.22-24	168	5.21–6.43	65
4.8-11	134, 179, 180, 182	4.11	188	7.26-34	65, 66
				7.26-28	66
4.8	179	1 Thessalonians		7.28-32	65
4.21	1	2.12	188	7.28-29	67, 68, 70
4.22	131			7.30	66
4.25-31	1	2 Thessalonians		7.47	66
4.26-27	134	1.5	188	11.1–12.34	67
4.27-31	134, 139			11.1	67

11.15	67	17.29-30	55	**4Q252**	
11.236-42	67	17.32-34	55	1.1–2.7	84
11.32	67			5.1-4	85-87, 155
11.34	67	*Testament of Judah*		5.2	85
11.37–12.1	47, 65	24.3	174	5.3	86
11.46	67				
12	68	**QUMRAN**		**CD**	
12.31-34	47, 65	*1QM*		3.1-20	117, 120-23
12.32	67, 68	1.1-7	91, 93		
12.33	68	1.5-8	87	3.4-5	120, 121
12.34	68	11.1-3	81	3.4	120
13	68	17.6-8	87	3.5-7	120
13.1-50	68			3.6-7	121
13.1-4	68	*1QSb*		3.9-12	120
13.3-13	47, 65	5.20-29	95	3.10-12	119-21
13.5-11	68	5.20	95	3.10	120
13.12-13	68	5.21-22	96	3.15-17	121
13.25-53	47, 65	5.21	95, 96	3.15-16	121
13.31-38	70	5.24	96	3.17	121
13.32	68	5.25	96	4.21	168
13.34-37	69	5.27-28	96	7.18-21	92
13.37	69	5.27	96		
13.38	69	5.28	96, 97	**TARGUMS**	
13.40-48	69			*Targum Neofiti Genesis*	
14.9	65	*1QbHap*		49.10	156
15–16	64	7.1	127		
		12.14–13.4	78	*Targum Onqelos Genesis*	
Jubilees				49.10	155
1.24	174	*4Q161*			
		1.20-25	89	**MISHNAH**	
Psalms of Solomon		1.23-25	89	*Sanhedrin*	
17	3, 4, 47, 49-52, 55, 56, 193, 199	2.1-7	89	11.1	10
		2.1	89		
		2.5-7	89	**JOSEPHUS**	
		2.8-16	89, 92	*Antiquities*	
17.1-20	53	2.14	92	18.194	176
17.1	50, 51	2.17-25	89		
17.5	53	2.17-24	92	**CLASSICAL SOURCES**	
17.7-9	53	2.22-25	92	Demosthenes	
17.11-18	49	3.1-10	89	*On the Crown*	
17.11	53	3.11-25	89, 92	18.235	
17.16-18	53	3.18-21	94		
17.20	53				
17.21-23	52	*4Q174*			
17.21	51, 54	1.1-4	82		
17.26-28	55	1.10-13	80, 83, 184		
17.28	52, 167	1.11	174		

INDEX OF AUTHORS

Abasciano, B.J. 48
Abegg, M.G. 94, 97
Alexander, T.D. 113, 147
Allen, L.C. 156, 167
Atkinson, K. 49, 50, 52–4

Babota, V. 70
Bachmann, V. 64
Baltzer, K. 130, 132, 134
Barclay, J.M.G. 38, 74, 105, 106, 115–17, 125
Barr, J. 41
Bauckham, R. 92, 184
Baur, F.C. 5, 9, 183, 191
Beale, G.K. 26, 136
Becker, J. 103, 110, 160, 171, 174, 180
Benson, M.E. 71
Berrin, S. 78, 79
Berthelot, K. 74
Betz, H.D. 10–12, 103, 105, 110, 114, 116–18, 127, 136, 163, 164, 173, 188, 189
Blenkinsopp, J. 88, 90–2, 130
Block, D.I. 156
Boccaccini, G. 77
Bogaert, P. 59, 60, 63
Bousset, W. 125
Brayford, S. 151
Bromiley, S. 999
Brondos, D.A. 134
Brooke, G.J. 78, 79, 81, 84
Brown, C. 999
Bruce, F.F. 1, 32, 103, 116, 118, 134, 136, 160, 163, 165, 168, 189
Brueggemann, W. 130
Burton, E. de Witt 1, 10, 109, 136, 146, 160, 171, 174

Callaway, P.R. 77
Campbell, J.G. 77, 119, 120
Caneday, A.B. 134
Capes, D.B. 184
Carson, D.A. 105
Cerfaux, L. 32, 33
Charles, R.H. 58–61

Charlesworth, J.H. 50, 77, 79, 95, 97
Chester, A. 68
Childs, B.S. 130, 132
Christensen, D.L. 124
Ciampa, R.E. 42, 43, 117, 128, 161, 162
Collins, A.Y. 37, 50
Collins, C.J. 112, 145–7
Collins, J.J. 37, 49, 50, 68, 69, 80
Conzelmann, H. 161
Cook, M. 97
Cosgrove, C.H. 105

Dahl, N.A. 33–5, 37, 145, 154
Darr, K.P. 167
Das, A.A. 10, 48, 102, 106, 108, 110, 116–18, 136, 160
Daube, D. 146
Davenport, G.L. 55
Davies, W.D. 1, 5, 8–10, 27, 31, 32, 136, 190, 191
de Boer, M.C. 1, 10, 103, 117, 136–40, 145, 150, 152, 158, 160, 163, 171, 179, 180, 188, 189
Denton, D.R. 7
Diffey, D.S. 151
Dimant, D. 77, 79
Docherty, S. 56
Doering, L. 57, 63
Donaldson, T.L. 73, 74
Doran, R. 70, 72, 73
Duling, D.C. 50, 145
Duncan, G.S. 176
Dunn, J.D.G. 15, 102, 105, 106, 109, 110, 116, 128, 146, 161, 172

Eastman, S.G. 102, 104
Egger-Wenzel, R. 70
Eisenman, R.H. 86
Elliott, N. 39
Embry, B. 55
Evans, C.A. 96

Fee, G.D. 160
Fensham, F.C. 122
Ferch, A.J. 69

Fishbane, M. 77
Fletcher-Louis, C. 184
Forman, M. 17–19, 136, 139
Foster, P. 48
Fuks, A. 74
Fung, R.Y.K. 106, 116, 127, 137

García Martínez, F. 5, 77, 80
Garlington, D.B. 1, 103, 136, 163, 164
George, T. 176
Golb, N. 77
Goldingay, J.E. 125
Goldstein, J.A. 70, 71, 73
Goodrich, J.K. 172, 175–8
Green, W.S. 28
Grindheim, S. 118, 121
Grossfeld, B. 155

Hafemann, S.J. 117, 175
Hahn, S.W. 146, 147
Hamilton, V.P. 156
Hammer, P.L. 6, 7, 154, 191
Hanhart, R. 50
Hardin, J.K. 178
Harmon, M.S. 42, 105, 112, 128, 130, 149
Harrington, D.J. 56, 64, 65, 70
Harris, J.R. 60
Hays, R.B. 42, 43, 105, 109, 117, 128, 129, 145, 146, 150, 163, 166, 168, 171, 177, 180, 187
Hengel, M. 128, 183
Henze, M. 56, 58, 61, 63
Hermisson, H.-J. 132
Hester, J.D. 16, 17, 135, 176
Hezser, C. 168
Hieke, T. 70
Hobbins, J.F. 56, 62
Hodge, C.J. 20, 21, 187
Hogan, K.M. 65, 67
Hooker, M.D. 159
Horsley, R.A. 39
Hossfeld, F.-L. 114
Hull, M.F. 161, 162
Hunn, D. 110, 114
Hurtado, L.W. 184

Janse, S. 153
Jassen, A.P. 89
Jervell, J. 106

Jervis, L.A. 145, 154
Jipp, J.W. 37, 43, 44
Jobes, K.H. 107, 134
Juel, D. 145, 150, 154

Kartzow, M.B. 165
Keesmaat, S.C. 42, 131, 175
Keiser, T.A. 130
Keown, G.L. 54
Kim, S. 116
Klausner, J. 60
Klein, R.W. 70
Klijn, A.F. 57
Knibb, M.A. 68
Knöppler, T. 133
Kramer, W.S. 184
Kwon, Y.-G. 139

Lambrecht, J. 116
Lange, A. 77
Lategan, B.C. 164, 167
Lee, A.H.I. 2, 45
Lee, C.C. 109
Lessing, R.R. 132
Lichtenberger, H. 76
Lied, L.I. 3, 56–9, 61, 63, 64
Lieu, J. 166
Lightfoot, J.B. 116, 118, 169, 171, 174, 179
Lincicum, D. 116, 117
Longenecker, B.W. 38, 67, 109, 128, 159, 180
Longenecker, R.N. 118, 128, 163, 165, 171, 174, 177, 183, 188
Lundbom, J.R. 54
Lyons, G. 105

Maier, J. 78
Martin, O.R. 25, 136, 164
Martin, T.W. 164
Martyn, J.L. 1, 10, 13, 45, 103, 109, 116, 127, 136, 140, 152, 163, 164, 173, 177, 185, 188, 189
Matera, F.J. 116, 160, 163, 164, 171, 173, 174, 179, 186
McCann, J.C. 114
McNamara, M. 156
Meeks, W.A. 163, 165
Metzger, B.M. 64, 66
Miller, E.L. 163

Moo, D.J. 14, 66, 103, 105, 106, 110, 116, 128, 137, 138, 146, 154, 164, 171, 173, 175, 177, 179, 186, 189
Morales, R.J. 19, 20, 102, 106, 107, 117–19, 124, 125, 129, 133, 138, 140, 142
Motyer, J.A. 92
Mussner, F. 105, 128, 173, 179

Nanos, M.D. 103
Nelson, R.D. 124
Neusner, J. 40
North, C. 132
Novakovic, L. 42
Novenson, M.V. 28, 30, 33, 35, 37, 40, 41, 145, 146, 150, 155, 185

Oakes, P. 103, 163, 164, 167
Oegema, G.S. 40, 49, 80, 96, 97, 155
Oepke, A. 171
Olley, J.W. 132
Oswalt, J. 134

Pate, M.C. 96
Paulsen, H. 159
Peppard, M. 186
Perkins, P. 161
Pomykala, K.E. 50, 86, 87
Pursiful, D.J. 155, 164, 170
Pyne, R.A. 146

Rabens, V. 105
Rahlfs, A. 50, 151
Ridderbos, H.N. 116
Robertson, O.P. 126
Rosner, B.S. 161, 162
Rusam, D. 179

Saller, R.P. 177
Sanders, E.P. 32, 49, 127
Sandmel, S. 46
Saukkonen, J.M. 84
Scalise, P.J. 54
Schlier, H. 103, 105, 106, 128, 163
Schnelle, U. 116
Schreiner, T.R. 102, 105, 106, 110, 116, 128, 163, 164, 171, 173, 175, 179, 181, 184, 187
Schröter, J. 146
Schüssler Fiorenza, E. 164
Schwartz, D.R. 53, 85

Schweitzer, A. 136
Scott, J.M. 18, 20, 39, 42, 112, 113, 117, 172, 174, 175, 186, 187
Sharp, D.B. 161
Smith, R.L. 126
Smothers, T.G. 54
Soards, M.L. 155, 164, 170
Spicq, C. 15
Sprinkle, P. 118, 121, 123
Stanley, C.D. 48, 116
Stegemann, H. 94
Steudel, A. 79
Stewart, A.E. 69
Stone, M.E. 65, 67–9
Stuckenbruck, L.T. 95, 97

Tamási, R. 58
Theissen, M. 22–4, 151
Thiselton, A.C. 161, 162
Tigchelaar, E.J.C. 5, 77, 80
Tooman, W.A. 80
Trick, B. 109, 111, 117, 120, 133, 135, 146, 148, 150, 153, 155, 157, 164, 179, 183, 186
Tromp, J. 53

Uzukwu, G.N. 165, 166

Vermès, G. 77–9

Wall, R.W. 106
Warren, N. 167
Watson, F. 5, 14, 15, 106, 110–12, 117, 123, 137, 138, 141, 152, 154
Watts, R.E. 126
Westermann, C. 132
Wevers, J.W. 151
Whitters, M.F. 57
Wilcox, M. 145
Wilder, W. 131, 175
Williams, S.K. 1, 10, 12, 13, 28, 136, 163–5
Willitts, J. 37, 51, 89, 92, 93, 118, 121, 128
Wilson, T.A. 103, 104, 131
Winninge, M. 53
Wise, M.O. 97
Witherington, B. 1, 10, 103, 105, 108, 116, 136, 137, 166, 169, 179
Wolter, M. 128

Wright, N.T. 7, 10, 20, 37, 38, 43, 71, 105, 111, 113, 117, 123, 146, 147, 162, 175, 184, 187

Xeravits, G.G. 77, 95, 96

Zenger, E. 114
Zimmerli, W. 91
Zimmermann, J. 79, 85, 91, 93, 95

www.ingramcontent.com/pod-product-compliance
Lightning Source LLC
Chambersburg PA
CBHW052037300426
44117CB00012B/1867